ASPIRE
SUCCEED
PROGRESS

# exam success

## Cambridge IGCSE® & O Level

# Chemistry

Great Clarendon Street, Oxford, OX2 6DP, United Kingdom

Oxford University Press is a department of the University of Oxford. It furthers the University's objective of excellence in research, scholarship, and education by publishing worldwide. Oxford is a registered trade mark of Oxford University Press in the UK and in certain other countries



First published in 2021



British Library Cataloguing in Publication Data
Data available

eBook: 9781382006378

Print book: 9781382006347

3 5 7 9 10 8 6 4 2

Paper used in the production of this book is a natural, recyclable product made from wood grown in sustainable forests.
The manufacturing process conforms to the environmental regulations of the country of origin.

Printed and bound by CPI Group (UK) Ltd, Croydon, CR0 4YY

**Acknowledgements**

The publisher and authors would like to thank the following for permission to use photographs and other copyright material:

Cover: Ruslana Bat/Shutterstock Images.

Artwork by Q2A Media Services Pvt. Ltd.



This Exam Success Guide refers to the Cambridge IGCSE® Chemistry (0620) and Cambridge O Level Chemistry (5070) Syllabuses published by Cambridge Assessment International Education.

# Contents

Answers for all exam-style questions are available at
www.oxfordsecondary.com/esg-for-caie-igcse

# Introduction

Matched to the latest Cambridge assessment criteria, this in-depth Exam Success Guide brings clarity and focus to exam preparation with detailed and practical guidance on raising attainment in IGCSE® Chemistry as well as Cambridge O Level Chemistry.

This Exam Success Guide:

- Is **fully matched** to the latest Cambridge IGCSE® syllabus as well as the Cambridge O Level syllabus.
- Includes a comprehensive list of **syllabus objectives** at the start of each chapter where you can build a record of your revision as well as **Key skills** features within the chapters to guide you through your revision and **Recap** features to review the key information. The syllabus objectives for O Level are the same as for IGCSE® but the numbering is slightly different. The syllabus sections are the same.
- Provides exam-style questions at the end of each chapter to equip you to **Raise your grade**. These questions have fully worked solutions with commentaries as part of the online resources.
- Will guide you through answering exam questions with extensive use of **Worked examples** with **Exam tips**.

# 'Supplement only' content

This book is intended for use by candidates studying both the Core and Supplement syllabuses.

- The syllabus objectives at the start of each chapter indicate **Supplement only** content in **bold**.
- Within each chapter, where content is in the Supplement syllabus but *not* in the Core syllabus, it is clearly shaded and indicated with a red 'Supplement' bar or an S icon.
- Raise your grade questions for the Supplement syllabus only are also clearly shaded and indicated with an S icon.
- For O Level, the syllabus is not divided into core and supplement, so all the contents of the book should be used.

# Particle theory

## Revision checklist

Tick these boxes to build a record of your revision. Columns 2 and 3 can be used if you want to make a record more than once.

| Core/**Supplement** syllabus content | | 1 | 2 | 3 |
|---|---|---|---|---|
| 1.1 | Describe the general properties of solids, liquids and gases; understand the term kinetic particle theory. | | | |
| 1.1 | Describe the structures of solids, liquids and gases in terms of particle separation, arrangement and motion. | | | |
| 1.1 | State the effect of temperature and pressure on the volume of gases. | | | |
| 1.2 | Describe the changes of state in terms of melting, boiling, evaporation, freezing and condensation. | | | |
| 1.2 | **Explain, using the kinetic particle theory, the effects of pressure and temperature on the volume of a gas.** | | | |
| 1.3 | Understand differences in physical state in terms of melting points and boiling points. | | | |
| 1.3 | **Explain changes of state using the kinetic particle theory.** | | | |
| 1.3 | **Interpret cooling curves and heating curves.** | | | |
| 1.4 | Define the terms solvent, solute, solution and saturated solution. | | | |
| 1.4 | State that concentration can be measured in $g/dm^3$ or $mol/dm^3$. | | | |
| 1.4 | Describe the chemical tests for water. | | | |
| 1.4 | State the meaning of the terms hydrated, anhydrous and water of crystallisation. | | | |
| 1.4 | Explain why distilled water is used in practical chemistry. | | | |
| 1.5 | Describe and explain diffusion using the kinetic particle theory. | | | |
| 1.5 | **Describe and explain the effect of molecular mass on the rate of diffusion in gases.** | | | |

# 1.1 Solids, liquids and gases

**You need to:**

- Describe the general properties of solids, liquids and gases; understand the term kinetic particle theory.
- Describe the structures of solids, liquids and gases in terms of particle separation, arrangement and motion.
- State the effect of temperature and pressure on the volume of gases.

**Recap**

The three physical **states** of matter are solids, liquids and gases.

*Solids* have a definite shape and volume but do not flow.

*Liquids* have a definite volume, take the shape of their container and can flow.

*Gases* have no particular volume and can spread everywhere.

**Worked example**

State two differences in the general properties of a solid and a liquid. [2]

A solid has a definite shape. A liquid takes the shape of its container. ✓

A solid cannot flow but a liquid can flow. ✓

**Exam tip**

**Watch out**

Take care not to muddle the general properties of solids, liquids and gases (flow, definite volume, presence of a surface) with the arrangement, motion and separation of the particles.

**Kinetic particle theory** is the idea that particles behave as hard spheres which can vibrate or move from place to place.

*Separation* of particles refers to how close the particles are.

*Arrangement* is either in fixed positions (in solids) or irregular (in liquids and gases).

*Motion* of particles in solids is only by vibration. In liquids the particles slide over each other. Gas particles bounce off each other.

**Exam tip**

Remember that in liquids the particles are close together. It is a common error to suggest they are some distance apart.

**Worked example**

Use the kinetic particle theory to describe the arrangement and motion of the particles in solid copper and liquid copper. [4]

In solid copper the particles are regularly arranged in fixed positions. ✓

In liquid copper the particles are arranged randomly – there is no particular arrangement. ✓

The particles in solid copper only vibrate. ✓

The particles in liquid copper slide over each other. ✓

**Exam tip**

Make sure that you know the difference between the words arrangement and separation when referring to particles. These are often confused.

## Apply

1. Make a table of the types of motion, separation and arrangement of the particles in solids, liquids and gases.

**Exam tip**

Remember that the motion in solids is vibration only. Movement from place to place only happens in liquids and gases.

An *increase in pressure* decreases the volume of a gas in a gas syringe.

An *increase in temperature* increases the volume of a gas in a gas syringe.

**Worked example**

A gas syringe has its end blocked.

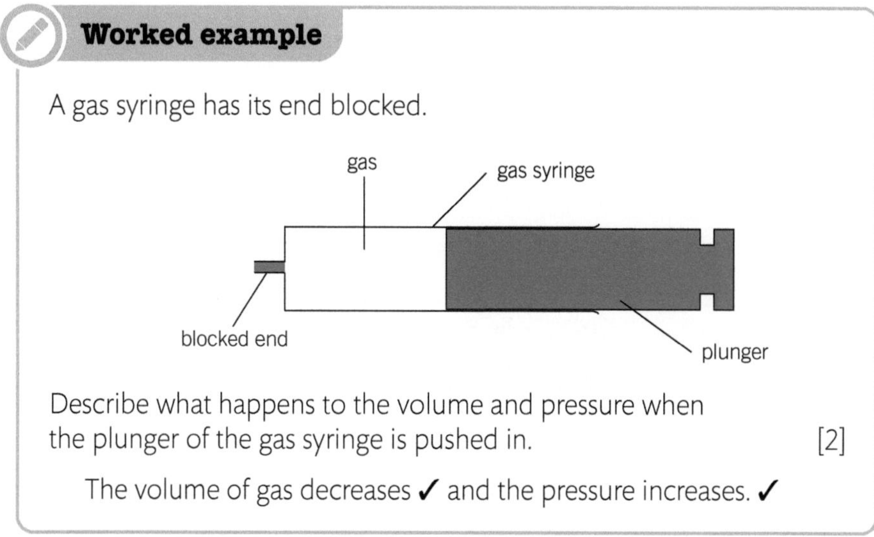


Describe what happens to the volume and pressure when the plunger of the gas syringe is pushed in. [2]

The volume of gas decreases ✓ and the pressure increases. ✓

**Recap**

- The kinetic particle theory is about the motion of particles under different conditions.
- We imagine the particles as tiny hard spheres to help us.

# 1.2 Using the kinetic particle theory

**You need to:**

- Describe the changes of state in terms of melting, boiling, evaporation, freezing and condensation.
- **Explain, using the kinetic particle theory, the effects of pressure and temperature on the volume of a gas.**

**Melting** is the change of state from solid to liquid.

**Boiling** is the change of state from liquid to gas at the boiling point.

**Evaporation** is the change in state from liquid to vapour below the boiling point.

**Condensation** is the change in state from gas to liquid.

**Freezing** is the change of state from liquid to solid.

**Worked example**

Name the changes of state labelled A, B and C. [3]

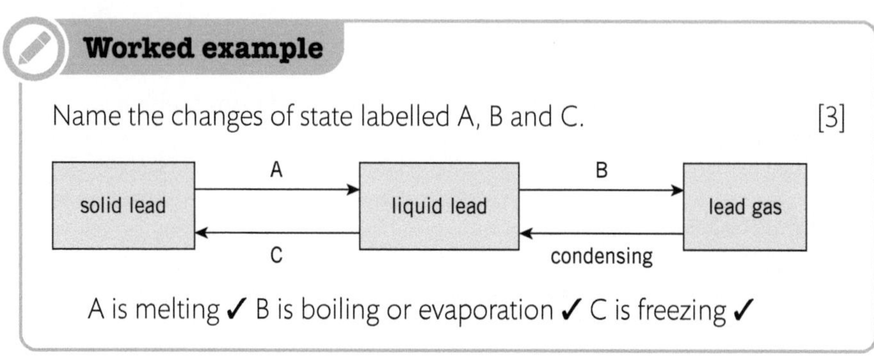


A is melting ✓ B is boiling or evaporation ✓ C is freezing ✓

**Key skills**

You need to be able to link scientific words such as condensation to the processes that they describe.

Supplement

*Energy is absorbed* during melting and boiling and released in condensing and freezing.

*The effect of pressure and temperature on the volume of a gas* depends on the frequency of particle collisions and the energy of the particles.

**Worked example**

Oxygen is a gas which turns into a liquid at −183 °C.

Describe and explain the change in energy of the oxygen particles which takes place when oxygen turns from a gas to a liquid. [2]

The oxygen particles have less kinetic energy ✓ because energy is given out during condensation. ✓

Use the kinetic particle theory to explain why the pressure of oxygen in a closed container decreases when the temperature decreases from 0 °C to −100 °C. [2]

The particles move more slowly at a lower temperature – they have less **kinetic energy**. ✓

So they hit the walls of the container less frequently. ✓

**Recap**

Energy is absorbed when a substance melts or boils. Energy is released when a substance condenses or freezes.

## Apply

2. State and explain using the kinetic particle theory what happens to the volume of a gas in a gas syringe when the temperature decreases. The pressure is constant.

# 1.3 Heating and cooling curves

**You need to:**

- **Understand differences in physical state in terms of melting points and boiling points.**
- **Explain changes of state using the kinetic particle theory; interpret cooling curves and heating curves.**

The *physical state* (solid, liquid or gas) can be deduced from melting and boiling point data.

**Exam tip**

**Watch out**

Take care with negative values: −20 °C is a lower temperature than −10 °C.

**Worked example**

Bromine melts at −7 °C and boils at 59 °C. Deduce the physical state of bromine at 5 °C. Give a reason for your answer. [2]

Liquid ✓ because 5 °C is above the melting point and below the boiling point. ✓

### Exam tip

When answering questions about the physical state of a substance given the melting and boiling points, it may help you to draw a diagram like this.

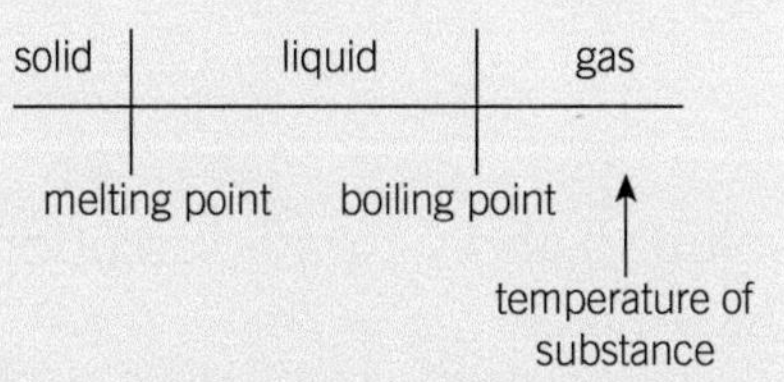


▲ **Physical state change**

*Energy changes* take place when there is a change of state.

A **cooling curve** shows how the temperature changes with time when a gas is slowly cooled to form a liquid or a liquid is slowly cooled to form a solid.

### Worked example

The temperature of gas **X** decreases as it cools. The cooling curve for gas **X** is shown.

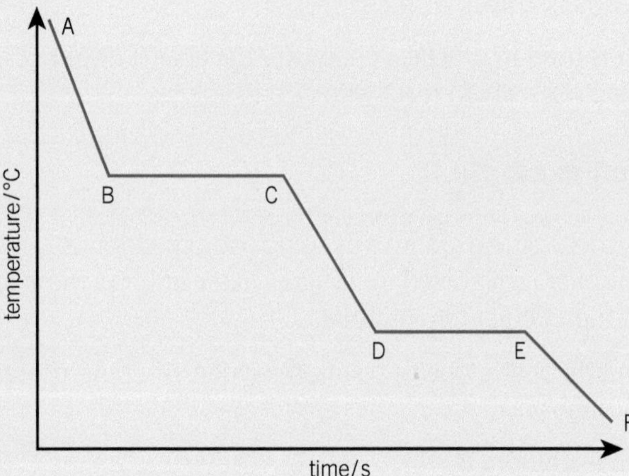


Deduce where **X** is freezing and explain using the kinetic particle theory the shape of the cooling curve between the points **A**, **B** and **C**. [5]

**X** freezes between **D** and **E**. ✓

Between **A** and **B** the temperature of the *gas* is decreasing ✓ because the particles are losing kinetic energy. ✓ Between **B** and **C** the gas is condensing ✓ so energy is being given out. ✓ The temperature remains constant because the decrease in energy of the molecules is balanced by the energy given out. ✓

(Note that there are more marking points than marks given for the question)

### Recap

The flat parts of a cooling curve or **heating curve** are where there is a change of state. For example, solid to liquid or gas to liquid.

## Apply

3. A pure liquid with a melting point of 45 °C is cooled from 60 °C to 30 °C. Describe and explain the cooling curve in terms of the kinetic particle theory.
4. The diagram shows a heating curve starting with a solid. Describe and explain this heating curve in terms of the kinetic particle theory.

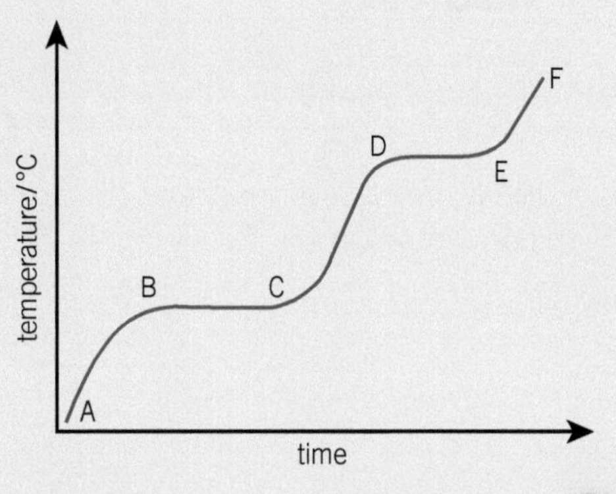

# 1.4 Solvents, solutes and solutions

**You need to:**

- Define the terms solvent, solute, solution and saturated solution; state that concentration can be measured in g/dm³ or mol/dm³.
- Describe the chemical tests for water; state the meaning of the terms hydrated, anhydrous and water of crystallisation; explain why distilled water is used in practical chemistry.

**Key skills**

You are expected to know the definitions for chemical terms such as saturated solution which appear in the syllabus.

A **solvent** is a substance which dissolves other substances.

A **solute** is a substance which dissolves in a solvent.

A **solution** is a mixture in which a solute is spread evenly throughout the solvent.

A **saturated solution** contains the maximum concentration of solute dissolved in a solvent at a particular temperature.

**Aqueous** means dissolved in water.

*Distilled water* is used in practical chemistry because it does not contain dissolved substances which react with added solutes.

**Exam tip**

**Watch out**

Make sure that you include key words in definitions. For example, in defining a saturated solution, the words 'maximum' and 'at a particular temperature' are important.

**Worked example**

A student does some experiments using sodium chloride solution. The sodium chloride is dissolved in distilled water until no more salt can dissolve at a particular temperature.

State the name of the type of solution formed when no more solute can dissolve. [1]

saturated solution. ✓

Suggest why distilled water is used instead of tap water. [1]

Substances present in tap water may interfere with the experiments. ✓

Give the chemical name for the solution formed when sodium chloride dissolves in water. [1]

aqueous sodium chloride. ✓

**Concentration** is mass (in grams) or moles of substance divided by volume of solution (in dm³).

*Concentration is measured* in g/dm³ or mol/dm³ (for the meaning of mol see Chapter 6).

**Exam tip**

**Watch out**

Make sure that you are working with the correct units of volume (cm³ or dm³) when answering questions about concentration.

**Key skills**

You need to be able to convert dm³ (**decimetres cubed**) to cm³ (centimetres cubed) by multiplying volume in dm³ by 1000.

You need to be able to convert cm³ to dm³ by dividing volume in cm³ by 1000.

**Worked example**

Calculate the concentration of aqueous sodium chloride in g/dm$^3$ when 15 g of sodium chloride is dissolved to make 200 cm$^3$ of solution. [2]

$$200\ \text{cm}^3 = \frac{200}{1000} = 0.20\ \text{dm}^3\ ✓$$

$$\text{concentration} = \frac{\text{mass}}{\text{volume in dm}^3}$$

$$\text{concentration} = \frac{15}{0.2} = 75\ \text{g/dm}^3\ ✓$$

## Apply

5. Calculate the concentrations in g/dm$^3$ or mol/dm$^3$ of:
   a. 24 g sodium chloride in 200 cm$^3$ of solution
   b. 56 g sodium hydroxide in 400 cm$^3$ of solution
   c. 0.50 g magnesium nitrate in 4 dm$^3$ of solution
   d. 0.20 mol sodium chloride in 250 cm$^3$ of solution

An **anhydrous solid** does not contain water.

A **hydrated solid** contains water.

**Water of crystallisation** is the water chemically combined in the structure of a crystal.

*Anhydrous copper(II) sulfate* turns from white to blue when water is added.

*Anhydrous cobalt(II) chloride* turns from blue to pink when water is added.

**Worked example**

The equation shows the reaction of anhydrous copper(II) sulfate with water.

$$CuSO_4 + 5H_2O \rightleftharpoons CuSO_4{\cdot}5H_2O$$

State the meaning of the term anhydrous. [1]

A solid which does not contain water. ✓

State the colour change when water is added to anhydrous copper(II) sulfate. [2]

From white ✓ to blue. ✓

State the name given to the water present in the structure of $CuSO_4{\cdot}5H_2O$. [1]

Water of crystallisation. ✓

**Recap**

- Hydrated crystals contain water of crystallisation.
- Solids without water of crystallisation are anhydrous.

**Recap**

$$\text{concentration (in g/dm}^3) = \frac{\text{mass (in g)}}{\text{volume (in dm}^3)}$$

**Exam tip**

The equation triangle may help you rearrange the equation for concentration. Cover the quantity you want to find. You will then see the form of equation to use.

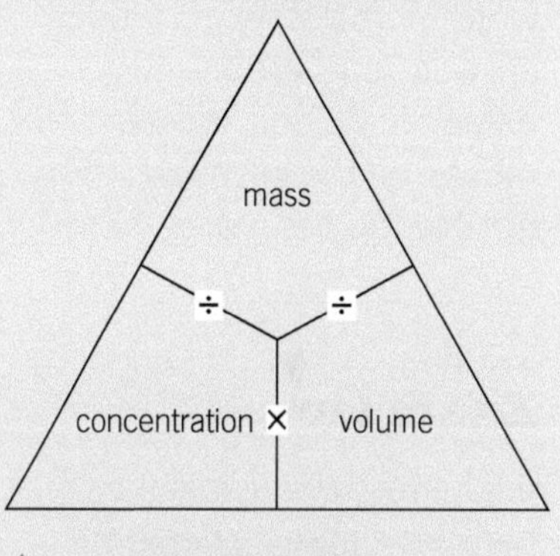


▲ Equation triangle

**Exam tip**

When making up solutions accurately, you dissolve the solid in a small amount of solvent then make it up to the volume required. You do not add the solid to the volume of solvent required.

**Key skills**

You need to be able to rearrange equations. For example, rearrange $\text{concentration} = \frac{\text{mass}}{\text{volume}}$ to make mass the subject:
mass = concentration × volume

You need to memorise the colour changes of particular reactions stated in the syllabus.

# 1.5 Diffusion

You need to:

- Describe and explain diffusion using the kinetic particle theory.
- **Describe and explain the effect of molecular mass on the rate of diffusion in gases.**

### Exam tip

**Watch out**

Make sure that you include the word, 'particles', when writing answers to questions about diffusion. Writing 'the gas moves' or 'the ink moves' will not get you the marks.

### Exam tip

It is better to write that the particles diffuse by random movement or random collisions rather than they '*move from a higher to a lower concentration*'. The words in italics suggest that movement only takes place in one direction rather than in all directions.

### Recap

Diffusion is the spreading out and mixing of different particles because of their random movement.

**Diffusion** is the spreading out and mixing of different particles because of their random movement.

### Worked example

A gas jar contains a blue liquid which easily turns into a gas at room temperature. After 1 hour, the blue colour of the gas has spread throughout the gas jar. Explain this using the kinetic particle theory. [3]

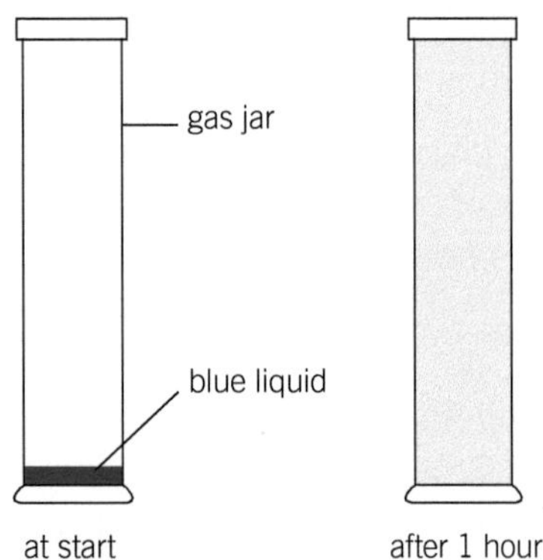


The particles of gas have moved ✓ randomly ✓ by diffusion ✓ so they have spread throughout the jar.

## Apply

6. Explain using the kinetic particle theory why it takes time for a smelly gas 20 m distant from you to reach your nose by diffusion.

The rate of diffusion is faster the lower the relative molecular mass of a substance. 

### Worked example

A dish containing a substance, **A**, that has a strong smell is placed at the front of a classroom. A student at the back of the room does not smell substance **A** at first. After 10 seconds the student can smell substance **A**. The experiment is repeated using a different substance **B** which has twice the relative molecular mass of **A** and a similar smell. Suggest how long it takes for the student to smell substance **B**. Explain your answer. [2]

**B** takes 15–20 seconds – it will be more than 10 seconds. ✓ Because the higher the molecular mass, the lower the rate of diffusion. ✓

## Questions

1. Describe the motion and separation of the particles in liquid bromine and bromine gas. [4]
2. Draw a sketch graph to show the effect of increasing pressure on the volume of gas in a syringe at constant temperature. [2]
3. State the names of these changes of physical state.
   a. solid to liquid
   b. gas to liquid
   c. liquid to gas below the boiling point [3]
4. Iodine melts at 114 °C and boils at 184 °C. Deduce the physical state of iodine at 100 °C. Give a reason for your answer. [2]
5. The equation shows the reaction of anhydrous cobalt(II) chloride with water.

$$CoCl_2 + 6H_2O \rightleftharpoons CoCl_2{\cdot}6H_2O$$

   a. State the meaning of the term anhydrous. [1]
   b. State the colour change in this reaction. [2]
   c. Give the chemical name of $CoCl_2{\cdot}6H_2O$. [1]
6. Choose words from the list to complete the following sentence.

   amount maximum minimum solute solution solvent volume water

   A saturated solution contains the .................... concentration of .................... dissolved in a .................... at a particular temperature. [3]
7. Calculate:
   a. The concentration, in g/dm$^3$, of 4 dm$^3$ of a solution containing 20 g of solid. [1]
   b. The concentration, in mol/dm$^3$, of 50 cm$^3$ of solution containing 2 mol of solid. [2]
   c. The mass of solid in 0.20 dm$^3$ of a solution of concentration 30 g/dm$^3$. [2]
   d. The volume of a solution, in cm$^3$, of concentration 12.5 g/dm$^3$ that contains 0.50 g of solute. [3]
8. Explain in terms of the kinetic particle theory why a drop of ink placed in water gradually spreads throughout the water. [3]

S

9. Use the kinetic particle theory to explain why the volume of gas in a syringe increases as the temperature increases. [3]
10. Part of a heating curve for water is shown.

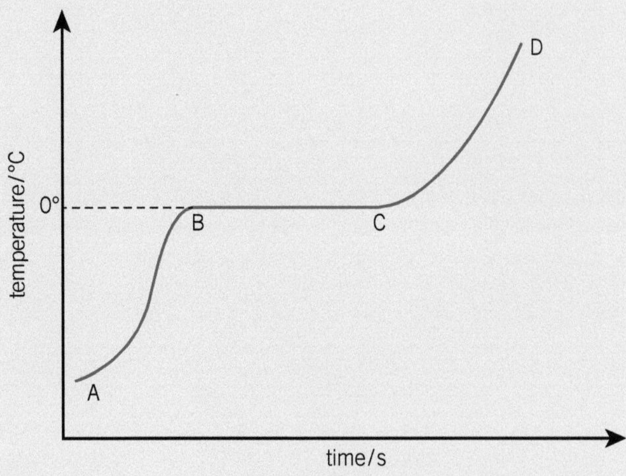

a. State which part of the curve shows ice being heated. Give a reason for your answer. [2]

b. Explain the shape of this curve in terms of kinetic particle theory. [4]

11. The rate of diffusion of two gases methane, $CH_4$, and ethane, $C_2H_6$ are compared. State and explain which of these gases diffuses faster. [2]

## Sample question

This question is about solids, liquids, gases and solutions.

1. a. Define the term solute. [1]

b. Iodine is soluble in hexane.

(i) State the meaning of the term soluble. [1]

(ii) Calculate the concentration of iodine in 150 $cm^3$ of a solution of iodine in hexane which contains 1.2 g of iodine. Give your answer in $g/dm^3$. [1]

(iii) A crystal of iodine is dropped into a beaker of hexane. After an hour the colour of the iodine has spread throughout the hexane. Explain this using the kinetic particle theory. [3]

c. Bromine melts at −7 °C and boils at 59 °C.

(i) Deduce the physical state of bromine at −15 °C. Give a reason for your answer. [2]

(ii) State the name of the change of state when liquid bromine changes to bromine gas. [1]

(iii) Describe the arrangement and motion of the particles in bromine gas. [2]

(iv) State two characteristics of a gas. [2]

S d. Hydrogen chloride (relative molecular mass 36.5) and hydrogen bromide (relative molecular mass 81) are both gases.

(i) Which of these compounds diffuses faster at the same temperature? Explain your answer using the kinetic particle theory. [2]

(ii) Describe and explain what happens when the volume of a sample of hydrogen chloride in a gas syringe is decreased at constant temperature. [3]

# Separating substances

## Revision checklist

Tick these boxes to build a record of your revision . Columns 2 and 3 can be used if you want to make a record more than once.

| Core/**Supplement** syllabus content | | 1 | 2 | 3 |
|---|---|---|---|---|
| 2.1 | Name suitable apparatus for measurement of time, temperature, mass and volume. | | | |
| 2.2 | Describe how paper chromatography separates soluble coloured substances using a suitable solvent. | | | |
| 2.2 | Interpret chromatograms to identify unknown substances and pure and impure substances. | | | |
| 2.2 | **Describe the use of locating agents to identify colourless substances after chromatography.** | | | |
| 2.2 | **State and use the equation** $R_f = \dfrac{\textbf{distance travelled by substance}}{\textbf{distance travelled by solvent}}$. | | | |
| 2.3 | Identify substances and assess their purity using melting point and boiling point data. | | | |
| 2.3 | Interpret chromatograms to identify unknown substances and pure and impure substances. | | | |
| 2.3 | Suggest separation and purification techniques given suitable information. | | | |
| 2.4 | Describe and explain methods of purification by filtration and crystallisation. | | | |
| 2.4 | Describe and explain methods of purification by the use of a suitable solvent. | | | |
| 2.4 | Define the terms filtrate and residue. | | | |
| 2.5 | Describe and explain methods of purification by simple distillation and fractional distillation. | | | |
| 2.5 | Suggest separation and purification techniques given suitable information. | | | |

# 2.1 Apparatus for measuring

**You need to:**

- Name suitable apparatus for measurement of time, temperature, mass and volume.

### Exam tip

When selecting apparatus for measuring volumes of liquids, think about the accuracy required. A burette or volumetric pipette is far more accurate than a measuring cylinder.

### Exam tip

**Watch out**

Take care not to use the word 'pipette' when selecting apparatus for measuring a volume of liquid accurately. 'Pipette' could refer to a dropping pipette. The correct term is volumetric pipette.

### Key skills

You need to be able to read time and values from diagrams of stopwatches, thermometers and burette scales.

### Recap

- Burettes and volumetric pipettes are used for measuring volumes of liquids accurately.
- 1 dm$^3$ = 1000 cm$^3$
- A gas syringe or inverted (upside-down) measuring cylinder full of water are used for measuring volumes of gases.

A **burette** or a **volumetric pipette** are used for measuring volumes of liquids accurately.

A **measuring cylinder** or **gas syringe** can be used to measure the volumes of gases.

*Volumes can be measured* in cm$^3$ or dm$^3$ (1 dm$^3$ = 1000 cm$^3$).

A *stopwatch or stopclock* is used to measure time.

A *thermometer* is used to measure temperature.

A *(top-pan) balance* is used to measure mass.

### Worked example

Choose from the list the piece of apparatus that is best used for measuring out 23.4 cm$^3$ of liquid. Give a reason for your answer. [2]

beaker    burette    gas syringe    gas jar    measuring cylinder

burette ✓ because it has accurate graduations / the volume 23.4 cm$^3$ is accurate to one decimal place ✓

Describe how to collect a gas using a measuring cylinder and a large beaker of water. [3]

Fill the measuring cylinder with water. ✓

Turn it upside down in the beaker of water. ✓

Put the end of a delivery tube below the upside-down measuring cylinder. ✓

## Apply

1. State the name of the apparatus used to:
   a. measure approximately 50 cm$^3$ of water into a beaker
   b. run 40.45 cm$^3$ of a liquid into a flask
   c. check the temperature of a solution
   d. measure the volume of a gas without using a measuring cylinder
   e. weigh 3.52 g of sodium chloride

# 2.2 Paper chromatography

**You need to:**

- Describe how paper chromatography separates soluble coloured substances using a suitable solvent; interpret chromatograms to identify unknown substances and pure and impure substances.
- **Describe the use of locating agents to identify colourless substances after chromatography; state and use the equation** $R_f = \frac{\text{distance travelled by substance}}{\text{distance travelled by solvent}}$.

**Chromatography** uses a beaker, chromatography paper and a solvent to separate a mixture of coloured compounds.

A **chromatogram** shows the separated compounds as separate spots.

Chromatography can be used to identify compounds by comparing the distance moved with known samples.

**Worked example**

The diagram shows the apparatus used to carry out chromatography. Give the correct names for **A–D**. [4]

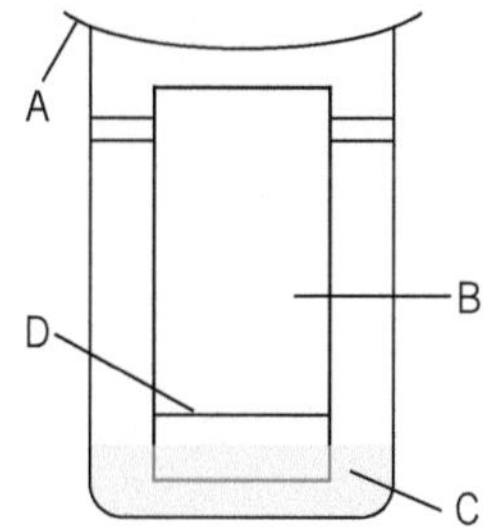


**A** = watchglass / cover ✓

**B** = filter paper / chromatography paper ✓

**C** = solvent ✓

**D** = baseline / origin line ✓

Describe how chromatography of a drop of a mixture of dyes (coloured substances) is performed to identify a particular dye in the mixture. You have access to pure dyes which may be in the mixture. [5]

A spot of the mixture is placed on the baseline. ✓

Spots of known pure dyes are put on the baseline. ✓

The chromatography paper is dipped into the solvent so the solvent level is below the spots / baseline. ✓

Let the solvent run up the paper. ✓

Then compare the level of the spots in the mixture with the level of the pure dyes. ✓

**Exam tip**

**Watch out**

When drawing chromatography apparatus, make sure that the baseline where the spot of mixture is placed is drawn above the solvent level. If it is below the solvent level, the spot of mixture will dissolve in the solvent.

**Exam tip**

When drawing chromatography apparatus, remember to draw the filter paper with the bottom dipping into the solvent. Don't forget to label these as well as the position of the spot on the baseline.

## Apply

2. a. State the terms used in chromatography for:
   (i) the liquid in which the coloured substance dissolves
   (ii) the line drawn in pencil on which the coloured spot is placed
   (iii) the line of the solvent as it moves up the paper

### Recap

- Paper chromatography is used to separate and identify a mixture of coloured substances.
- The coloured substances are separated when the solvent moves up the chromatography paper.
- Locating agents are used to react with colourless compounds and make them visible. 
- $R_f = \frac{\text{distance travelled by substance}}{\text{distance travelled by solvent}}$

b. The diagram shows a chromatogram.

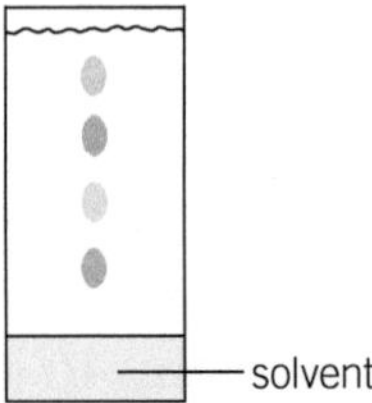


(i) How many different substances have been separated?

(ii) Mark with an **X** the place where the spot should be placed at the start of the chromatography.

### Exam tip

You do not need to know the names of specific locating agents.

S **Locating agents** are used following chromatography to show the position of compounds which are colourless.

The ***R*$_f$ value** is the distance travelled by a substance during chromatography divided by the distance travelled by the solvent.

### Worked example

Which of the following substances require the use of a locating agent after undergoing chromatography? Give a reason for your answer. [2]

a dye copper(II) sulfate green colouring from leaves sugar solution

Sugar solution ✓

because it is the only one without a colour – all the others are coloured. ✓

After chromatography, the distance of a substance **X** from the baseline is 2.6 cm. The **solvent front** is 4.0 cm from the baseline. Deduce the $R_f$ value of **X**. [1]

$\frac{2.6}{4.0} = 0.65$ ✓

# 2.3 Is that chemical pure?

**You need to:**

- Identify substances and assess their purity using melting point and boiling point data.
- Interpret chromatograms to identify unknown substances and pure and impure substances.
- Suggest separation and purification techniques given suitable information.

A **pure** substance has a sharp melting point and boiling point.

**Impurities** in a compound lower its melting point and raise its boiling point.

An **impure compound** may show more than one spot on a chromatogram.

**Worked example**

Substance **Z** has a melting point between 117 °C and 121 °C.

Suggest whether **Z** is pure or impure. Give a reason for your answer. [1]

Impure because the melting point is a range and not a definite value. ✓

State two other ways of determining whether a substance is pure or impure. [2]

The boiling point is increased if the substance is impure. ✓

An impure substance shows several spots on a chromatogram. ✓

**Exam tip**

Remember that there are three ways of telling whether a substance is impure: melting or boiling points are not sharp; there is an increase in boiling point or decrease in melting point; there is more than one spot on a chromatogram.

**Recap**

- Impurities lower the melting point and raise the boiling point of a compound.
- A pure compound has a sharp melting point and boiling point and gives only a single spot when chromatographed.

## Apply

3. State two effects of impurities on:
   a. the boiling point of a compound
   b. the melting point of a compound

# 2.4 Separation and purification

**You need to:**

- **Describe and explain methods of purification by filtration and crystallisation.**
- **Describe and explain methods of purification by the use of a suitable solvent.**
- **Define the terms filtrate and residue.**

**Filtration** is used to separate a solid from a liquid.

A **filtrate** is the liquid or solution that has passed through a filter.

A **residue** is the solid which remains after filtration, evaporation or **distillation**.

**Crystallisation** involves heating to evaporate water from the solution until the solution is saturated. The saturated solution is then allowed to cool and deposit crystals.

### Exam tip

You are expected to be able to define the terms filtration, filtrate, residue and crystallisation and use these when discussing how to separate mixtures of substances.

### Worked example

Sulfur is a solid which is insoluble in water. Suggest how to separate the sulfur and water from a mixture of sulfur and water. In your answer use the words filtrate and residue. [3]

Filter the mixture. ✓ The sulfur is the residue ✓ which remains on the filter paper. The water is the filtrate ✓ because it goes through the filter paper.

### Exam tip

**Watch out**

When describing how to dry crystals do not write 'heat in an oven' or 'put in a desiccator'. If you do these the water of crystallisation will be removed.

### Worked example

Describe how to make pure dry crystals of copper(II) sulfate from a solution of copper(II) sulfate. [3]

Heat the solution to evaporate some of the water until the point of crystallisation ✓ is reached. Then let the solution cool and form crystals. Filter off the crystals ✓ and dry them between filter papers. ✓

*Solvent extraction* is used to separate two solids of different solubility by using different solvents.

### Recap

- Filtration separates the residue (solid) from the filtrate (solution passing through a filter).
- Crystallisation involves heating a solution until the solution is saturated (to the **crystallisation point**) and then cooling to form crystals.
- A mixture of two solids can be separated if one is soluble in a particular solvent and the other is not.

### Worked example

Hexane is a liquid that does not mix with water. Solid X is soluble in hexane but slightly soluble in water. Salt is soluble in water but insoluble in hexane. Suggest how to prepare pure solid X from a solution of X and salt using hexane. Give a reason why the method you chose works. [4]

Shake the solution with hexane. ✓

Separate the solution of X in hexane from the aqueous solution using a separating funnel. ✓

Evaporate the hexane from the solution of X. ✓

Reason: solid X will dissolve in the hexane but the salt will not. ✓

## Apply

4. Link the terms **A** to **E** with the definitions **1** to **5**.

| | |
|---|---|
| **A** filtrate | **1.** The separation of a solid from a solution |
| **B** residue | **2.** The separation of a substance from aqueous solution by shaking with an immiscible solvent |
| **C** crystallisation | **3.** The solid left on a filter paper after filtration |
| **D** filtration | **4.** The liquid which passes through a filter |
| **E** solvent extraction | **5.** An example is the formation of hydrated copper(II) sulfate from a solution of copper(II) sulfate |

# 2.5 More about separation and purification

**You need to:**

- Describe and explain methods of purification by simple distillation and fractional distillation.
- Suggest separation and purification techniques given suitable information.

**Simple distillation** is used to separate a solvent from dissolved solids or to separate liquids of greatly different boiling points.

**Fractional distillation** is used to separate a mixture of liquids with boiling points which are close to each other.

**Worked example**

Fractional distillation is used to separate a mixture of liquids by using the difference in their boiling points to separate them. Describe and explain how the apparatus shown can be used to obtain a sample of each of the liquids present in a mixture of two liquids. [5]

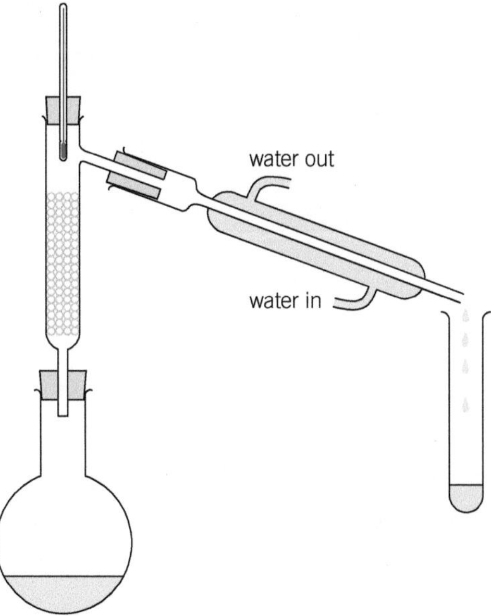


When the flask is heated, ✓ the liquid with the lower boiling point turns to a vapour first. ✓ It moves up the column faster. ✓ When it reaches the **condenser**, it condenses ✓ and is collected in a test tube. The second liquid condenses later ✓ and is then collected in another test tube.

One or more of the processes of *filtration*, *crystallisation* or *distillation* can be used to separate substances.

**Purification of mixtures** often involves a combination of filtration, evaporation and distillation.

### Exam tip

Remember:

- Distillation involves boiling then condensation.
- Substances with a lower boiling point distil off first.

### Exam tip

If you want to separate a mixture of liquids the method is 'fractional distillation'. Remember to include the essential word 'fractional'. Just 'distillation' on its own is not enough.

### Key skills

You need to be able to select the correct method of separating and purifying a mixture given information. When doing this you need to know the physical state of the substances to be separated and their **solubilities**.

**Recap**

- Simple distillation is used to separate two substances which have a very large difference in their boiling points.
- Fractional distillation is used to separate a mixture of substances (generally liquids) which have boiling points which are quite close to each other. For example, 45 °C, 54 °C, 60 °C.
- Mixtures can be purified and separated using one or more of chromatography, filtration, evaporation, distillation or solvent extraction.

**Worked example**

Sand is **insoluble** in water. Cobalt(II) chloride crystals are soluble in water. Suggest how you can separate a mixture of sand and cobalt(II) chloride crystals, to obtain a pure sample of both sand and cobalt(II) chloride crystals. [6]

Add water and stir until all the cobalt chloride is dissolved. ✓ Filter off the sand ✓ and wash it with water. ✓ Take the filtrate of cobalt chloride solution and evaporate to the point of crystallisation. ✓ Then allow the saturated solution to crystallise by leaving it at room temperature. ✓ Once crystals are formed filter them off. ✓

## Apply

5. Suggest methods for separating these mixtures:
   a. separating a mixture of two liquids with different boiling points
   b. getting salt from a solution of salt in water
   c. getting both salt and water from a solution of salt in water
   d. extracting bromine from a solution of bromine in water without using distillation
   e. separating a mixture of small solid particles and water

## Questions

**1. a.** State the method used to separate:

**(i)** copper(II) sulfate crystals from aqueous copper(II) sulfate [1]

**(ii)** a mixture of sand and water [1]

**(iii)** a mixture of two liquids which have boiling points of 60 °C and 68 °C [1]

**2. a.** Explain how simple distillation separates sodium chloride (salt) from a solution of sodium chloride in water. [4]

**b. (i)** Name a physical property that can be used to check that the sodium chloride is pure. [1]

**(ii)** Describe how you can use the value of this physical property to determine whether the sodium chloride is pure. [1]

**3.** A student uses chromatography to separate a mixture of coloured substances.

**a.** Draw and label a diagram of the apparatus the student should use. On your diagram include the solvent and an **X** to show where the spot of mixture should be placed. [4]

**b.** Explain why the baseline on the chromatogram must not be drawn in ink. [1]

S **c.** A student wants to identify a colourless amino acid after chromatography has been carried out. Describe exactly how the student can do this. [5]

## Sample question

This question is about separating substances.

1. **a.** State the meaning of the terms:

   **(i)** residue [1]

   **(ii)** filtrate [1]

   **b.** Iodine is a solid which is soluble in solvent **G**. Zinc is a solid which is insoluble in solvent **G**. Solvent **G** has a boiling point below that of iodine. Suggest how to separate a mixture of solid zinc and solid iodine to produce separate samples of solid iodine and solid zinc. [4]

   **c.** A student wants to separate a mixture of two liquids.

   **(i)** State the method used to separate the liquids. [2]

   **(ii)** Name the physical property on which this separation method depends. [1]

   **d.** A student wants to separate the different coloured compounds present in a plant leaf.

   **(i)** Suggest how the student can obtain a solution of the coloured compounds. [3]

   **(ii)** Name the process used to separate coloured compounds. [1]

   **S e.** The results from part **(d)** are shown.

   **(i)** Why is it difficult to determine exactly how many coloured substances were separated? [1]

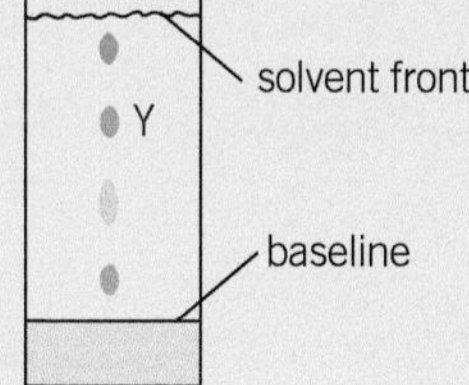


   **(ii)** Calculate the $R_f$ value of substance **Y**. [1]

# Atoms, elements and compounds

## Revision checklist

Tick these boxes to build a record of your revision. Columns 2 and 3 can be used if you want to make a record more than once.

| Core/**Supplement** syllabus content | | 1 | 2 | 3 |
|---|---|---|---|---|
| 3.1 | Describe the structure of the atom. | | | |
| 3.1 | State the relative charges and relative masses of a proton, neutron and electron. | | | |
| 3.1 | Define proton number (atomic number). | | | |
| 3.1 | Describe the Periodic Table as an arrangement of elements in order of increasing proton number. | | | |
| 3.2 | Define mass number, nucleon number and isotopes. | | | |
| 3.2 | **Know that isotopes have the same chemical properties because they have the same electronic configuration.** | | | |
| 3.2 | **Know how to calculate the accurate relative atomic mass from the abundances of the isotopes.** | | | |
| 3.3 | Describe the electronic configuration (electronic structure) of the first 20 elements in the Periodic Table. | | | |
| 3.3 | State that the number of outer shell electrons is equal to the group number in Groups I to VII. | | | |
| 3.3 | State that the number of occupied electron shells is equal to the period number. | | | |
| 3.3 | Explain why the noble gases are unreactive by reference to their stable outer shell of electrons. | | | |
| 3.4 | Describe the differences between elements, compounds and mixtures. | | | |
| 3.5 | Describe the general physical properties of metals and non-metals. | | | |
| 3.5 | Describe the general chemical properties of metals and non-metals. | | | |

# 3.1 Inside the atom

**You need to:**

- Describe the structure of the atom.
- State the relative charges and relative masses of a proton, neutron and electron; define proton number (atomic number).
- Describe the Periodic Table as an arrangement of elements in order of increasing proton number.

## Inside the atom

An **atom** is the smallest uncharged particle that can undergo a **chemical change**.

The **nucleus** of an atom contains protons and neutrons.

**Protons** have a positive charge and a **relative mass** of 1.

**Neutrons** are uncharged and have a relative mass of 1.

**Electrons** are found outside the nucleus in electron shells (energy levels).

Electrons have a negative charge and have a relative mass of $\frac{1}{1836}$ $\left(\text{roughly } \frac{1}{2000}\right)$.

### Worked example

Complete the table to show the relative mass and relative charge of a proton, neutron and electron. [6]

| | Proton | Neutron | Electron |
|---|---|---|---|
| Relative mass | 1 ✓ | 1 ✓ | about $\frac{1}{2000}$ ✓ |
| Relative charge | +1 ✓ | 0 ✓ | −1 ✓ |

*Atoms are uncharged* because the number of protons = the number of electrons.

**Proton number (atomic number)** is the number of protons in the nucleus of an atom.

The **Periodic Table** is an arrangement of elements in order of increasing proton number.

### Worked example

An atom has 26 protons. State the number of electrons in this atom. [1]

26 ✓

Where in an atom are the protons found? [1]

In the nucleus. ✓

Describe how proton number changes from element to element in the Periodic Table. [1]

Across the Table from one element to the next, it increases by one proton. ✓

### Exam tip

**Watch out**

- When writing the relative charge, make sure that you include the + or – sign.
- It is a common error to write '–' for the charge on the neutron. It can be interpreted as a negative sign.

### Exam tip

Remember that you can use the Periodic Table to find the number of protons in an atom.

### Recap

The nucleus of an atom contains positively charged protons (relative mass 1) and uncharged neutrons (relative mass 1). Outside the nucleus are the negatively charged electrons in shells.

## Apply

1. Name the parts of an atom with the following descriptions:
   a. the centre of the atom that contains only neutrons and protons
   b. a particle that is about two thousand times lighter in mass than a proton
   c. a particle in an atom that has a negative charge
   d. a particle that increases in number by one as you go across a period in the Periodic Table
   e. a particle in an atom which does not have a charge

# 3.2 Isotopes

**You need to:**

- Define mass number, nucleon number and isotopes.
- **Know that isotopes have the same chemical properties because they have the same electronic configuration.**
- **Be able to calculate the accurate relative atomic mass from the abundances of the isotopes.**

### Exam tip

You will always be given the mass number of an atom in a question. Note that the Periodic Table does *not* show mass numbers. The larger number is the relative atomic mass.

### Key skills

You should be able to interpret symbols such as $^{12}_{6}C$.

### Exam tip

Remember that in atom symbols such as $^{12}_{6}C$ the number at the top is the mass number (number of protons + neutrons) and the number at the bottom is the number of protons.

**Mass number** is the number of protons + neutrons in the nucleus. *Symbols such as* $^{12}_{6}C$ give information about the number of protons, neutrons and electrons in an atom.

### Worked example

Complete the table to show the number of protons, neutrons and electrons in the atoms shown. [9]

| Atom | Protons | Neutrons | Electrons |
|---|---|---|---|
| $^{37}_{17}Cl$ | 17 ✓ | 20 ✓ | 17 ✓ |
| $^{192}_{76}Os$ | 76 ✓ | 116 ✓ | 76 ✓ |
| $^{15}_{7}N$ | 7 ✓ | 8 ✓ | 7 ✓ |

### Recap

Number of neutrons = mass number − proton number.

## Apply

2. a. Deduce the number of protons, neutrons and electrons in each of these atoms.
   (i) $^{19}_{9}F$ (ii) $^{60}_{28}Ni$ (iii) $^{226}_{88}Ra$
   b. Deduce the number of protons, neutrons and electrons in each of these ions. Note that if the ion is positive it has lost one or more electrons and if it is negative it has gained one or more electrons.
   (i) $^{134}_{56}Ba^{2+}$ (ii) $^{41}_{19}K^{+}$ (iii) $^{32}_{16}S^{2-}$

**Isotopes** are atoms with the same number of protons but different numbers of neutrons. 

*Isotopes have the same chemical properties* because they have the same electronic configuration.

### Worked example

State which of the following two pairs are isotopes. Explain why. [2]

$^{37}_{17}Cl$  $^{32}_{16}S$  $^{40}_{19}K$  $^{134}_{56}Ba$  $^{40}_{22}Ca$  $^{32}_{15}P$  $^{136}_{56}Ba$  $^{35}_{17}Cl$

$^{37}_{17}Cl$ and $^{35}_{17}Cl$ and $^{134}_{56}Ba$ and $^{136}_{56}Ba$ ✓ because they have the same number of protons but different numbers of neutrons ✓

Explain why isotopes have the same chemical properties. [1]

They have exactly the same electronic structure ✓

*Accurate* **relative atomic masses** are found by using the mass and **percentage abundance** of each isotope.

### Worked example

The element europium has two isotopes, $^{151}_{63}Eu$ (abundance = 47.8%) and $^{153}_{63}Eu$ (abundance 52.2%). Calculate the relative atomic mass of europium to one decimal place. [2]

$(151 \times 47.8) + (153 \times 52.2) = 15204.4$ ✓

$\frac{15204.4}{100} = 152.0$ ✓

### Exam tip

When defining isotopes, the word 'atoms' is essential. Writing 'elements' instead of atoms is incorrect.

### Key skills

You have to be able to work out a weighted average in the calculation of accurate relative atomic mass.

### Exam tip

**Watch out**

In the Periodic Table, it is the top number above each element symbol that is the proton number *but* in writing symbols showing the number of protons and mass number the proton number is the lower number.

### Key skills

You need to be able to recognise the meaning of the numbers and charges in symbols such as $^{37}_{17}Cl$.

# 3.3 Electronic structure and the Periodic Table

**You need to:**

- Describe the electronic configuration (electronic structure) of the first 20 elements in the Periodic Table.
- State that the number of outer shell electrons is equal to the group number in Groups I to VII.
- State that the number of occupied electron shells is equal to the period number.
- Explain why the noble gases are unreactive by reference to their stable outer shell of electrons.

**Recap**

- Group number is the same as the number of electrons in the outer shell of an atom.
- Period number is the same as the number of electron shells which contain electrons.
- The first electron shell has a maximum of two electrons. The second shell has a maximum of eight electrons.

**Key skills**

You have to be able to work out patterns of numbers of electrons in each shell.

**Exam tip**

Make sure that you can draw the electronic configuration (in rings) of the first 20 elements in the Periodic Table as well as writing them in the form 2,8,8,2.

**Electronic configuration** is the arrangement of the electrons in shells.

The *maximum number of electrons* in the first shell is two. For elements up to calcium, the second and third shells have a maximum of eight electrons.

The *number of outer shell electrons* is the same as the group number in Groups I to VII.

The *number of occupied* **electron shells** is the same as the **period** number.

**Worked example**

Deduce the electronic configuration of these atoms. The proton numbers are given in brackets.

chlorine (17) [1]

2,8,7 ✓

lithium (3) [1]

2,1 ✓

State the group number and period number of chlorine. [2]

Group VII ✓ Period 3 ✓

State the name of the element which has the electronic configuration 2,8,8,2. [1]

calcium ✓

The **chemical properties** of an element depends on their electronic configuration, especially the number of outer shell electrons.

**Noble gases** *are unreactive* because they have a full outer shell of electrons which is a stable electronic configuration.

**Worked example**

State which of these electronic configurations is that of a noble gas. Explain your answer.

2   2,2   2,6   2,8,4   2,8,8   2,8,8,2   [3]

2 and 2,8,8 ✓ because they both have a full outer shell of electrons ✓ which is a stable electronic configuration ✓

**Recap**

Two electrons in the first shell or eight electrons in the second or third shells is a stable electronic configuration.

## Apply

3. a. Deduce the electronic configurations of these atoms. Use the Periodic Table to help you.

   (i) argon   (ii) boron   (iii) helium   (iv) aluminium   (v) calcium

   b. State which of the elements in part (a) are in the same group of the Periodic Table.

   c. State which of the elements in part (a) have complete outer electron shells.

   d. State which elements in part (a) are in the same period of the Periodic Table.

# 3.4 Elements, compounds and mixtures

**You need to:**

- Describe the differences between elements, compounds and mixtures.

An **element** is a substance that contains only one type of atom. All the atoms have the same proton number.

A **compound** is a substance that contains two or more different types of atom bonded (joined) together.

**Mixtures** contain two or more different substances which are not bonded together.

The *substances in a mixture* can be present in any proportion.

The substances in *a mixture can be separated* by physical means, e.g. distillation.

**Key skills**

You need to be able to recognise the important words in definitions of chemical terms used in the syllabus.

**Worked example**

State whether the diagrams **A** to **D** show elements, compounds or mixtures. In each case explain you answers. The different shadings show different types of atom. [6]

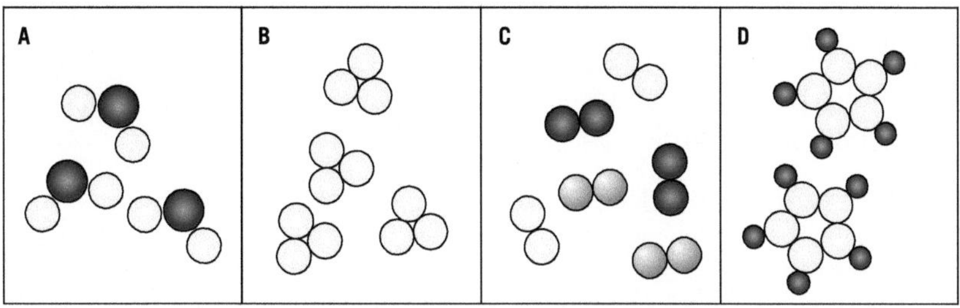

### Exam tip

- Make sure that you learn the definitions of elements, compounds and mixtures in detail.
- For example, remember that there are two parts to the definition of a compound: (1) different types of atoms (2) bonded together.

**A** and **D** are compounds ✓ because in each molecule two different types of atom are bonded together. ✓

**B** is an element ✓ because it's made up of only one type of atom. ✓

**C** is a mixture of elements ✓ because there are three different types of substances (molecules) present. ✓

### Exam tip

**Watch out**

When writing the definition of a compound make sure that you don't use the word 'mixture'. It is a common error to suggest that 'a mixture of different atoms is bonded together'.

### Recap

- Elements only have one type of atom.
- Compounds have two or more types of atom bonded together.
- Elements and compounds can form mixtures. The substances in a mixture are not bonded together.

## Apply

4. State whether the descriptions below refer to elements, compounds or mixtures.
   a. There can be different amounts of iron and chromium in an alloy of iron.
   b. The formula for hexane is always $C_6H_{14}$.
   c. The atoms in the sample have the same number of protons.
   d. Oxygen can be separated from nitrogen by fractional distillation.
   e. The carbon and oxygen in carbon dioxide are always present in the ratio of one carbon atom to two oxygen atoms.

# 3.5 Metals and non-metals

**You need to:**

- Describe the general physical properties of metals and non-metals.
- Describe the general chemical properties of metals and non-metals.

**Physical properties** are properties such as melting point and density which do not depend on chemical reactions.

*All metals* are good electrical and thermal **conductors** and are malleable (can be hammered into different shapes), ductile (can be drawn into wires) and lustrous (shiny).

*Most metals* are hard, have a high density and have high melting points but Group I metals are soft and have low densities.

**Density** is mass (in grams) divided by volume (in $cm^3$).

*All non-metals* are poor electrical and thermal conductors, are not malleable or ductile and are generally not shiny.

**Graphite** *is a non-metal* which conducts electricity.

**Worked example**

The list shows some physical properties. State which of these properties are characteristic of all metals.

good electrical conductor    hard    high density

high boiling point    malleable    [2]

good electrical conductor ✓ and malleable ✓

Calculate the density of 6.00 $cm^3$ of red phosphorus which has a mass of 14.04 g. Give you answer to two decimal places. Include the units. [2]

$\frac{14.04}{6.00}$ = 2.34 ✓ $g/cm^3$ ✓

*Metal oxides and most metals* react with acids.

*Most non-metals* do not react with acids.

*Most non-metal oxides* react with alkalis.

**Worked example**

An acid does not react with element **G**, but does react with the oxide of **G**. Suggest whether **G** is a metal or non-metal. Give a reason for your answer. [1]

It is a metal because not all metals react with acids but all metal oxides react with acids. ✓

## Apply

5. a. State which of these physical properties describe metals and which describe non-metals.
   - (i) poor electrical conductor
   - (ii) breaks apart when hit
   - (iii) can be drawn into wires
   - (iv) good thermal conductor
   - (v) have a dull surface
   - (vi) can be bent and moulded without breaking

   b. Name a non-metal which conducts electricity.

   c. Calculate the density of a cube of a solid which has a mass of 52 g. Each side of the cube is 2 cm.

### Exam tip

**Watch out**

Take care not to confuse physical and chemical properties. Make sure you choose the right type of property when answering questions. Chemical properties are about chemical reactions; physical properties are things such as ductility, boiling point and conductivity.

### Exam tip

When asked about the physical properties of metals choose conductivity, melting and boiling points, ductility, malleability or lustre because these apply to all metals.

**Recap**

- All metals are good electrical and thermal conductors, ductile, malleable and lustrous.
- Metal oxides and most metals react with acids.
- The properties of non-metals are usually the opposite of those of metals.

## Questions

1. **a.** State the relative charge and mass of a neutron. [2]
   **b.** Where are the electrons found in the atom? [2]
   **c.** Explain why atoms are uncharged. [2]
2. **a.** Define mass number. [1]
   **b.** An atom has 41 electrons and a mass number of 93.
   Deduce the number of neutrons and protons in this atom. [2]
   **c.** An ion is described by the symbol $^{127}_{53}I^{-}$.
   **(i)** State the number of electrons in this ion. [1]
   **(ii)** An atom in the same group of the Periodic Table has the electronic configuration 2,8,7.
   State the group number and period number of this atom. Explain your answers. [4]
   **(iii)** Explain why the element having atoms with the electronic configuration 2,8 is unreactive. [1]
3. **a.** Define the term *compound.* [2]
   **b.** Explain two differences between a compound of iron and sulfur and a mixture of iron and sulfur. [2]
4. **a.** State three physical properties shown by all metals. [3]
   **b.** The oxide of element **D** reacts with an alkali but not with an acid. State what can be deduced about element **D** from this information. [1]
   **c.** Element **D** has a low density and is not ductile. State the meaning of the terms:
   **(i)** density [1]
   **(ii)** ductile [1]

## Sample question

This question is about magnesium and oxygen.

1. **a.** Deduce the electronic configuration of magnesium. [1]
   **b.** Oxygen is a non-metal. It forms an ion that can be written as $^{18}_{8}O^{2-}$.
   **(i)** Deduce the number of protons, neutrons and electrons in this ion. [3]
   **(ii)** Describe the position, relative charge and relative mass of the electrons in an oxygen atom. [4]
   **c.** Magnesium is a silvery solid. Oxygen is a colourless gas. They are both elements.
   **(i)** Define the term *element.* [1]
   **(ii)** Describe two differences between a compound of magnesium and oxygen and a mixture of magnesium and oxygen. [2]
   **(iii)** Suggest whether magnesium will react with acids or alkalis or both. Give a reason for your answer. [2]
   S **d.** **(i)** Define the term *isotopes.* [2]
   **(ii)** The element magnesium has three isotopes. The mass numbers and abundances are: Mg-24 = 78.60%, Mg-25 = 10.11% and Mg-26 = 11.29%
   Calculate the relative atomic mass of magnesium to two decimal places. Show your working. [3]

Raise your grade

# Structure and bonding

## Revision checklist

Tick these boxes to build a record of your revision. Columns 2 and 3 can be used if you want to make a record more than once.

| Core/**Supplement** syllabus content | | 1 | 2 | 3 |
|---|---|---|---|---|
| 4.1 | Describe the formation of positive ions by electron loss and negative ions by electron gain. | | | |
| 4.1 | Describe an ionic bond as an electrostatic force of attraction between oppositely charged ions. | | | |
| 4.1 | Describe the formation of ionic bonds between elements from Groups I and VII including the use of dot-and-cross diagrams. | | | |
| 4.1 | **Draw dot-and-cross diagrams for the formation of ions between other metallic and non-metallic elements.** | | | |
| 4.2 | Describe the formation of single covalent bonds as a pair of electrons shared between two atoms leading to a noble gas electron configuration. | | | |
| 4.2 | Describe the formation of single covalent bonds in $H_2$, $Cl_2$, $H_2O$, $CH_4$, $NH_3$ and HCl using dot-and-cross diagrams. | | | |
| 4.3 | **Describe the electronic configuration in covalent molecules including $N_2$, $O_2$, $C_2H_4$, $CH_3OH$ and $CO_2$.** | | | |
| 4.4 | Describe the properties of ionic compounds (high melting and boiling points and good electrical conductivity when aqueous or molten). | | | |
| 4.4 | Describe in terms of structure and bonding the properties of simple molecular compounds (low melting and boiling points and poor electrical conductivity). | | | |
| 4.4 | **Describe the giant lattice structure of ionic compounds.** | | | |
| 4.4 | **Explain in terms of structure and bonding the properties of ionic compounds.** | | | |
| 4.4 | **Explain in terms of structure and bonding the properties of simple molecular compounds.** | | | |
| 4.5 | Describe the giant covalent structures of graphite and diamond. | | | |
| 4.5 | Relate the structures of graphite and diamond to their uses. | | | |
| 4.5 | **Describe the giant covalent structure of silicon(IV) oxide.** | | | |
| 4.5 | **Describe the similarity in properties between diamond and silicon(IV) oxide, related to their structures.** | | | |
| 4.6 | **Describe metallic bonding as the electrostatic attraction between the positive ions in a metallic lattice and a 'sea' of delocalised electrons.** | | | |
| 4.6 | **Explain in terms of structure and bonding why metals are good electrical conductors and are malleable and ductile.** | | | |

# 4.1 Ionic bonding

**You need to:**

- Describe the formation of positive ions by electron loss and negative ions by electron gain.
- Describe an ionic bond as an electrostatic force of attraction between oppositely charged ions.
- Describe the formation of ionic bonds between elements from Groups I and VII including the use of dot-and-cross diagrams.
- **Draw dot-and-cross diagrams for the formation of ions between other metallic and non-metallic elements.**

**Ions** are positively or negatively charged particles formed when atoms or groups of atoms gain or lose electrons.

*Positive ions* are formed when atoms lose one or more electrons.

*Negative ions* are formed when atoms gain one or more electrons.

The *electronic configuration of ions* is that of the nearest noble gas.

### Exam tip

Remember how the ionic charge varies with the position of the element in the Periodic Table: Group I is +, Group II is 2+, Group III is 3+, Group V is 3−, Group VI is 2−, Group VII is −.

### Worked example

Complete these equations by showing the electrons on one or the other side of the equation. Use $e^-$ as a symbol for one electron and $2e^-$ as the symbol for two electrons.

$Ca \rightarrow Ca^{2+}$ [1]

$Ca \rightarrow Ca^{2+} + 2e^-$ ✓

$O \rightarrow O^{2-}$ [1]

$O + 2e^- \rightarrow O^{2-}$ ✓

$K \rightarrow K^+$ [1]

$K \rightarrow K^+ + e^-$ ✓

Complete these equations by writing the formula of the ion.

$Al \rightarrow$ ...... $+ 3e^-$ [1]

$Al \rightarrow Al^{3+} + 3e^-$ ✓

$Cl + e^- \rightarrow$ ...... [1]

$Cl + e^- \rightarrow Cl^-$ ✓

### Key skills

You need to be able to draw dot-and-cross diagrams clearly showing the origin of the electrons in each ion as dots or crosses.

### Exam tip

Remember that:

- You do not get stable ions with more than 3+ or 3− charges.
- The electron configuration of ions is that of the nearest noble gas.

**Dot-and-cross diagrams** show the electronic configuration for compounds using • for the electrons from one atom and × for the electrons from another atom.

An **ionic bond** is the electrostatic force of attraction between positive and negative ions.

**Worked example**

Write the electronic configuration of each of these atoms and ions in numbers.

aluminium atom and aluminium ion [2]

Atom is 2,8,3 ✓

Ion is 2,8 ✓

oxygen atom and oxide ion [2]

Atom is 2,6 ✓

Ion is 2,8 ✓

**Worked example**

Draw a dot-and-cross diagram for sodium oxide, $Na_2O$, to show both the sodium ions and the oxide ion. Show all the electrons. [4]

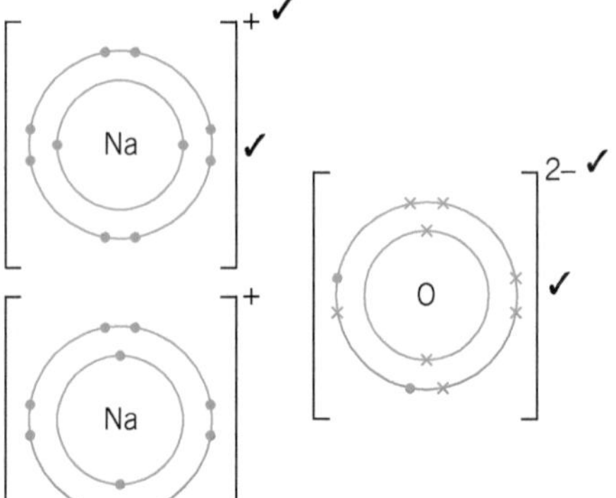


## Exam tip

When drawing the electronic configurations of ions, remember to put the charge at the top right of the ion just outside the square brackets. Take care not to put the charge in the middle of the ion.

**Recap**

- Positive ions are formed by loss of electrons and negative ions are formed by gain of electrons.
- Each ion in a simple ionic structure has the nearest noble gas configuration.

## Apply

1. a. Write the formula for:
   (i) a sulfide ion
   (ii) a calcium ion

   b. Draw a dot-and-cross diagram for the ionic compound magnesium fluoride, $MgF_2$, to show both the magnesium ion and the fluoride ions. Show all the electrons.

# 4.2 Covalent bonding (1): simple molecules

**You need to:**

- Describe the formation of single covalent bonds as a pair of electrons shared between two atoms leading to a noble gas electron configuration.
- Describe the formation of single covalent bonds in $H_2$, $Cl_2$, $H_2O$, $CH_4$, $NH_3$ and HCl using dot-and-cross diagrams.

### Exam tip

When drawing dot-and-cross diagrams, remember to pair up the electrons in the overlap area first. Take care not to put them outside this area.

### Exam tip

When drawing dot-and-cross diagrams, remember to pair up the electrons as dots and crosses in the bonds to show where each electron has come from.

### Recap

- A covalent bond is formed when two atoms share a pair of electrons.
- In dot-and-cross diagrams for many molecules, there are eight electrons around each atom, except for hydrogen atoms, where there are two electrons.

A *single* **covalent bond** is formed when atoms share a pair of electrons so that the outer electrons of each atom have the noble gas configuration.

The *symbol for a covalent bond* is a line drawn between two atoms, e.g. H–Br.

The *electronic configuration of a simple covalent* **molecule** can be shown using a dot-and-cross diagram.

### Worked example

Draw a dot-and-cross diagram for ammonia, $NH_3$. Show only the outer shell electrons. [2]

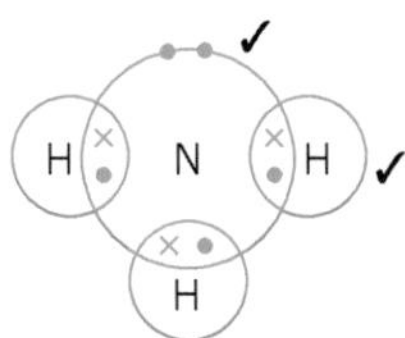


Three hydrogen atoms with paired electrons ✓

Eight electrons around the N atom ✓

## Apply

2. Draw dot-and-cross diagrams for these molecules. Show only the outer shell electrons.

   a. hydrogen, $H_2$

   b. hydrogen chloride, HCl

   c. methane, $CH_4$

Supplement

# 4.3 Covalent bonding (2): more complex molecules

**You need to:**

- **Describe the electronic configuration arrangement in covalent molecules including $N_2$, $O_2$, $C_2H_4$, $CH_3OH$ and $CO_2$.**

A *double covalent bond* is formed when two pairs of electrons are shared between two atoms.

A *triple covalent bond* is formed when three pairs of electrons are shared between two atoms.

The *symbol for a double covalent bond* is =, e.g. O=O.

The *symbol for a triple covalent bond* is ≡, e.g. N≡N.

**Worked example**

Draw a dot-and-cross diagram for ethene, $C_2H_4$. Show only the outer shell electrons. [2]

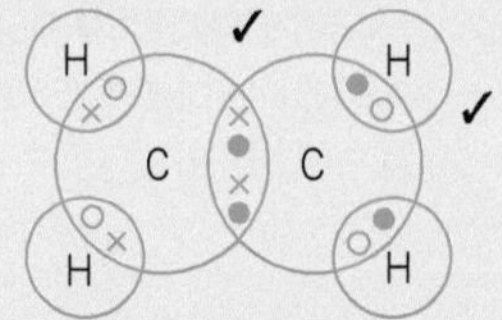


Two C atoms with two sets of paired electrons between them ✓
Two H atoms with paired electrons with each carbon atom ✓

## Apply

3. Draw dot-and-cross diagrams for these molecules. Show only the outer shell electrons.

   a. oxygen, $O_2$

   b. methanol, $CH_3OH$

   c. arsenic tribromide, $AsBr_3$ (As is in Group V)

### Exam tip

When drawing dot-and-cross diagrams of molecules with three or four different atoms you can also use symbols such as o or □ to distinguish electrons from different atoms.

**Recap**

- A double covalent bond is formed when two atoms share two pairs of electrons.
- A triple covalent bond is formed when two atoms share three pairs of electrons.

### Exam tip

When drawing dot-and-cross diagrams of molecules with double or triple bonds, remember to draw the atoms large enough so that you can put two or three pairs of electrons into the overlap area.

# 4.4 Ionic or simple molecular?

**You need to:**

- Describe the properties of ionic compounds (high melting and boiling points and good electrical conductivity only when aqueous or molten).
- Describe in terms of structure and bonding the properties of simple molecular compounds (low melting and boiling points and poor electrical conductivity).
- **Describe the giant lattice structure of ionic compounds.**
- **Explain in terms of structure and bonding the properties of ionic compounds.**
- **Explain in terms of structure and bonding the properties of simple molecular compounds.**

**Key skills**

You need to be able to recognise values of physical properties such as melting point as being relatively high or low. For example, 700 °C is a high melting point but 100 °C is a relatively low melting point.

**Exam tip**

**Watch out**

Make sure that you don't muddle structure and bonding. Structure is about the arrangement of the particles. Bonding is about how they are joined (bonded) together.

**Exam tip**

Remember that compounds of Group I or Group II metals with Group VI or Group VII elements are likely to be ionic compounds.

*Ionic structures* have high melting and boiling points and only conduct electricity when molten or in aqueous solution.

*Simple molecular structures* have low melting and boiling points and do not conduct electricity in any physical state.

**Worked example**

Compound **A** melts at 37 °C. Compound **B** does not conduct electricity when solid but conducts when dissolved in water. Describe the structure of compounds **A** and **B** and give one other physical property of **A** and **B**. [4]

**A** has a simple molecular structure ✓ and
**B** has an ionic structure. ✓

**A** is a poor electrical conductor as it is a simple molecule. ✓
**B** has a high melting point. ✓

**Recap**

- Ionic compounds have high melting and boiling points and conduct electricity only when molten and in aqueous solution.
- Simple **covalent compounds** have low melting and boiling points and are poor electrical conductors in any state.

## Apply

4. State which of these properties are those of ionic compounds and which are those of simple molecular compounds.
   a. low boiling point
   b. conduct electricity when molten
   c. high melting point
   d. do not conduct electricity when solid but do conduct when in aqueous solution

An **ionic lattice** is a regular arrangement of alternating positive and negative ions in three dimensions.

*Ionic structures have high melting and boiling points* because a lot of energy is needed to break the strong ionic bonds.

*Ionic structures do not conduct electricity when solid* because the ions cannot move.

*Ionic structures conduct electricity when molten or in aqueous solution* because the ions can move from place to place.

*Simple molecular structures have low melting and boiling points* because the forces between the molecules are weak.

*Simple molecular structures do not conduct electricity* because they do not have mobile ions or delocalised electrons.

**Worked example**

Explain in terms of structure and bonding why sodium chloride, NaCl, has a high melting point. [2]

Sodium chloride has a giant ionic structure ✓ so it needs a lot of thermal energy to break the strong ionic bonds. ✓

Explain in terms of structure and bonding why sulfur, $S_8$, is a poor conductor of electricity. [2]

Sulfur has a simple molecular structure ✓ and does not contain any mobile ions or delocalised electrons. ✓

## Apply

5. a. Explain in terms of structure and bonding why ethanol, $C_2H_5OH$, has a low melting point.

   b. Explain in terms of structure and bonding why calcium chloride, $CaCl_2$, is a good conductor of electricity when dissolved in water.

### Exam tip

The melting and boiling points of simple molecular structures are low because the forces between the molecules (**intermolecular forces**) are weak.

### Exam tip

**Watch out**

Take care not to use the term intermolecular forces when writing about ionic structures.

### Exam tip

**Watch out**

Make sure that you don't muddle the moving particles that are responsible for the conduction of electricity. In ionic structures it's the ions but in metals it's the delocalised electrons.

# 4.5 Giant covalent structures

**You need to:**

- Describe the giant covalent structures of graphite and diamond.
- Relate the structures of graphite and diamond to their uses.
- **Describe the giant covalent structure of silicon(IV) oxide.**
- **Describe the similarity in properties between diamond and silicon(IV) oxide, related to their structures.**

**Key skills**

When you revise you need to be able to make sure that you can distinguish between key words such as covalent and ionic and the physical properties related to these words. Making a mind map (spider diagram) can help here.

**Recap**

- Diamond and graphite are both giant covalent structures.
- Diamond has a structure of interlinked tetrahedrons. Graphite is a layered structure.
- Graphite conducts electricity well but diamond does not.

**Exam tip**

When explaining electrical conduction in graphite, remember that it is the delocalised electrons which move along the layers. Just stating that 'the electrons move' is not sufficient because it is not detailed enough.

*Diamond is a* **giant covalent structure** with each C atom forming four covalent bonds with other C atoms (tetrahedral arrangement).

*Diamond is used* as a cutting tool because it is hard (the network of strong covalent bonds is difficult to break).

*Graphite is a giant covalent structure* with each carbon atom forming three covalent bonds with other C atoms (layered structure).

*Graphite is used as a lubricant* because the layers can easily be rubbed off due to the weak bonding between the layers.

*Graphite conducts electricity* because some of the electrons can move along the layers.

**Worked example**

Describe the structure of graphite and explain in terms of its structure why it is used as a lubricant. [4]

Graphite is made up of layers ✓ of carbon atoms ✓ which are arranged in hexagons. Each carbon atom forms bonds with three other carbon atoms. ✓ It is used as a lubricant because the bonding between each layer is weak so the layers can be rubbed off easily. ✓

## Apply

6. a. Name two giant structures made up of carbon atoms.
   b. Explain what is meant by the term giant covalent structure.
   c. Explain why the tips of some high-speed drills include diamond in their structure.

*Silicon dioxide* has a giant covalent structure similar to diamond.

The *physical properties of silicon dioxide* include high melting point, hard and poor electrical conductor.

**Worked example**

Describe the structure of silicon dioxide, $SiO_2$, and explain in terms of bonding why it has a high melting point. [5]

It is a giant covalent structure. ✓ Each oxygen atom is attached to two silicon atoms ✓ and each silicon atom is attached to four other atoms. ✓ It has a high melting point because it has a large network ✓ of strong covalent bonds. ✓

**Exam tip**

**Watch out**

Take care not to use the term intermolecular forces when writing about giant covalent structures.

**Recap**

Giant covalent structures have high melting and boiling points because they have a network of strong covalent bonds.

# 4.6 Metallic bonding

**You need to:**

- **Describe metallic bonding as the electrostatic attraction between the positive ions in a metallic lattice and a 'sea' of delocalised electrons.**
- **Explain in terms of structure and bonding why metals are good electrical conductors and are malleable and ductile.**

**Metallic bonding** is the strong electrostatic attraction between positive metal ions and the sea of delocalised electrons.

**Delocalised electrons** are electrons which are not associated with any particular atom.

**Worked example**

The structure shown by the dotted lines represents a metal. Complete and label the diagram to show metallic structure. [4]

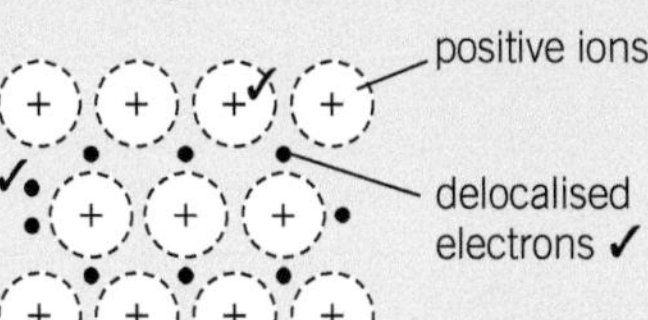


+ drawn in circle ✓ labelled positive ions ✓ dots (or e⁻) drawn between the circles ✓ labelled delocalised (or mobile) electrons ✓

**Key skills**

You need to be able to develop methods for learning the meaning of key words in the syllabus such as 'electrostatic' or 'lattice'.

**Exam tip**

**Watch out**

It is a common error to suggest that in a metallic structure the attractive forces are between the ions instead of between the ions and delocalised electrons.

Supplement

*Metals conduct electricity* because the delocalised electrons are able to move through the metallic **lattice**.

*Metals are* **malleable** *and* **ductile** because the layers of metal atoms are able to slide when a force is applied.

### Exam tip

When writing about electrical conductivity in metals the answer 'it has free electrons' is too vague to gain a mark. A more accurate answer is 'there are mobile electrons (or delocalised electrons) moving between the ions'.

### Worked example

Explain why metals are malleable. [2]

The layers can slide ✓ when a force is applied and strong metallic bonds reform ✓ in new positions.

### Recap

- A metallic structure is positive metal ions in a sea of delocalised electrons.
- Metals are malleable and ductile because the layers of ions can slide.
- Metals conduct electricity because of the sea of mobile electrons.

## Apply

7. a. Describe the structure of metals.

   b. Explain why metals conduct electricity.

## Questions

**1.** Define the term ionic bond. [2]

**2.** State the number of electrons and protons in each of these ions:

**a.** $Al^{3+}$ [2]

**b.** $O^{2-}$ [2]

**c.** $H^{+}$ [2]

**d.** $I^{-}$ [2]

**3.** Complete these equations by adding electrons to one or other side of the equation.

**a.** $Mg \rightarrow Mg^{2+}$ [1]

**b.** $N \rightarrow N^{3-}$ [1]

**4.** Draw dot-and-cross diagrams for:

**a.** sodium chloride, NaCl, showing all the electrons [4]

**b.** chlorine, $Cl_2$, showing only the outer shell electrons [2]

**5.** Describe two differences in the physical properties of ionic and simple covalent compounds. [4]

**6.** Describe two differences in the structures of diamond and graphite. [4]

S **7.** Hydrogen sulfide, $H_2S$, has a boiling point of –61 °C.

**a.** Describe the structure and bonding in hydrogen sulfide. [2]

**b.** Draw a dot-and-cross diagram for hydrogen sulfide. [2]

**8. a.** Define the term ionic lattice. [2]

**b.** State the name of two other types of structure with high melting points which have a lattice. [2]

**9. a.** Define metallic bonding. [2]

**b.** Explain why metals conduct electricity. [1]

## Sample question

This question is about structure and bonding.

**1.** Magnesium is a metal. Bromine is a simple covalent molecule.

Magnesium reacts with bromine to form the ionic compound magnesium bromide.

**a.** Draw a dot-and-cross diagram for magnesium bromide. Show only the electrons in the outer shell. [4]

**b.** Magnesium reacts with water above 100 °C. Draw a dot-and-cross diagram for water. [2]

**c.** Magnesium bromide and diamond are both giant structures.

**(i)** Describe the structure and bonding in diamond. [2]

**(ii)** State one use of diamond. [1]

S **(iii)** Explain why diamond does not conduct electricity but graphite does. [2]

**(iv)** Diamond is one form of carbon. Carbon burns in air to form carbon dioxide.

Draw a dot-and-cross diagram for carbon dioxide. [2]

**d.** Metals such as magnesium and iron are ductile.

**(i)** Explain why metals are ductile by referring to their structure and bonding. [3]

**(ii)** Use ideas about metallic bonding to suggest why magnesium has a higher melting point than sodium. [2]

# Formulae and equations

## Revision checklist

Tick these boxes to build a record of your revision. Columns 2 and 3 can be used if you want to make a record more than once.

| Core/**Supplement** syllabus content | | **1** | **2** | **3** |
|---|---|---|---|---|
| 5.1 | State the formulae of the elements and compounds given in the syllabus. | | | |
| 5.1 | Deduce the formula of a simple compound from the relative number of atoms present. | | | |
| 5.2 | Describe molecular formula as the number and type of different atoms in one molecule. | | | |
| 5.2 | Deduce the formula of a simple compound from the relative number of atoms present in a model or diagram. | | | |
| 5.2 | Draw and interpret the displayed formula of a molecule. | | | |
| 5.2 | **Describe empirical formula as the simplest whole number ratio of the different atoms or ions in a compound.** | | | |
| 5.2 | **Determine the formula of an ionic compound from the number and charges of the ions present.** | | | |
| 5.3 | Construct word equations and symbol equations. | | | |
| 5.4 | Construct symbol equations with state symbols. | | | |
| 5.4 | **Construct balanced ionic equations.** | | | |
| 5.4 | **Deduce the symbol equation for a reaction given relevant information.** | | | |

# 5.1 Chemical formulae

**You need to:**

- State the formulae of the elements and compounds given in the syllabus.
- Deduce the formula of a simple compound from the relative number of atoms present.

In *compounds made up of a metal and non-metal*, the non-metal part comes second and generally ends in -ide.

The *ending -ate* in a compound generally shows that there is oxygen and two other elements present.

The *formula of a compound containing two elements* can often be deduced from the position of each element in the Periodic Table.

**Key skills**

Learning how some elements change the end of their names when they form compounds is essential in order to progress in chemistry.

**Worked example**

Name these compounds.

KCl [1]

potassium chloride ✓

$NaNO_3$ [1]

sodium nitrate ✓

$CaCO_3$ [1]

calcium carbonate ✓

ZnO [1]

zinc oxide ✓

$Na_2SO_4$ [1]

sodium sulfate ✓

Deduce the formulae of these compounds.

magnesium bromide [1]

$MgBr_2$ ✓

aluminium chloride [1]

$AlCl_3$ ✓

magnesium hydroxide [1]

$Mg(OH)_2$ ✓

calcium nitrate [1]

$Ca(NO_3)_2$ ✓

**Exam tip**

When writing symbols for elements with two letters, make sure that the second letter is a small one. For example, cobalt is Co, *not* CO.

**Exam tip**

Take care with writing formulae such as $CO_2$ or $O^{2-}$. Writing $CO^2$ or $O_{2-}$ is incorrect.

## Apply

1. a. Name these compounds:

   (i) $Na_2O$ (ii) $Ba(OH)_2$ (iii) $NaHCO_3$
   (iv) $CuI_2$ (v) $CuSO_4$

   b. Deduce the formulae of these compounds:

   (i) calcium chloride
   (ii) magnesium oxide
   (iii) aluminium oxide
   (iv) aluminium sulfate
   (v) ammonium sulfate (the ammonium ion is $NH_4^+$)

**Exam tip**

When writing formulae involving groups such as $SO_4$, $NO_3$, $CO_3$ and OH, the atoms in these group must always be kept together. We often use brackets to keep them together in examples such as $Mg(NO_3)_2$ and $Fe(OH)_3$.

**Recap**

- In compounds of the ending of the non-metal part changes from -ine to -ide.
- Compounds ending in -ate have oxygen in the non-metallic part as well as another element, e.g. sulfate, $SO_4$, nitrate, $NO_3$, carbonate, $CO_3$.

**Recap**

Each chemical element has its own particular symbol.

# 5.2 Working out the formula

**You need to:**

- Describe molecular formula as the number and type of different atoms in one molecule.
- Deduce the formula of a simple compound from the relative number of atoms present in a model or diagram.
- Draw and interpret the displayed formula of a molecule.
- **Describe empirical formula as the simplest whole number ratio of the different atoms or ions in a compound.**
- **Determine the formula of an ionic compound from the number and charges of the ions present.**

The **molecular formula** shows the number and type of each atom in a molecule.

The **displayed formula** shows all of the atoms and all of the bonds in a molecule.

### Exam tip

**Watch out**

When writing molecular formulae, make sure that you don't write the same atoms more than once. For example, $C_2H_5OH$ is incorrect. The H has been written twice. The correct answer is $C_2H_6O$.

### Exam tip

When deducing the molecular formula from a displayed formula it is useful to cross out each atom as you count them so that you do not miss any.

### Recap

- Molecular formulae show the number and type of atoms in a molecule.
- Displayed formulae show all of the atoms and all of the bonds.

### Worked example

Deduce the molecular formulae of these compounds. [3]

```
    H             H H          H     H
    |             | |           \   /
H—C—O—H        H—C—C—H           N—N
    |             | |           /   \
    H          H—C—C—H         H     H
                  | |
                  H H
```

$CH_4O$ ✓   $C_4H_8$ ✓   $N_2H_4$ ✓

Write the displayed formulae for these compounds.

$NH_3$ [1]

```
  H
  |
  N
 / \
H   H
```

$C_2H_6$ (structure is $CH_3CH_3$) [1]

```
   H H
   | |
H—C—C—H
   | |
   H H
```

$H_2O$ [1]

```
H—O—H
```

## Apply

2. a. Deduce the molecular formulae of these compounds.

(i)
```
   H    O
   |   //
H—C—C
   |   \
   H    O—H
```

(ii)
```
   F
F \ | / F
    S
F / | \ F
   F
```

(iii)
```
   H
   |
H—C—O—H
   |
H—C—O—H
   |
H—C—O—H
   |
   H
```

(iv)
```
        O
        ||
  H   _C_    H
    C     C
  H /       \ H
     C — C
  H / |   | \ H
     H   H
```

b. Write the displayed formulae for these compounds.

(i) $PCl_3$

(ii) $SnCl_4$

(iii) $CH_2=CH_2$

(iv) $H_3C-CHO$ (there is a CO double bond)

**Key skills**

You need to be able to work out the formulae of simple compounds from the position of the different elements in the Periodic Table or from the charges on the ions.

The **empirical formula** is the simplest whole number ratio of the different atoms in a compound.

The *formula of an ionic compound* is always the empirical formula.

The *formula of an ionic compound can be found* by balancing the positive and negative charges.

**Recap**

- Empirical formulae show the simplest ratio of atoms.
- In ionic compounds the charges of the ions balance, e.g. in $MgCl_2$ one $Mg^{2+}$ ion is balanced by two $Cl^-$ ions.

**Worked example**

Deduce the empirical formulae of these compounds.

$C_6H_3Cl_3$ [1]

divide by 3 = $C_2HCl$ ✓

$Al_2Cl_6$ [1]

divide by 2 = $AlCl_3$ ✓

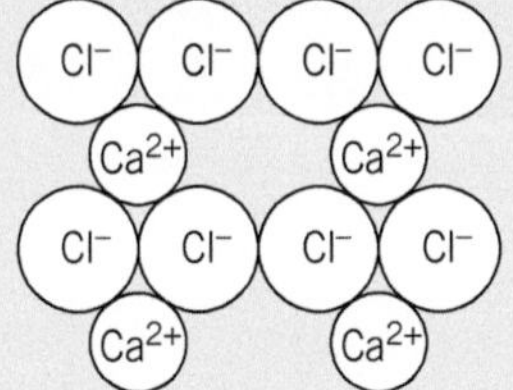


$8Cl^- : 4Ca^{2+} = CaCl_2$ ✓

The formulae of some ions are shown.

$Al^{3+}$ $Cl^-$ $K^+$ $Na^+$ $NO_3^-$ $OH^-$ $SO_4^{2-}$ $Zn^{2+}$

Use these ions to deduce the formulae of these compounds:

zinc hydroxide [1]

$Zn(OH)_2$ ✓

potassium nitrate [1]

$KNO_3$ ✓

sodium sulfate [1]

$Na_2SO_4$ ✓

aluminium chloride [1]

$AlCl_3$ ✓

Supplement

## Apply

3. a. Deduce the empirical formulae of these compounds.

   (i) $H_2O_2$

   (ii) $CH_3CH_2CH_2COOH$

   (iii) $C_6H_4N_2O_4$

   b. The formulae of some ions are shown.

   $Al^{3+}$ $Br^-$ $CO_3^{2-}$ $Cu^{2+}$ $K^+$ $Mg^{2+}$ $NO_3^-$ $OH^-$ $PO_4^{3-}$

   Use these ions to deduce the formulae of these compounds:

   (i) aluminium bromide

   (ii) potassium carbonate

   (iii) magnesium phosphate

   (iv) copper hydroxide

   (v) aluminium nitrate

# 5.3 Chemical equations

**You need to:**

- Construct word equations and symbol equations.

**Key skills**

Learning how to balance chemical equations is one of the most basic skills. Remember to balance each type atom (or group of atoms) one by one until the equation is completely balanced.

**Word equations** show the names of the reactants on the left and the products on the right (after the arrow).

**Worked example**

Construct word equations for these reactions.

The reaction of methane with oxygen to produce carbon dioxide and water. [1]

methane + oxygen → carbon dioxide + water ✓

The reaction of (aqueous) potassium bromide with chlorine to produce (aqueous) potassium chloride and bromine. [1]

potassium bromide + chlorine → potassium chloride + bromine ✓

**Exam tip**

You are expected to know the formulae of simple molecules mentioned in the syllabus, especially $H_2$, $Cl_2$, $O_2$, $N_2$, $CO_2$ and HCl.

## Apply

4. Construct word equations for these reactions:

   a. the reaction of sodium with water to produce sodium hydroxide and hydrogen

   b. the reaction of iron(II) chloride with potassium hydroxide to produce iron(II) hydroxide

   c. the effect of heating magnesium nitrate to produce magnesium oxide, nitrogen dioxide and oxygen

In a *symbol equation* there is the same number of each type of atom on each side of the equation.

*Symbol equations are balanced* by writing large numbers in front of particular **reactants** or products.

**Worked example**

Copy and complete these symbol equations:

$CuCl_2$ + ..........NaOH → $Cu(OH)_2$ + 2NaCl [1]

$CuCl_2 + 2NaOH \rightarrow Cu(OH)_2 + 2NaCl$ ✓

..........Na + $Cl_2$ → ..........NaCl [1]

Balance the chlorine atoms: ..........Na + $Cl_2 \rightarrow$ 2NaCl

Balance the sodium atoms: $2Na + Cl_2 \rightarrow 2NaCl$ ✓

..........P + ..........$O_2$ → ..........$P_2O_3$ [1]

Balance the phosphorus atoms: 2P + ..........$O_2$ → ..........$P_2O_3$

Balance the oxygen atoms: $2P + 1\frac{1}{2}O_2 \rightarrow 1P_2O_3$

Multiply through by 2 to get rid of the ½: $4P + 3O_2 \rightarrow 2P_2O_3$ ✓

**Worked example**

Construct the symbol equation for the reaction of hydrogen with chlorine to produce hydrogen chloride. [2]

Write the formulae: $H_2 + Cl_2 \rightarrow HCl$

Balance the hydrogen atoms: $H_2 + Cl_2 \rightarrow 2HCl$

✓ for correct formulae ✓ for correct balance dependent on the formulae being correct

The chlorine atoms are also balanced automatically in this case.

Construct the symbol equation for the reaction of ethane, $C_2H_6$, with oxygen to form carbon dioxide and water. **S** [2]

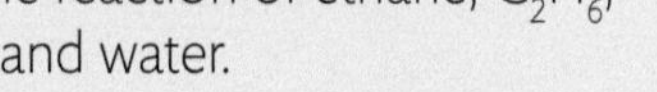

Write the formulae: $C_2H_6 + O_2 \rightarrow CO_2 + H_2O$

Balance the carbon atoms: $C_2H_6 + O_2 \rightarrow 2CO_2 + H_2O$

Balance the hydrogen atoms: $C_2H_6 + O_2 \rightarrow 2CO_2 + 3H_2O$

Balance the oxygen atoms: $C_2H_6 + 3\frac{1}{2}O_2 \rightarrow 2CO_2 + 3H_2O$

Multiply through by 2 to get rid of the ½:
$2C_2H_6 + 7O_2 \rightarrow 4CO_2 + 6H_2O$

✓ for correct formulae ✓ for correct balance dependent on the formulae being correct

Construct the symbol equation for the reaction of magnesium hydroxide with nitric acid, $HNO_3$, to produce magnesium nitrate and water. [2]

Write the formulae: $Mg(OH)_2 + HNO_3 \rightarrow Mg(NO_3)_2 + H_2O$

Balance the nitrate group: $Mg(OH)_2 + 2HNO_3 \rightarrow Mg(NO_3)_2 + H_2O$

Balance the hydrogen atoms: $Mg(OH)_2 + 2HNO_3 \rightarrow Mg(NO_3)_2 + 2H_2O$

Note that the oxygen atoms are also balanced.

✓ for correct formulae ✓ for correct balance dependent on the formulae being correct

**Exam tip**

**Watch out**

Take care naming compounds. $NH_4Cl$ is ammonium chloride *not* ammonia chloride.

**Exam tip**

**Watch out**

When balancing **chemical equations** never change the formula of the compounds or elements in the equation. For example, you must not change KCl to $KCl_2$.

**Exam tip**

When counting atoms, remember that $2Fe(OH)_2$ means two Fe atoms and two (OH) groups.

**Recap**

- Symbol equations are balanced by changing only the numbers in front of each compound or element.
- You balance one atom (or group of atoms) at a time and then another atom (or group of atoms) until you get the whole equation balanced.

**Exam tip**

In equations involving burning compounds of carbon and hydrogen such as $C_5H_{12}$, balance the carbon first, then the hydrogen. Balance the oxygen last.

## Apply

5. a. (i) Write the word equation for the reaction of iron(III) oxide with carbon monoxide to produce iron and carbon dioxide.

(ii) Copy and complete the symbol equation for the reaction in part (a)(i).

$Fe_2O_3$ + ..............CO → ..............Fe + $3CO_2$

b. Construct a balanced chemical equation for the reaction of hydrogen and oxygen to produce water.

c. Construct a balanced chemical equation for the reaction of sodium with oxygen to produce sodium peroxide, $Na_2O_2$.

d. Convert these symbol equations into a word equation.

(i) $H_2SO_4 + 2NH_3 \rightarrow (NH_4)_2SO_4$

(ii) $Fe(NO_3)_2 + 2NaOH \rightarrow Fe(OH)_2 + 2NaNO_3$

S e. Construct the symbol equations for these reactions:

(i) the reaction of nitrogen with hydrogen to produce ammonia, $NH_3$

(ii) the reaction of calcium with hydrochloric acid, HCl, to produce calcium chloride and hydrogen

(iii) the reaction of aluminium with oxygen to produce aluminium oxide, $Al_2O_3$

(iv) the reaction of calcium carbonate with nitric acid to produce calcium nitrate, $Ca(NO_3)_2$, carbon dioxide and water

(v) the reaction of chlorine with potassium bromide, KBr, to produce potassium chloride and bromine

(vi) the reaction of propane, $C_3H_8$, with oxygen to produce carbon dioxide and water

# 5.4 More about equations

**You need to:**

- Construct symbol equations with state symbols.
- **Construct balanced ionic equations.**
- **Deduce the symbol equation for a reaction given relevant information.**

The **state symbols** are (s) for solid, (l) for liquid, (g) for gas and (aq) for aqueous solution.

**Worked example**

A solution of hydrochloric acid in water reacts with solid calcium carbonate to produce aqueous calcium chloride, carbon dioxide and water. Copy and complete the equation by writing in the state symbols.

$CaCO_3 + 2HCl \rightarrow CaCl_2 + CO_2 + H_2O(l)$ [2]

$CaCO_3(s) + 2HCl(aq) \rightarrow CaCl_2(aq) + CO_2(g) + H_2O(l)$

State symbols of reactants correct ✓ state symbols of products correct ✓

## Apply

6. Copy and complete these equations using the correct state symbols.
   a. When chlorine is bubbled into a solution of potassium iodide in water, aqueous potassium chloride and aqueous iodine are produced.

      $Cl_2 + 2KI \rightarrow I_2 + 2KCl$
   b. Sodium reacts with water to produce aqueous sodium hydroxide and hydrogen.

      $2Na + 2H_2O \rightarrow 2NaOH + H_2$

Supplement

**Ionic equations** are simplified symbol equations showing the ions that take part in a reaction and the products formed from these ions.

**Spectator ions** are ions that are present in the reaction mixture but do not take part in the reaction.

**Worked example**

Construct the ionic equation for the reaction of aqueous iron(III) chloride with aqueous sodium hydroxide to form a precipitate of iron(III) hydroxide and aqueous sodium chloride. Include state symbols. [3]

$$FeCl_3(aq) + 3NaOH(aq) \rightarrow Fe(OH)_3(s) + 3NaCl(aq)$$

Write the ions present in the aqueous solutions:

$$Fe^{3+} + 3Cl^- + 3Na^+ + 3OH^- \rightarrow Fe(OH)_3(s) + 3Na^+ + 3Cl^-$$

Cancel the spectator ions:

$$Fe^{3+} + \cancel{3Cl^-} + \cancel{3Na^+} + 3OH^- \rightarrow Fe(OH)_3(s) + \cancel{3Na^+} + \cancel{3Cl^-}$$

Write the species remaining including state symbols:

$$Fe^{3+}(aq) + 3OH^-(aq) \rightarrow Fe(OH)_3(s)$$

correct formulae for ions and $Fe(OH)_3$ ✓

correct balance ✓

correct state symbols ✓

**Key skills**

You need to be able to recognise which compounds are ionic in order to construct ionic equations.

### Exam tip

**Watch out**

When constructing an ionic equation make sure that the charges balance as well as the atoms and ions.

### Exam tip

When writing ionic equations first identify the reactants and products that are solids, liquids or simple molecules such as chlorine. These will appear in the final equation. It is only then that you can separate the other compounds into ions.

**Supplement**

**Recap**

- Spectator ions do not appear in an ionic equation. They are the ions that cancel out on each side of the equation.
- Substances which have state symbols (s) or (l) in an equation remain in an ionic equation.

### Exam tip

When writing ionic equations involving acids, you need to know that acids contain $H^+$ ions.

## Apply

7. Construct the ionic equations from the full equations shown.

   a. $Cl_2(aq) + 2KI(aq) \rightarrow I_2(aq) + 2KCl(aq)$

   b. $NaOH(aq) + HCl(aq) \rightarrow NaCl(aq) + H_2O(l)$

   c. $Cu(NO_3)_2(aq) + 2KOH(aq) \rightarrow Cu(OH)_2(s) + 2KNO_3(aq)$?

## Questions

1. Name these compounds.
   - **a.** $K_2CO_3$ [1]
   - **b.** $Pb(NO_3)_2$ [1]
   - **c.** $CaI_2$ [1]
2. Give the formulae for
   - **a.** magnesium sulfate [1]
   - **b.** aluminium chloride [1]
3. Write both the molecular formula and the displayed formula for the compound with the structure $CH_3{-}CH_2{-}CH_3$ in which the three carbon atoms are connected. [2]
4. Copy and balance these equations:
   - **a.** ..............Na + ..............$H_2O \rightarrow 2NaOH + H_2$ [1]
   - **b.** $2Ag_2O \rightarrow$ ..............Ag + $O_2$ [1]
   - **c.** ..............Fe(..............) + ..............$H_2O(g) \rightarrow Fe_3O_4(s) + 4H_2$(..............) [3]

**S** The structure of compound **A** is shown.

Deduce the empirical formula of this compound. [1]

6. Construct chemical equations for these reactions. Include state symbols.

   a. the reaction of solid zinc carbonate, $ZnCO_3$, with hydrochloric acid, HCl, to produce zinc chloride, carbon dioxide and water [3]

   b. the reaction of aqueous sodium hydroxide with dilute sulfuric acid, $H_2SO_4$, to form aqueous sodium sulfate and water [3]

7. Construct ionic equations for these reactions.

   a. $3KOH(aq) + AlCl_3(aq) \rightarrow Al(OH)_3(s) + 3KCl(aq)$ [2]

   b. $Mg(s) + 2HCl(aq) \rightarrow MgCl_2(aq) + H_2(g)$ [2]

## Sample question

This question is about formulae and equations.

1. a. (i) Define the term molecular formula. [1]

   (ii) Deduce the molecular formula of the structure shown.

```
        H   H
H\      |   |      /H
  N — C — C — N
H/      |   |      \H
        C   H
       / \\
H — O     O
```

[1]

   (iii) Name the type of formula shown in part **(a)(ii)**. [1]

   b. The compounds $K_2SO_4$ and $ZnBr_2$ are salts.

   (i) Name these two compounds. [2]

   (ii) Give the formulae of the two ions present in $K_2SO_4$. [2]

   c. Write a word equation for this reaction.

   $Ca(NO_3)_2 + 2NaOH \rightarrow Ca(OH)_2 + 2NaNO_3$ [2]

   d. Calcium reacts with water to produce calcium hydroxide and hydrogen.

   (i) Copy and complete the chemical equation for this reaction.

   $Ca(s) + ......H_2O(l) \rightarrow Ca(OH)_2(aq) + ......(g)$ [2]

   (ii) State the meaning of the symbols (s) and (aq). [2]

   e. Construct the chemical equation for the reaction of carbon with oxygen to form carbon monoxide, CO. [2]

S f. (i) Define empirical formula. [1]

   (ii) The molecular formula of a compound is $C_9H_6O_6$. Deduce the empirical formula of this compound. [2]

   g. Solid potassium chlorate(V), $KClO_3$, decomposes when heated to produce potassium chloride and oxygen. Construct the chemical equation for this reaction. Include state symbols. [3]

   h. Magnesium reacts with aqueous silver nitrate:

   $Mg(s) + 2AgNO_3(aq) \rightarrow Mg(NO_3)_2(aq) + 2Ag(s)$

   Construct the ionic equation for this reaction. [2]

# Chemical calculations

## Revision checklist

Tick these boxes to build a record of your revision. Columns 2 and 3 can be used if you want to make a record more than once.

| Core/**Supplement** syllabus content | | 1 | 2 | 3 |
|---|---|---|---|---|
| 6.1 | Define relative atomic mass. | | | |
| 6.1 | Define relative molecular mass and relative formula mass. | | | |
| 6.2 | Calculate reacting masses using simple proportions. | | | |
| 6.2 | **Define the mole and the Avogadro constant.** | | | |
| 6.2 | **Use the mole in simple calculations to find relative molecular mass (including molar mass) and relative atomic mass.** | | | |
| 6.2 | **Use the number of moles and the Avogadro constant to calculate the number of particles present.** | | | |
| 6.3 | **Calculate stoichiometric reacting masses.** | | | |
| 6.3 | **Calculate percentage composition by mass.** | | | |
| 6.4 | **Understand the terms limiting reactant and excess reactant.** | | | |
| 6.5 | **Use the molar gas volume in calculations involving gases.** | | | |
| 6.5 | **Convert $cm^3$ to $dm^3$.** | | | |
| 6.5 | **Calculate the relative atomic mass or relative molecular mass of a substance.** | | | |
| 6.6 | **Calculate percentage yield.** | | | |
| 6.6 | **Calculate percentage purity.** | | | |
| 6.7 | **Calculate empirical formula.** | | | |
| 6.7 | **Calculate molecular formula.** | | | |
| 6.8 | **Calculate solution concentration and volumes of solutions using data provided.** | | | |
| 6.8 | **Use experimental data to calculate the concentration of a solution in a titration.** | | | |

# 6.1 Masses and molecules

**You need to:**

- Define relative atomic mass and relative molecular mass (including molar mass).
- Define relative molecular mass and relative formula mass.

**Relative atomic mass**, $A_r$, is the average mass of the isotopes of an element compared to $\frac{1}{12}$th the mass of an atom of carbon-12.

**Relative molecular mass**, $M_r$, is the sum of the relative atomic masses in the formula of one molecule.

**Relative formula mass**, also $M_r$, is the sum of the relative 'atomic masses' in the empirical formula of an ionic compound.

**Key skills**

You need to be able to add and multiply correctly to calculate $M_r$ values, including the use of brackets.

**Worked example**

Calculate the relative molecular mass of these compounds. Use the relative atomic masses in the Periodic Table to help you.

$Cl_2$ [1]

$2 \times 35.5 = 71$ ✓

$C_2H_6O$

$(2 \times 12) + (6 \times 1) + (1 \times 16) = 46$ ✓

$Mg(NO_3)_2$ [1]

$Mg + (2\ N) + (2 \times 3\ O)$

$24 + (2 \times 14) + (6 \times 16) = 148$ ✓

**Exam tip**

You may be asked to define terms such as relative atomic mass and relative molecular mass in an exam. Make sure that you know the essential details of these definitions.

**Recap**

Relative molecular mass is deduced by adding all the relative atomic masses of the atoms in one molecule or formula unit of a compound.

**Exam tip**

**Watch out**

When calculating relative molecular masses for simple molecules remember that molecules such as oxygen and nitrogen have two atoms. Don't write 16 for the $M_r$ for $O_2$ instead of 32.

## Apply

1. Calculate the relative molecular mass of these compounds. Use the relative atomic masses in the Periodic Table to help you.
   a. $CHCl_3$
   b. $Mg(OH)_2$
   c. $Na_2SO_4$
   d. $Al(NO_3)_3$
   e. $CuSO_4{\cdot}5H_2O$ (work out $5H_2O$ separately from the $CuSO_4$, then add them together)

**Exam tip**

If a formula has brackets, first add the atomic masses inside the brackets. Then multiply by the number outside the brackets. Finally, add the atomic masses which are not bracketed.

# 6.2 Chemical calculations and the mole

**You need to:**

- Calculate reacting masses using simple proportions.
- **Define the mole and the Avogadro constant.**
- **Use the mole in simple calculations to find relative molecular mass and relative atomic mass; use the moles and the Avogadro constant to calculate the number of particles present.**

The *masses of substances reacting or the mass of product formed* can be calculated using simple proportions.

**Worked example**

When 8 g of hydrogen is burned in excess oxygen, 72 g of water is formed.

Calculate the mass of water formed when 2 g of hydrogen is burned. [1]

8 g $H_2$ gives 72 g $H_2O$

So 2 g gives $\frac{2}{8} \times 72 = 18$ g $H_2O$ ✓

## Apply

2. a. When 2.4 g of magnesium reacts with excess hydrochloric acid 9.5 g of magnesium chloride is formed.

   Calculate the mass of magnesium chloride formed when 14.4 g of magnesium reacts with excess hydrochloric acid.

   b. When 16 g of methane reacts with excess oxygen 36 g of water is formed.

   Calculate the minimum mass of methane needed to form 1.8 g of water.

**Exam tip**

If you have difficulty rearranging the mole equation, this triangle may help.

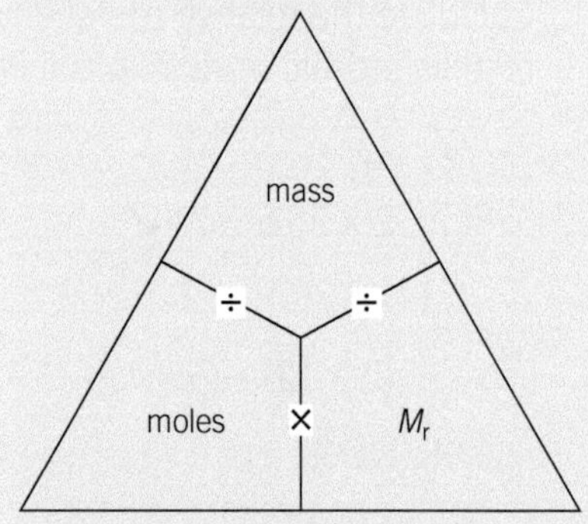


Cover the quantity you want to find. You will see the correct form of the equation to use.

A **mole** is the amount of substance that contains $6.02 \times 10^{23}$ defined particles (atoms, molecules or ions).

$$\text{Number of moles} = \frac{\text{mass of substance (in grams)}}{\text{mass of 1 mole of the substance (in grams)}}$$

**Worked example**

Calculate the number of moles in 16 g of sodium hydroxide, NaOH. [2]

Mass of 1 mole of sodium hydroxide = 23 + 16 + 1 = 40 ✓

Moles = $\frac{16}{40} = 0.4$ mol ✓

Calculate the mass of 0.48 moles of magnesium sulfate, $MgSO_4$. [2]

Mass of 1 mole of magnesium sulfate = 24 + 32 + (4 × 16) = 120 g ✓

Rearrange the equation to make mass the subject:

Mass (in g) = moles × mass of 1 mole

= 0.48 × 120 = 57.6 g ✓

Recap

$$\text{Number of moles} = \frac{\text{mass of substance (in grams)}}{\text{mass of 1 mole of the substance (in grams)}}$$

Key skills

You need to be able to rearrange chemical relationships such as moles = mass / $M_r$ to make mass or $M_r$ the subject.

## Apply

3. a. Calculate the amount in moles of:
   (i) 9.25 g of calcium hydroxide, $Ca(OH)_2$
   (ii) 5.0 g of calcium carbonate, $CaCO_3$
   (iii) 42.6 g of chlorine molecules, $Cl_2$
   (iv) 28.35 g of zinc nitrate, $Zn(NO_3)_2$

   b. Calculate the mass of:
   (i) 2 moles of sodium sulfate, $Na_2SO_4$
   (ii) 3.5 moles of magnesium oxide, MgO
   (iii) 0.02 moles of ammonium sulfate, $(NH_4)_2SO_4$

   c. Calculate the relative molecular mass of iodine molecules if 0.9 moles of iodine has a mass of 228.6 g.

**Exam tip**

When using moles, make sure that it is clear the type of particle present. For example, 160 g of bromine, $Br_2$, is 1 mole of bromine molecules but 2 moles of bromine atoms.

The **Avogadro constant** is the number ($6.02 \times 10^{23}$) of defined particles present in a mole of these particles.

$$\text{Number of defined particles} = \text{number of moles of the defined particles} \times \text{Avogadro constant}$$

Key skills

You need to be able to understand the meaning of and work with powers to the base ten such as $6 \times 10^{23}$.

**Worked example**

Calculate the number of chlorine atoms in 0.025 moles of chlorine molecules, $Cl_2$. Avogadro constant $6.02 \times 10^{23}$ per mol. [2]

In 0.025 mol of $Cl_2$ molecules there are $0.025 \times 2 = 0.05$ mol of Cl atoms. ✓

Number of chlorine atoms = moles × Avogadro constant = $0.05 \times 6.02 \times 10^{23}$

$= 3.01 \times 10^{22}$ Cl atoms ✓

## Apply

4. a. Calculate the number of iron atoms in 0.2800 g of iron. Avogadro constant $6.02 \times 10^{23}$ per mol.

   b. Calculate a value for the Avogadro constant if there are $1.21 \times 10^{24}$ atoms of sodium in 46 g of sodium.

Supplement

# 6.3 More chemical calculations

**You need to:**

- **Calculate stoichiometric reacting masses.**
- **Calculate percentage composition by mass.**

The **stoichiometry** of a reaction is the ratio of each reactant and product in the balanced chemical equation.

When calculating **reacting masses**, we use the relative molecular mass, $M_r$, of the reactants and / or products as well as the stoichiometry of the equation.

**Key skills**

You need to be able to work through mathematical problems involving several stages.

**Worked example**

Calculate the maximum mass of iron formed when 385 g of iron(III) oxide reacts with excess carbon monoxide. $A_r$ values Fe = 56, O = 16

$Fe_2O_3 + 3CO \rightarrow 2Fe + 3CO_2$ [3]

**Method 1**

1. Calculate the relevant formula masses for iron(III) oxide and iron:

   $Fe_2O_3 = (2 \times 56) + (3 \times 16) = 160 \qquad Fe = 56$ ✓

2. Multiply each formula mass by the number of moles in the equation (the stoichiometry):

   1 mol $Fe_2O_3 \rightarrow$ 2 mol Fe

   160 g $Fe_2O_3 \rightarrow 2 \times 56$ g Fe = 112 g ✓

3. Use simple proportion to calculate the mass of iron produced:

   385 g $Fe_2O_3 \rightarrow \frac{385}{160} \times 112 = 269.5$ g Fe ✓

**Method 2**

1. Calculate the number of moles of iron oxide: $\frac{385}{160} = 2.40625$ mol ✓
2. Use the stoichiometry of the equation to deduce the moles of iron:

   1 mol $Fe_2O_3 \rightarrow$ 2 mol Fe

   2.40625 mol $\rightarrow 2 \times 2.40625 = 4.8125$ mol Fe ✓

3. Calculate the mass of iron (mass = mol × $A_r$)

   $4.8125 \times 56 = 269.5$ g Fe

**Recap**

To calculate the mass of named product from the mass of named reactant you need to know:

- the relative formula masses of the reactant and product
- the ratio of the reactant and product in the chemical equation.

**Key skills**

You need to be able to understand significant figures.

**Exam tip**

**Watch out**

When calculating reacting masses, make sure that you are working with the correct reactants or products and take account of the number of moles of each in the chemical equation.

## Apply

5. a. 0.755 g of tin(IV) oxide is reduced by excess carbon.

$$SnO_2 + 2C \rightarrow Sn + 2CO$$

Calculate the maximum mass of carbon that will react with all the tin(IV) oxide.

$A_r$ values Sn = 119, C = 12, O = 16

b. Red lead oxide, $Pb_3O_4$, reacts with excess carbon:

$$Pb_3O_4 + 4C \rightarrow 3Pb + 4CO$$

Calculate the mass of $Pb_3O_4$ needed to produce 31.05 g of lead. Give your answer to three significant figures.

$A_r$ values Pb = 207, O = 16

c. Propane reacts with excess oxygen to produce carbon dioxide and water.

$$C_3H_8 + 5O_2 \rightarrow 3CO_2 + 4H_2O$$

Calculate the maximum mass of water formed when 11 g of propane is burned.

$A_r$ values C = 12, O = 16, H = 1

### Exam tip

In calculations, it's useful to put the $M_r$ values or moles below the appropriate reactants or products in the symbol equation so that it's clear which compounds you are working with and can take account of the ratio of the moles which react.

**Percentage composition by mass** = $\dfrac{\text{mass of a particular element in a mole of a compound}}{\text{mass of one mole of the compound}}$

### Worked example

Calculate the percentage composition by mass of sodium in sodium sulfate, $Na_2SO_4$.

$A_r$ values Na = 23, S = 32, O = 16 [2]

Calculate the mass of sodium in a mole of $Na_2SO_4$: 2 × 23 = 46 g

Calculate the mass of a mole of $Na_2SO_4$: (2 × 23) + 32 + (4 × 16) = 142 ✓

Percentage composition by mass = $\dfrac{46}{142} \times 100$ = 32.4% (to three significant figures) ✓

### Recap

% composition by mass of H in $H_2O$ = $\dfrac{\text{mass of 2H in 1 mole of water}}{\text{mass of 2H + O in 1 mole of water}}$

### Exam tip

**Watch out**

When calculating percentage composition by mass make sure that you have included all the atoms of a particular type in the top part of the equation. For example, in $(NH_4)_2SO_4$ there are two N atoms.

## Apply

6. Calculate the percentage by mass of:

$A_r$ values K = 39, N = 14, H = 1, S = 32, O = 16, P = 31, Cl = 35.5

a. oxygen in potassium nitrate, $KNO_3$

b. nitrogen in ammonium sulfate, $(NH_4)_2SO_4$

c. chlorine in phosphorus(V) chloride, $PCl_5$

# 6.4 Amount of product

**You need to:**

- **Understand the terms limiting reactant and excess reactant.**

### Exam tip

In chemical calculations involving limiting reactants, make sure that you take into account the ratio of the numbers of moles which react.

- The limiting reactant is the reactant that is not in excess.
- When determining which reactant is limiting, the ratio of the reactants in the equation must be taken into account.

### Exam tip

**Watch out**

In questions about limiting or excess reactants, look out for the ratio of each reactant in the chemical equation.

### Exam tip

When doing calculations with several steps, do not round the figures between each step. This can lead to the incorrect answer.

The **excess reactant** is the reactant which is not completely used up when the reaction has finished.

The **limiting reactant** is the reactant which is not in excess and is used up completely when the reaction has finished.

When calculating which reactant is limiting we calculate the number of moles of each reactant and then take into account the stoichiometry of the reaction. The stoichiometry is the ratio of the moles of particular reactants and products in the equation.

### Worked example

A student reacts 4.60 g of sodium with 4.00 g of sulfur: $2Na + S \rightarrow Na_2S$

Deduce which reactant is in excess and by how much in moles.
$A_r$ values Na = 23, S = 32 [3]

1. Calculate the number of moles of each reactant.

   $$Na = \frac{4.6}{23} = 0.200 \text{ mol}$$

   $$S = \frac{4.0}{32} = 0.125 \text{ mol} ✓$$

2. From the equation determine the ratio in which the Na and S react.

   $2Na + S \rightarrow Na_2S$

   2 moles 1 mole

3. Determine which is in excess (larger number of moles) or limiting (smaller number of moles) taking into account this stoichiometry:

   To react completely with 0.200 moles Na it needs

   $\frac{1}{2} \times 0.200$ moles = 0.100 mol of S. ✓

   There are 0.125 mol of S present so S is in excess by
   0.125 – 0.100 = 0.025 mol ✓

## Apply

7. Determine by calculation which reactant is limiting.

   $A_r$ values Mg = 24, O = 16, C = 12, H = 1, P = 31, Cl = 35.5

   a. 26 g of Mg reacts with 16 g of $O_2$ $2Mg + O_2 \rightarrow 2MgO$

   b. 80 g of $C_3H_8$ reacts with 320 g of $O_2$ $C_3H_8 + 5O_2 \rightarrow 3CO_2 + 4H_2O$

   c. 34 g of P react with 110 g of $Cl_2$ $2P + 3Cl_2 \rightarrow 2PCl_3$

# 6.5 Gas volume calculations

**You need to:**

- **Use the molar gas volume in calculations involving gases.**
- **Convert $cm^3$ to $dm^3$.**
- **Calculate the relative atomic mass or relative molecular mass of a substance.**

**Room temperature and pressure (r.t.p.)** is 20 °C and 1 atmosphere (atm) pressure.

*One atmosphere* = 101 kilopascals (kPa)

*One mole of any gas* occupies 24 $dm^3$ at r.t.p.

*Volume of gas at r.t.p. in $dm^3$* = moles of gas × 24

**Worked example**

Calculate the volume in $dm^3$ of 1.54 g of carbon dioxide at r.t.p. [3]

1. Calculate moles $CO_2 = \dfrac{1.54}{12 + (2 \times 16)}$ ✓ = 0.035 mol ✓

   Calculate volume (volume in $dm^3$ × molar gas volume)

   = 0.035 × 24 = 0.84 $dm^3$ ✓

Calculate the mass of butane in 60 $cm^3$ of butane gas, $C_4H_{10}$. [2]

1. Change volume in $cm^3$ to $dm^3$. 60 $cm^3 = \dfrac{60}{1000} = 0.06\ dm^3$
2. Calculate number of moles using $\dfrac{\text{volume in } dm^3}{\text{molar gas volume}}$

   $= \dfrac{0.06}{24} = 0.0025$ mol ✓
3. Calculate mass (mass = moles × $M_r$)

   $M_r = (4 \times 12) + (10 \times 1) = 58$ ✓ mass = 0.0025 × 58 = 0.145 g ✓

## Apply

8. Calculate:

   a. the volume of 42.6 g of chlorine gas at r.t.p.

   b. the volume of 4 moles of carbon dioxide at r.t.p.

   c. the mass of 48 $cm^3$ of ethene, $C_2H_4$, at r.t.p.

   d. the mass of 144 $dm^3$ of oxygen at r.t.p.

**Exam tip**

When working with gas volumes, make sure that you convert $cm^3$ into $dm^3$ when using the **molar gas volume** (24 $dm^3$/mol).

**Recap**

- One mole of any gas at room temperature and pressure occupies 24 $dm^3$.
- Volume of gas in $dm^3$ = moles of gas × 24.

**Key skills**

You need to be able to rearrange chemical relationships such as:

$$\text{moles of gas} = \frac{\text{volume of gas in } dm^3}{\text{molar gas volume}}$$

to make volume the subject.

Supplement

The *relative atomic mass of a metal* can be determined using the number of moles of gas produced from a known number of moles of metal when it reacts with excess acid.

**Worked example**

0.02 g of Mg reacts with excess hydrochloric acid to produce 20 $cm^3$ of hydrogen at r.t.p.

$$Mg + 2HCl \rightarrow MgCl_2 + H_2$$

Calculate the relative atomic mass of magnesium. [3]

1. Calculate the volume of hydrogen in $dm^3$: $\frac{20}{1000} = 0.02\ dm^3$
2. Calculate moles of $H_2$: $\frac{0.02}{24} = 8.33 \times 10^{-4}$ mol ✓
3. Check the stoichiometry of the equation: 1 mol Mg produces 1 mol hydrogen

   So moles Mg = $8.33 \times 10^{-4}$ mol
4. Use simple proportion to calculate $A_r$:

   $8.33 \times 10^{-4}$ mol has a mass of 0.02 g

   So 1 mole has a mass of $0.02 \times \frac{1}{8.33 \times 10^{-4}}$ ✓ = 24.0 ✓

## Apply

9. 0.668 g of $CaCO_3$ reacts with excess hydrochloric acid to produce 160 $cm^3$ of carbon dioxide at r.t.p.:

   $$CaCO_3 + 2HCl \rightarrow CaCl_2 + CO_2 + H_2O$$

   Calculate the relative formula mass of calcium carbonate.

# 6.6 Yield and purity

**You need to:**

- **Calculate percentage yield.**
- **Calculate percentage purity.**

**Experimental yield** is the mass of a specific product found by experiment from a known amount of limiting reactant.

**Theoretical yield** is the maximum mass of a specific product found by calculation from a known amount of limiting reactant.

$$\textbf{Percentage yield} = \frac{\text{experimental yield}}{\text{theoretical yield}} \times 100$$

**Worked example**

A student reacts 30.0 g of aluminium powder with excess chlorine. The mass of aluminium chloride produced is 135.3 g.

$$2Al + 3Cl_2 \rightarrow 2AlCl_3$$

Calculate the percentage yield of aluminium chloride to two significant figures.

$A_r$ Al = 27, Cl = 35.5 [3]

1. Calculate relative formula masses. Al = 27, $AlCl_3$ = 27 + (3 × 35.5) = 133.5 ✓
2. Calculate the theoretical yield using simple proportion taking into account the stoichiometry of the equation:

$$1 \text{ mol Al} \rightarrow 1 \text{ mol } AlCl_3$$

$$30.0 \text{ g} \rightarrow 30.0 \times \frac{133.5}{27} = 148.33 \text{ g} ✓$$

3. Calculate the percentage yield: $\frac{135.3}{148.33} \times 100 = 91\%$ ✓

## Apply

10. A student reacts 11.0 g of propane with excess oxygen. The mass of carbon dioxide produced is 125.4 g.

$$C_3H_8 + 5O_2 \rightarrow 3CO_2 + 4H_2O$$

Calculate the percentage yield of carbon dioxide to two significant figures.

$A_r$ C = 12, H = 1, O = 16

### Exam tip

Always show your working in calculations with more than one mark. If you make an error at the start, you can still get marks for 'error carried forward' if the rest of your working is correct.

**Percentage purity** = $\frac{\text{mass of pure substance}}{\text{mass of impure substance}} \times 100$

**Worked example**

When 3.0 g of impure calcium carbonate is heated, 1.1 g of carbon dioxide is formed.

$$CaCO_3 \rightarrow CaO + CO_2$$

Calculate the percentage purity of the calcium carbonate to one decimal place.

Assume that the impurities do not give off carbon dioxide when heated. [3]

$A_r$ Ca = 40, C = 12, O = 16

1. Calculate the $M_r$ values.

| $CaCO_3$ | $\rightarrow$ | $CaO + CO_2$ |
|---|---|---|
| 40 + 12 + (3 × 16) | | 12 + (2 × 16) |
| 100 | | 44 ✓ |

2. Calculate the theoretical mass of calcium carbonate used to make 1.1 g of $CO_2$ using simple proportion.

To get 1.1 g of $CO_2$ we need $1.1 \times \frac{100}{44} = 2.5$ g of $CaCO_3$ ✓

3. Calculate the percentage purity.

$\frac{\text{mass of pure substance}}{\text{mass of impure substance}} \times 100$ $\frac{2.5}{3.0} \times 100 = 83.3\%$ ✓

Supplement

## Apply

11. Calculate the percentage purity:

    $A_r$ Al = 27, O = 16

    a. 20 g of impure aluminium oxide contains 0.19 moles of aluminium oxide.

    b. When 10.2 g of impure sodium hydrogencarbonate is heated, 0.042 moles of carbon dioxide is formed. Assume that the impurities do not give off carbon dioxide when heated.

    $$2NaHCO_3 \rightarrow Na_2CO_3 + CO_2 + H_2O$$

# 6.7 Empirical formula and molecular formula

**You need to:**

- **Calculate empirical formula.**
- **Calculate molecular formula.**

### Key skills

You need to be able to work out the nearest simple ratio of values such as 0.68, 0.137 and 0.033 (in this case 2:4:1).

### Recap

Empirical formula is found by:

- dividing the mass of each element in a compound by its relative atomic mass and then
- finding the simplest ratio of each element.

*Empirical formula* is calculated by taking the mass (or percentage by mass) of each element in a compound and dividing each by its atomic mass to get the simplest ratio of the elements.

### Worked example

A compound contains 3.84 g of carbon, 0.64 g of hydrogen and 11.40 g of chlorine by mass.

Calculate the empirical formula of this compound. $A_r$ C = 12, H = 1, Cl = 35.5 [3]

1. Divide mass (or percentage by mass) by the relative atomic mass.

   $$C = \frac{3.84}{12} = 0.32 \qquad H = \frac{0.64}{1} = 0.64 \qquad Cl = \frac{11.40}{35.5} = 0.32 \checkmark$$

2. Divide the result of each by the lowest figure of the three.

   $$C = \frac{0.32}{0.32} \qquad H = \frac{0.64}{0.32} \qquad Cl = \frac{0.32}{0.32} \checkmark$$

3. Find the simplest ratio and write the empirical formula.

   C = 1 H = 2 Cl = 1

   Empirical formula is $CH_2Cl$ ✓

## Apply

12. Deduce the empirical formula of the following:

    $A_r$ C = 12, H = 1, Sn = 119, Cl = 35.5, O = 16

    a. A compound of carbon and hydrogen contains 85.7% carbon and 14.3% hydrogen by mass.

    b. A chloride of tin contains 23.8 g of tin and 28.4 g of chlorine.

    c. A compound of carbon, hydrogen and oxygen contains 4.8 g of carbon, 0.6 g of hydrogen and 3.2 g of oxygen.

*Molecular formula is deduced* using the empirical formula and the relative molecular mass of a compound.

**Worked example**

A compound has the empirical formula $CH_2$ and a relative molecular mass of 70.

Deduce the molecular formula of this compound. $A_r$ C = 12, H = 1 [2]

1. Find the empirical formula mass: 12 + (2 × 1) = 14
2. Divide relative molecular mass by empirical formula mass: $\frac{70}{14} = 5$ ✓
3. Multiply the number of all the atoms in the empirical formula by the number obtained in step 2:

$$5 \times CH_2 = C_5H_{10}$$ ✓

### Exam tip

**Watch out**

In the first stage of an empirical formula calculation, it is a common error to divide by the molecular mass rather than the atomic mass. Make sure that you don't use 2 for hydrogen or 32 for oxygen.

### Exam tip

When calculating empirical formulae make sure that you don't round the figures during your working.

## Apply

13. Deduce the molecular formulae of the following:

    $A_r$ C = 12, H = 1, Br = 80, O = 16, Al = 27

    a. A compound has the empirical formula $C_2HBr$ and a relative formula mass of 315.

    b. A compound has the empirical formula $CH_2O$ and a relative formula mass of 60.

    c. A compound has the empirical formula $AlCl_3$ and a relative formula mass of 267.

# 6.8 Titrations

**You need to:**

- **Calculate solution concentration and volumes of solutions using data provided.**
- **Use experimental data to calculate the concentration of a solution in a titration.**

**Concentration of solution** $= \frac{\text{amount of solute in moles}}{\text{volume of solution in dm}^3}$

Supplement

**Key skills**

You need to be able to rearrange chemical relationships such as concentration = $\frac{\text{moles}}{\text{volume}}$ to make moles or volume the subject.

**Worked example**

Calculate the concentration in mol/dm$^3$ of a solution that contains 1.5 g of sodium hydroxide, NaOH, in 50 cm$^3$ of solution. [2]

1. Convert mass to moles: $\frac{1.5}{40}$ = 0.0375 mol ✓
2. Change cm$^3$ to dm$^3$: 50 cm$^3$ = $\frac{50}{1000}$ = 0.05 dm$^3$
3. Calculate concentration: $\frac{0.0375}{0.05}$ = 0.75 mol/dm$^3$ ✓

Calculate the volume of a solution of calcium chloride of concentration 0.200 mol/dm$^3$ which contains 13.32 g of calcium chloride, $CaCl_2$. [2]

1. Convert mass to moles: $\frac{13.32}{111}$ = 0.12 mol ✓
2. Rearrange the concentration equation to make volume the subject:

$$\text{volume in dm}^3 = \frac{\text{moles}}{\text{concentration in mol/dm}^3} = \frac{0.12}{0.200} = 0.6 \text{ dm}^3 ✓$$

## Exam tip

When doing titration calculations you may need to convert cm$^3$ to dm$^3$ or dm$^3$ to cm$^3$ in particular parts of the calculation.

## Exam tip

Some students prefer to do titration calculations using the formula:

$$\frac{m_1 \times V_1}{n_1} = \frac{m_2 \times V_2}{n_2}$$

where *m* is the concentration, *V* is the volume and *n* is the molar ratio in the equation of the acid (1) and alkali (2).

**Recap**

We can find the concentration of an acid or alkali by:

- first calculating the number of moles of the solution for which we know the concentration and volume
- then deducing the number of moles of the other solution using the ratio of acid and alkali in the chemical equation
- then calculating concentration from the moles in step 2 and the volume of the other solution.

## Apply

14. a. Calculate the concentrations in mol/dm$^3$ of:
    (i) 11.1 g of $CaCl_2$ in 400 cm$^3$ of solution
    (ii) 24 g of ethanoic acid, $CH_3COOH$, in 600 cm$^3$ of solution

    b. Calculate the mass of solute needed to make these solutions:
    (i) 50 cm$^3$ of aqueous copper(II) sulfate, $CuSO_4$, of concentration 0.2 mol/dm$^3$
    (ii) 200 cm$^3$ of aqueous magnesium nitrate, $Mg(NO_3)_2$, of concentration 2.0 mol/dm$^3$

    c. Calculate the volume of these solutions in cm$^3$:
    (i) a solution containing 2.80 g of potassium hydroxide, KOH, of concentration 0.5 mol/dm$^3$
    (ii) a solution containing 1.5 mol of sulfuric acid, $H_2SO_4$, of concentration 0.5 mol/dm$^3$

An acid–base **titration** is a method used to find the concentration of an acid or alkali by running acid from a burette into a known volume of alkali in a flask until the indicator in the flask changes colour.

**Worked example**

25.00 $cm^3$ of aqueous sodium hydroxide is neutralised by 12.40 $cm^3$ of sulfuric acid of concentration 0.2000 mol/$dm^3$.

$$2NaOH + H_2SO_4 \rightarrow Na_2SO_4 + 2H_2O$$

Calculate the concentration, in mol/$dm^3$, of the aqueous sodium hydroxide. [3]

1. Calculate moles of reactant for which both concentration and volume are known:

   $$\text{moles} = \text{concentration (mol/dm}^3) \times \frac{\text{volume (cm}^3)}{1000}$$

   $$\text{moles of } H_2SO_4 = 0.2000 \times \frac{12.40}{1000} = 2.480 \times 10^{-3} \text{ mol } H_2SO_4 \checkmark$$

2. Use the mole ratio in the balanced equation to calculate moles of NaOH.

   1 mol $H_2SO_4$ reacts with 2 mol NaOH

   So, $2.480 \times 10^{-3}$ mol $H_2SO_4$ reacts with $2 \times (2.480 \times 10^{-3})$ $= 4.960 \times 10^{-3}$ mol NaOH ✓

3. Calculate concentration of NaOH:

   $$\text{concentration of NaOH} = \text{moles} \times \frac{1000}{\text{volume (cm}^3)}$$

   $$= 4.960 \times 10^{-3} \times \frac{1000}{25.00} = 0.1984 \text{ mol/dm}^3 \checkmark$$

**Key skills**

You need to be able to work through mathematical problems involving several stages.

**Exam tip**

You may find that exam questions about titrations are written so that each step is given in sequence, e.g. moles of acid → moles of alkali from the equation → concentration of alkali.

**Exam tip**

**Watch out**

Make sure that you write your answer to the correct number of significant figures if asked. It's easy to forget this after doing an extended calculation.

## Apply

15. a. 20.0 $cm^3$ of aqueous potassium hydroxide of concentration 0.400 mol/$dm^3$ is neutralised by 27.5 $cm^3$ of hydrochloric acid.

$$KOH + HCl \rightarrow KCl + H_2O$$

Calculate the concentration, in mol/$dm^3$, of the hydrochloric acid. Give your answer to two significant figures.

b. 20.0 $cm^3$ of aqueous sodium hydroxide is neutralised by 15.0 $cm^3$ of sulfuric acid of concentration 0.500 mol/$dm^3$.

$$2NaOH + H_2SO_4 \rightarrow Na_2SO_4 + 2H_2O$$

Calculate the concentration, in mol/$dm^3$, of the aqueous sodium hydroxide.

c. A solution of aqueous barium hydroxide contains 3.46 g of barium hydroxide. This solution is neutralised by 22.5 $cm^3$ of dilute hydrochloric acid.

$$Ba(OH)_2 + 2HCl \rightarrow BaCl_2 + 2H_2O$$

Calculate the concentration, in mol/$dm^3$, of the dilute hydrochloric acid.

## Questions

**1. a.** Complete the definition of relative atomic mass using words from the list.

S

atom average carbon compound element hydrogen molecule total

Relative atomic mass is the ........................ mass of the isotopes of an ........................ compared to $\frac{1}{12}$th the mass of an ........................ of ........................ -12. [4]

**b.** **(i)** Define relative molecular mass. [1]

**(ii)** Give the symbol for relative molecular mass. [1]

**(iii)** Calculate the relative molecular mass of potassium sulfate, $K_2SO_4$. [1]

**c.** Calculate the concentration, in mol/dm$^3$, of a solution containing 0.2 moles of sodium chloride in 500 cm$^3$ of solution. [1]

**d.** Calculate the volume of a solution containing 0.5 moles of sodium hydroxide of concentration 0.25 mol/dm$^3$. [1]

**e.** Calculate the volume of 6.16 g of carbon dioxide at r.t.p. [2]

**f.** **(i)** Calculate the mass of carbon that reacts with excess lead oxide, $Pb_3O_4$, to form 62.1 g of lead.

$$Pb_3O_4 + 4C \rightarrow 3Pb + 4CO$$ [3]

**(ii)** Calculate the percentage by mass of lead in $Pb_3O_4$. [2]

**(iii)** A compound of lead contains 59.3% lead and 40.7% chlorine by mass. Calculate the empirical formula of this compound. [2]

**g.** When 9.50 g of impure sodium hydrogencarbonate is heated, 0.035 moles of carbon dioxide is formed. Assume that the impurities do not give off carbon dioxide when heated.

$$2NaHCO_3 \rightarrow Na_2CO_3 + CO_2 + H_2O$$

Calculate the percentage purity of the impure sodium hydrogencarbonate. [3]

**h.** 40.0 cm$^3$ of aqueous potassium hydroxide is neutralised by 12.4 cm$^3$ of dilute sulfuric acid of concentration 0.200 mol/dm$^3$. Calculate the concentration, in mol/dm$^3$, of the aqueous potassium hydroxide. [3]

## Sample question

This question is about sodium and compounds of sodium.

**1.** **a.** **(i)** Sodium has a relative atomic mass of 23. Define relative atomic mass. [3]

**(ii)** Calculate the number of sodium atoms in 0.46 g of sodium. [2]

**b.** Calculate the percentage by mass of sodium in sodium carbonate, $Na_2CO_3$. [2]

S

**c.** Sodium carbonate is formed when sodium hydrogencarbonate is heated:

$$2NaHCO_3 \rightarrow Na_2CO_3 + CO_2 + H_2O$$

**(i)** Calculate the maximum mass of sodium carbonate formed when 21.0 g of sodium hydrogencarbonate is completely decomposed. [3]

**(ii)** Calculate the volume of carbon dioxide formed when 21.0 g of sodium hydrogencarbonate is completely decomposed. [2]

**(iii)** A sample of 14.0 g of impure sodium hydrogencarbonate contains 0.1 moles of sodium carbonate as an impurity. Calculate the percentage purity of the sodium hydrogencarbonate. [3]

**d.** Sodium carbonate reacts with dilute hydrochloric acid.

$$Na_2CO_3 + 2HCl \rightarrow 2NaCl + CO_2 + H_2O$$

**(i)** 10.0 cm$^3$ of aqueous sodium carbonate of concentration 0.150 mol/dm$^3$ is neutralised by 32.5 cm$^3$ of dilute hydrochloric acid.

Calculate the concentration of the dilute hydrochloric acid. Give your answer to three significant figures. [3]

**(ii)** In a separate experiment, a student added 13.25 g of sodium carbonate to 50 cm$^3$ of hydrochloric acid of concentration 4.0 mol/dm$^3$.

Show by calculation that hydrochloric acid is the limiting reactant. [4]

**e.** **(i)** A compound of sodium, sulfur and oxygen contains 29.1% sodium and 40.5% sulfur by mass. Calculate the empirical formula of this compound. [3]

**(ii)** Another compound of sodium has the empirical formula $NaCO_2$. The relative formula mass of this compound is 134. Deduce the molecular formula of this compound. [2]

# Electricity and chemistry

## Revision checklist

Tick these boxes to build a record of your revision. Columns 2 and 3 can be used if you want to make a record more than once.

| Core/**Supplement** syllabus content | | 1 | 2 | 3 |
|---|---|---|---|---|
| 7.1 | Describe electrical conductors and electrical insulators. | | | |
| 7.1 | Describe the reasons for the use of copper and steel-cored aluminium for electrical cables and why plastics and ceramics are used as insulators. | | | |
| 7.1 | Define electrolysis. | | | |
| 7.1 | Identify the anode, cathode and electrolyte in an electrolytic cell. | | | |
| 7.2 | Describe the electrode products and observations made during the electrolysis of molten lead(II) bromide and concentrated sulfuric acid. | | | |
| 7.2 | State that metals or hydrogen are formed at the cathode and non-metals other than hydrogen are formed at the anode during electrolysis. | | | |
| 7.2 | Predict the identity of the electrolysis products of a specified binary compound in the molten state. | | | |
| 7.3 | Describe the electrode products and observations made during the electrolysis of dilute sulfuric acid. | | | |
| 7.3 | **Predict and identify the electrolysis products of aqueous halides in dilute or concentrated aqueous solution.** | | | |
| 7.4 | **Describe the charge transfer during electrolysis.** | | | |
| 7.4 | **Construct ionic half-equations for the reactions at the anode and cathode during electrolysis.** | | | |
| 7.5 | **Identify the electrode products and describe the observations made during the electrolysis of aqueous copper(II) sulfate using graphite electrodes and copper electrodes.** | | | |
| 7.5 | **Describe the purification of copper by electrolysis.** | | | |
| 7.6 | Know that metal objects are electroplated to improve their appearance and resistance to corrosion. | | | |
| 7.6 | Describe how metals are electroplated. | | | |
| 7.7 | **Describe the extraction of aluminium from purified bauxite.** | | | |
| 7.7 | **Construct ionic half-equations for reactions at the anode and cathode during the electrolysis of molten aluminium oxide.** | | | |

# 7.1 Conductors and electrolysis

**You need to:**

- Describe electrical conductors and electrical insulators.
- Describe the reasons for the use of copper and steel-cored aluminium for electrical cables and why plastics and ceramics are used as insulators.
- Define electrolysis.
- Identify the anode, cathode and electrolyte in an electrolytic cell.

**Electrical conductors** are substances that allow electricity to flow through them easily.

*Copper is used in electrical wiring* because it is a very good conductor of electricity.

*Steel-cored aluminium cables are used in high-voltage power lines* because (i) aluminium is a good conductor and (ii) steel strengthens the cable.

**Insulators** such as plastics and ceramics are poor electrical conductors.

### Exam tip

When answering questions about insulators, it is better to describe them as 'poor conductors' rather than 'non-conductors' because many do conduct to a very small extent.

### Key skills

Look out for words such as 'each' in a question. In this case, it tells you that you have to write about four materials in the diagram.

### Worked example

The structures of household electrical wiring (a) and an overhead electrical cable (b) are shown.

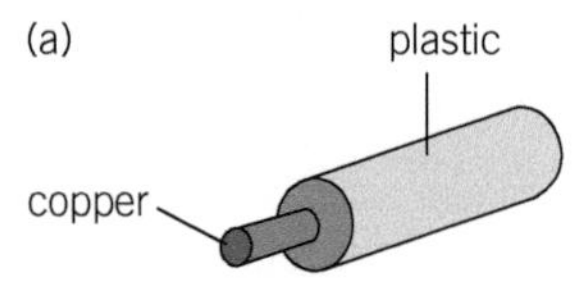


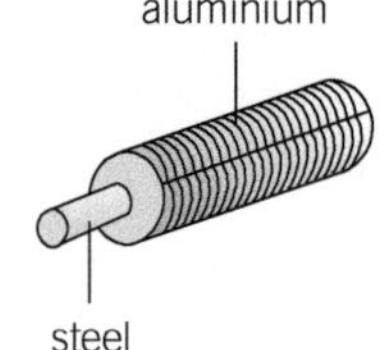


Explain how the physical properties of each material is related to its use in electrical wiring. [4]

Copper is a good conductor of electricity. ✓

Plastic is an insulator, so is a poor conductor of electricity. ✓

Aluminium is a good conductor of electricity. ✓

Steel strengthens the cable (and so stops it from breaking). ✓

### Exam tip

**Watch out**

It is a common mistake to suggest that the steel core in aluminium electricity cables just conducts electricity. It is there mainly to strengthen the cable.

### Recap

- Metals are good conductors of electricity.
- Most non-metals are poor conductors of electricity.

## Apply

1. a. Name one non-metallic element that conducts electricity.

   b. Name two other elements that conduct electricity.

   c. Describe two differences between a high-voltage electricity cable and the electrical wiring in a house.

**Electrolysis** is the **decomposition** of an ionic compound when molten or in an aqueous solution by the passage of an electric current.

An **electrolyte** is a molten or aqueous ionic compound that conducts electricity and decomposes during electrolysis.

**Electrodes** are rods that carry the electric current to and from the electrolyte.

The **anode** is the positive electrode.

The **cathode** is the negative electrode.

### Exam tip

Remember that electrolytes include:

- molten or aqueous ionic salts such as sodium iodide and magnesium chloride
- acids such as sulfuric acid and hydrochloric acid.

### Worked example

Complete and label the diagram of an electrolysis cell to show:

the anode and the cathode

the power supply

the electrolyte [3]

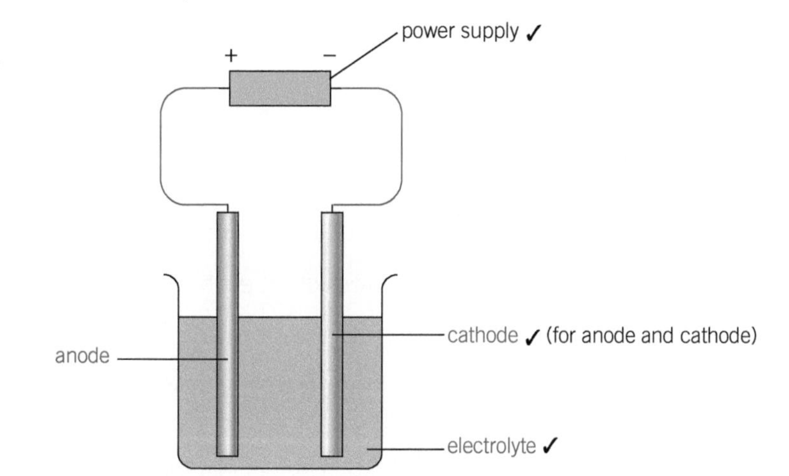


### Key skills

You should be prepared to draw and label diagrams of electrolysis apparatus in the examination.

### Exam tip

**Watch out**

When labelling the electrodes, make sure that the lines or arrows pointing to the electrodes finish at the electrode itself and don't end at the electrolyte.

### Recap

- Decomposition is the breakdown of a substance into two or more different substances.
- Graphite or platinum electrodes are used in electrolysis because they do not react with the electrolyte.
- The anode is the positive electrode and the cathode is the negative electrode.

### Exam tip

When drawing connecting wires to the electrolysis apparatus, make sure that the wire from the + end of the power supply goes to the anode and the wire from the - end of the power supply goes to the cathode.

## Apply

2. Link the words **A** to **D** with the phrases **1** to **4**.

**A** cathode **B** electrolyte **C** anode **D** electrolysis

**1** an example is molten sodium bromide

**2** the negative electrode

**3** the breakdown of a substance by the passage of electricity

**4** the positive electrode

### Exam tip

Remember that ionic solids do not conduct electricity because the ions cannot move (see Chapter 4).

# 7.2 The products of electrolysis

**You need to:**

- Describe the electrode products and observations made during the electrolysis of molten lead(II) bromide and concentrated sulfuric acid.
- State that metals or hydrogen are formed at the cathode and non-metals other than hydrogen are formed at the anode during electrolysis.
- **Predict and identify the electrolysis products of aqueous halides in dilute or concentrated aqueous solution.**

*Electrolysis of molten lead(II) bromide* produces a red-brown gas at the anode and a silvery grey metal at the cathode.

*Electrolysis of a molten* **binary ionic compound** produces a metal at the cathode and a non-metal at the anode.

*Electrolysis of a dilute aqueous ionic solution* produces hydrogen at the cathode and oxygen at the anode.

**Worked example**

Molten zinc bromide is electrolysed.

Give the observations and name the products at each electrode. [4]

Anode: bromine ✓ is formed which is a red-brown gas. ✓

Cathode: zinc ✓ is formed which forms a grey layer ✓ on the electrode.

Explain why solid zinc bromide does not conduct electricity. [1]

The ions cannot move in the solid. ✓

**Exam tip**

If you see the word observation it means you have to write about what you see (or feel or hear) *not* the name of the substance formed.

**Recap**

- A binary ionic compound contains only one type of positive ion and one type of negative ion, e.g. potassium chloride, magnesium bromide.
- During electrolysis of a molten binary compound a metal is formed at the cathode and a non-metal at the anode.

**Exam tip**

**Watch out**

Makes sure that you never write '-ides' as products of electrolysis. For example, when chlorides are electrolysed the product is chlorine.

## Apply

3. a. In what physical states must an ionic compound be for it to be electrolysed?

   b. Name the molecules formed when molten compounds containing these ions are electrolysed:

   (i) chloride (ii) oxide (iii) iodide

   c. Complete this statement about the products of electrolysis using words from the list.

   anode cathode hydrogen metals nitrogen non-metals

   Metals or .......................... are formed at the cathode and .......................... other than hydrogen are formed at the .......................... during electrolysis.

   d. Name the products formed at the anode and cathode when these molten compounds are electrolysed.

   (i) lead(II) chloride

   (ii) aluminium oxide

# 7.3 Electrolysis of aqueous solutions

**You need to:**

- Describe the electrode products and observations made during the electrolysis of dilute sulfuric acid.
- State that metals or hydrogen are formed at the cathode and non-metals other than hydrogen are formed at the anode during electrolysis.
- State the products of electrolysis of concentrated aqueous sodium chloride.
- **Describe the electrode products and observations made during the electrolysis of dilute and concentrated aqueous solutions of the halides.**

*Electrolysis of dilute sulfuric acid* produces bubbles of oxygen at the anode and bubbles of hydrogen at the cathode.

*Electrolysis of concentrated aqueous sodium chloride* produces chlorine at the anode and hydrogen at the cathode.

**Exam tip**

Remember that when molten sodium chloride is electrolysed sodium is formed at the cathode, but when aqueous sodium chloride is electrolysed hydrogen is formed at the cathode.

**Worked example**

Dilute sulfuric acid is electrolysed using **inert electrodes**.

Suggest why magnesium cannot be used as an electrode. [1]

It reacts with sulfuric acid ✓

State the **products** formed at the positive and negative electrodes. [2]

Positive electrode: oxygen ✓ Negative electrode: hydrogen. ✓

**Recap**

In aqueous ionic solutions, hydrogen is formed at the cathode if ions of a reactive metal are present, and oxygen at the anode, if chloride, bromide or iodide ions are not present.

## Apply

4. a. Name two elements that can be used as inert electrodes when acids are electrolysed.

   b. Name a piece of apparatus that you can use to collect the gases when acids are electrolysed.

   c. Name the products at each electrode when concentrated aqueous sodium chloride is electrolysed.

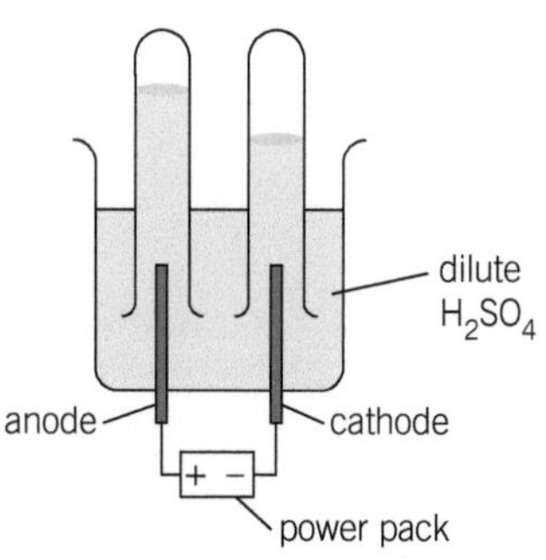


**Apparatus for electrolysis of dilute sulfuric acid, $H_2SO_4$**

Supplement

Electrolysis of dilute aqueous ionic solutions (other than halides) produces hydrogen at the cathode and oxygen at the anode.

The products of the electrolysis of aqueous solutions of halides depend on the reactivity of the halogens and the concentration of the solution.

Electrolysis of very dilute sodium chloride produces hydrogen at the cathode and oxygen or a mixture of oxygen and chlorine at the anode.

Less reactive elements are more likely to be discharged (formed) at the electrodes than more reactive elements.

**Worked example**

Electrolysis of a dilute solution of potassium sulfate produces hydrogen at the cathode.

Explain why hydrogen is formed at the cathode rather than potassium. [4]

Potassium is higher than hydrogen in the reactivity series. ✓ So potassium ions are less likely to be discharged than hydrogen ions. ✓ The hydrogen comes from the water ✓ which contains small amounts of $H^+$ ions. ✓

Give the formula of the product formed at the anode. [1]

$O_2$ ✓

**Recap**

- A very dilute aqueous solution contains an excess of water molecules and so the $H^+$ and $OH^-$ ions present in water form hydrogen and oxygen.
- Hydrogen is discharged at the cathode in preference to metals above hydrogen in the reactivity series when an aqueous solution of a metal halide is electrolysed.

## Apply

5. a. Suggest the names of the products formed at each electrode when the following aqueous solutions are electrolysed:
   (i) concentrated aqueous magnesium chloride
   (ii) concentrated aqueous potassium bromide
   (iii) very dilute potassium chloride

   b. Describe the observations at each electrode when a dilute solution of potassium iodide is electrolysed.

# 7.4 Explaining electrolysis

**You need to:**

- **Describe the charge transfer during electrolysis.**
- **Construct ionic half-equations for the reactions at the anode and cathode.**

*Charge transfer in the external circuit* involves movement of electrons in the direction:

anode → positive pole of the power supply and negative pole of the power supply → cathode.

*Negative ions move* towards the positive electrode during electrolysis.

*Positive ions move* towards the negative electrode during electrolysis.

**Worked example**

Complete and label the diagram of an electrolysis cell to show:

the anode and the cathode

an arrow labelled **C** to show the direction of the movement of the electrons in the external circuit

an arrow labelled **D** to show the direction of the movement of the positive ions. [3]

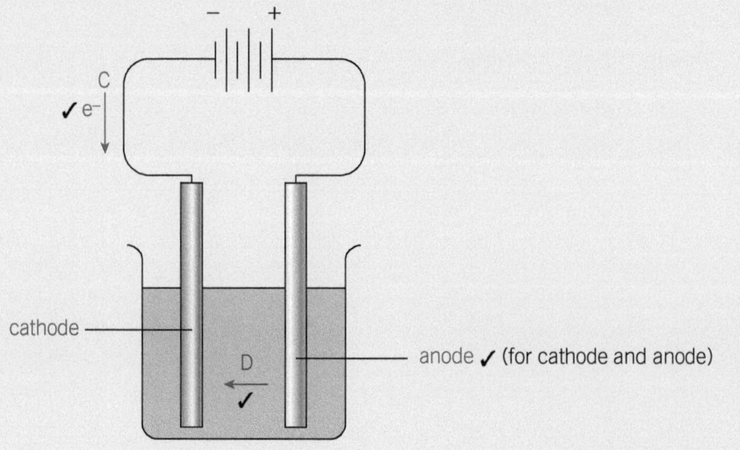

**Recap**

Positive ions gain electrons at the cathode (reduction) and negative ions lose electrons at the anode (oxidation).

**Exam tip**

Remember that in an electrolyte, it is the ions that move *not* the electrons.

**Exam tip**

<u>C</u>ations (+ ions) move to the <u>c</u>athode. <u>A</u>nions (- ions) move to the <u>a</u>node.

**Exam tip**

It is useful to remember that reduction always happens at a cathode and oxidation at the anode. For more information about oxidation and reduction, see Chapter 9.

## Apply

6. a. (i) Give the formulae of all the ions present in solution when dilute aqueous sodium chloride is electrolysed.

   (ii) State the direction of movement of each of these ions during electrolysis.

   b. Describe how charge is transferred in the external circuit during electrolysis.

Supplement

**Key skills**

Learning how to write and balance half-equations involving loss or gain of electrons is a skill you will need to use in several places in the course.

*Ions lose* electrons at the anode.

*Ions gain* electrons at the cathode.

**Ionic half-equations** show the gain or loss of electrons when atoms are formed from ions.

**Worked example**

Write ionic half-equations for the formation of these products during electrolysis.

Include state symbols.

hydrogen [3]

$2H^+(aq) + 2e^- \rightarrow H_2(g)$

Correct reactant and product including electrons ✓ correct balance ✓ correct state symbols ✓

bromine [3]

$2Br^-(aq) \rightarrow Br_2(aq) + 2e^-$

Correct reactant and product including electrons ✓ correct balance ✓ correct state symbols (allow: $Br_2(g)$) ✓

**Exam tip**

**Watch out**

Remember to balance the electrons in an ionic half-equation.

**Exam tip**

Another way of writing the half-equation at the anode to show electron loss is:

$2Br^-(aq) - 2e^- \rightarrow Br_2(aq)$

But stick to one method or the other so that you don't get muddled.

## Apply

7. Write ionic half-equations for the reactions at both the anode and cathode during the electrolysis of:
   a. dilute hydrochloric acid
   b. molten zinc bromide
   c. dilute sulfuric acid
   d. molten lithium oxide

**Exam tip**

**Watch out**

Remember that the formula for an oxide ion is $O^{2-}$. It is often written incorrectly.

# 7.5 Purifying copper

**You need to:**

- **Identify the electrode products and describe the observations made during the electrolysis of aqueous copper(II) sulfate using graphite electrodes and copper electrodes.**
- **Describe the purification of copper by electrolysis.**

*Copper is purified* using an impure copper anode and a pure copper cathode.

*Electrolysis of copper using inert electrodes* produces copper at the cathode and oxygen at the anode

*Electrolysis of copper using copper electrodes produces* copper at the cathode but the anode reacts as Cu is converted to $Cu^{2+}$ ions which go into solution.

**Worked example**

Copper(II) sulfate is electrolysed using copper electrodes.

Write the equation for the reaction occurring at the anode. [2]

$Cu + 2e^- \rightarrow Cu^{2+} + 2e^-$

Correct reactant and product including electrons ✓
correct balance ✓

Describe any observations at the anode. [1]

The anode gets thinner ✓

Explain why the electrolyte does not change in depth of colour during the electrolysis. [2]

The coloured copper ions removed from the solution at the cathode ✓ are replaced by copper ions formed at the anode. ✓

**Key skills**

You need to understand the difference in meaning of command words such as describe and explain to maximise your marks.

**Recap**

When copper(II) sulfate is electrolysed the anode product is copper ions when a copper electrode is used but oxygen if an inert electrode is used.

## Apply

8. Copper(II) sulfate is electrolysed using graphite electrodes.
   a. Write the equation for the reaction occurring at the cathode.
   b. Describe any observations at the cathode.
   c. Explain why the electrolyte gradually loses its blue colour during the electrolysis.

### Exam tip

Remember that in electrolysis, the electrodes are usually inert (graphite or platinum). If the anode is not inert it will react and decrease in size.

# 7.6 Electroplating

**You need to:**

- Know that metal objects are electroplated to improve their appearance and resistance to corrosion.
- Describe how metals are electroplated.

**Electroplating** is a process that uses electrolysis to coat one metal with another.

*Electroplating is used* to improve the appearance of an object and to improve its resistance to **corrosion**.

The *plating (coating) metal* is made the anode of an electrolysis cell.

The *object to be plated* is made the cathode of an electrolysis cell.

**Recap**

In electroplating, the object to be plated is made the cathode and the metal used for the plating is the anode.

### Exam tip

Remember that the **P**lating metal is the **P**ositive electrode (anode) and the object to be electroplated is the cathode.

### Exam tip

For the Supplement syllabus, you may be asked to write ionic half-equations for electroplating.

**Worked example**

Draw a diagram of the apparatus used to electroplate a steel spoon with silver.

On your diagram label the anode, the cathode, the electrolyte and the name of a suitable electrolyte. [5]

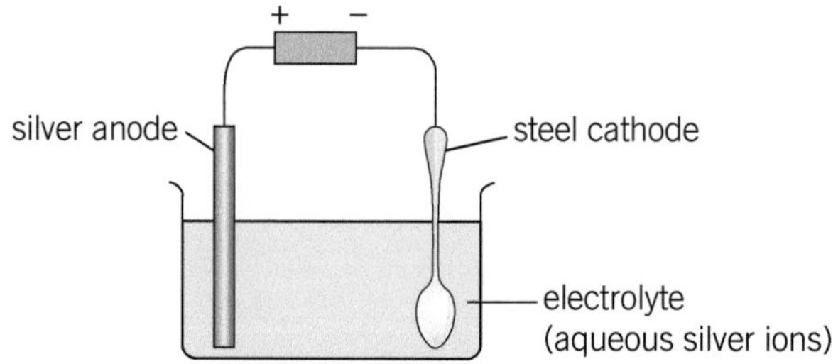


Two electrodes dipping into a liquid connected correctly to a power supply ✓

silver anode ✓ steel / spoon cathode ✓

electrolyte labelled ✓ electrolyte named as silver ions or named soluble silver compound, e.g. silver nitrate ✓

Write half-equations for the reactions at the anode and cathode. [2]

Anode: $2O^{2-} \rightarrow O_2 + 4e^-$ ✓

Cathode: $Al^{3+} + 3e^- \rightarrow Al$ ✓

## Apply

9. Draw a diagram of the apparatus used to electroplate a copper rod with nickel.

   On your diagram label the anode, the cathode, the electrolyte and the name of a suitable electrolyte.

# 7.7 Extracting aluminium

**You need to:**

- **Describe the extraction of aluminium from purified bauxite.**
- **Construct ionic half-equations for reactions at the anode and cathode during the electrolysis of molten aluminium oxide.**

The *aluminium electrolysis cell* has carbon anodes and a carbon cathode.

The *electrolyte* is molten aluminium oxide, dissolved in molten cryolite.

*Cryolite* helps dissolve the aluminium oxide and lowers the melting point of the electrolyte.

The *anodes are replaced* regularly because they react with the oxygen formed during electrolysis.

**Worked example**

The diagram shows an electrolysis cell for the extraction of aluminium.

Label the anode, the cathode, where the aluminium collects and the electrolyte. [4]

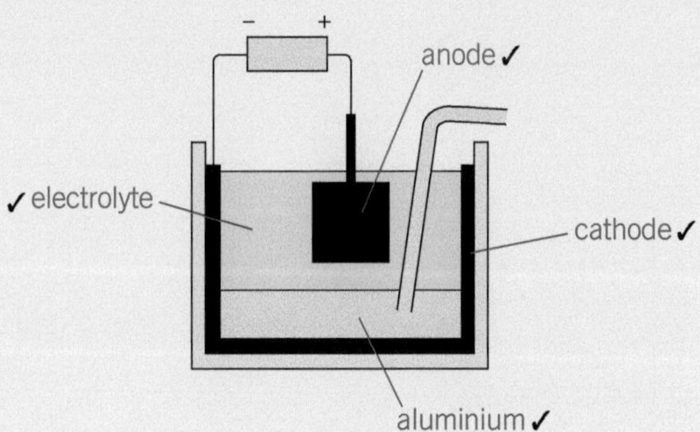


Explain why a mixture of cryolite and aluminium oxide is used as the electrolyte instead of aluminium oxide alone. [2]

Cryolite dissolves the aluminium oxide ✓ and lowers the melting point of the electrolyte. ✓ The melting point of aluminium oxide on its own is very high so too much energy would be used.

Write half-equations for the reactions at the anode and cathode. [2]

Anode: $2O^{2-} \rightarrow O_2 + 4e^-$ ✓

Cathode: $Al^{3+} + 3e^- \rightarrow Al$ ✓

**Exam tip**

You do not have to know the details of the purification of $Al_2O_3$ but you may be asked questions about purification techniques when given suitable information.

**Exam tip**

You do not have to learn the diagram of the cell used to extract aluminium but you should be able to label the different parts.

**Recap**

In the production of aluminium:

- carbon electrodes are used with an electrolyte of aluminium oxide dissolved in cryolite
- the carbon anodes are renewed regularly because they react with the oxygen produced at the anode.

## Apply

10. a. Name the main ore of aluminium.

    b. Name the electrolyte used in the extraction of aluminium.

    c. Name the element used for the electrodes in the extraction of aluminium and explain why the anodes have to be replaced from time to time.

    d. Write an ionic half-equation for the reaction at the cathode during the electrolysis of aluminium.

## Questions

1. Which of these substances are insulators?

   ceramic steel zinc plastic magnesium [2]

2. Copy and complete this definition of electrolysis using some of the words from the list.

   aqueous covalent current decomposition
   hexane ionic oxidation spark

   Electrolysis is the .................... of an .................... compound when molten or in .................... solution by the passage of an electric .................... [4]

3. Which of these substances can be electrolysed? Explain why.
   - **a.** molten zinc chloride
   - **b.** dilute nitric acid
   - **c.** solid carbon dioxide
   - **d.** molten sulfur
   - **e.** aqueous potassium sulfate
   - **f.** solid sodium chloride
   - **g.** molten zinc [3]

4. Name the products formed at the anode and cathode when the following are electrolysed and give the observations at each electrode.
   - **a.** molten calcium bromide [4]
   - **b.** concentrated aqueous sodium chloride [4]
   - **c.** dilute sulfuric acid [4]

5. Electroplating is carried out to make objects more attractive.
   - **a.** Give one other advantage of electroplating. [1]
   - **b.** Copy and complete these sentences about electroplating.
     - **(i)** The object to be electroplated is made the .................... electrode. [1]
     - **(ii)** The plating metal is connected to the .................... pole of the power supply. [1]
     - **(iii)** The electrolyte is an aqueous .................... solution of a compound of the plating metal. [1]

S

6. **a.** Write ionic half-equations for the reaction at each electrode when the following are electrolysed:
   - **(i)** molten zinc oxide [4]
   - **(ii)** concentrated aqueous calcium chloride [4]
   - **(iii)** aqueous potassium sulfate [4]

7. **a.** Describe and explain the direction of movement of ions and electrons during electrolysis. [5]

   **b.** State where **(i)** oxidation and **(ii)** reduction happens during electrolysis. [2]

8. Give the formula and direction of movement of the ions in the electrolyte during the production of aluminium by electrolysis. State whether these ions lose or gain electrons at the electrodes. [4]

## Sample question

This question is about electrolysis.

1. **a.** State the meaning of the term electrolysis. [2]

   **b.** Give two reasons why graphite electrodes are used in electrolysis. [2]

   **c.** **(i)** Name the products at the anode and cathode when molten nickel bromide is electrolysed. [2]

   **(ii)** Describe the observations at the anode and cathode when molten nickel bromide is electrolysed. [2]

   **(iii)** A steel knife can be electroplated with nickel. Describe using a labelled diagram how this is done. [5]

   S **d.** Copper(II) sulfate can be electrolysed using inert electrodes.

   Write ionic half-equations for the reactions occurring at the anode and cathode during this electrolysis. Include state symbols. [6]

   **e.** When a very dilute aqueous solution of potassium chloride is electrolysed, hydrogen is produced at the cathode and oxygen at the anode. Explain why the electrode products are not potassium and chlorine. [4]

   **f.** Aluminium is extracted from a mixture of molten aluminium oxide and cryolite.

   **(i)** Write ionic half-equations for the reactions at the cathode and anode. [4]

   **(ii)** Describe and explain the observations at the anode during the electrolysis. [3]

# Chemical energetics

## Revision checklist

Tick these boxes to build a record of your revision. Columns 2 and 3 can be used if you want to make a record more than once.

| Core/**Supplement** syllabus content | | 1 | 2 | 3 |
|---|---|---|---|---|
| 8.1 | Identify physical and chemical changes and understand the differences between them. | | | |
| 8.1 | Describe the meaning of the terms exothermic and endothermic. | | | |
| 8.1 | **Describe the transfer of thermal energy in a reaction as an enthalpy change, Δ*H*.** | | | |
| 8.1 | **Exothermic reactions have negative enthalpy changes and endothermic reactions have positive enthalpy changes.** | | | |
| 8.2 | Interpret reaction pathway diagrams for exothermic and endothermic reactions. | | | |
| 8.2 | **Define activation energy.** | | | |
| 8.2 | Draw and label reaction pathway diagrams to include activation energy. | | | |
| 8.3 | **Describe bond breaking as an endothermic process and bond making as an exothermic process.** | | | |
| 8.3 | **Calculate the overall energy change of a reaction using bond energies and determine if the reaction is exothermic or endothermic.** | | | |
| 8.4 | Name the fossil fuels coal, natural gas and petroleum. | | | |
| 8.4 | Name methane as the main constituent of natural gas. | | | |
| 8.4 | Write word equations for the complete combustion of carbon-containing fuels. | | | |
| 8.4 | Describe the transfer of thermal energy by burning fuels. | | | |
| 8.4 | State that carbon monoxide is formed from the incomplete combustion of carbon-containing fuels. | | | |
| 8.4 | **Construct chemical equations for the complete combustion of carbon-containing fuels.** | | | |
| 8.5 | State that a hydrogen–oxygen fuel cell uses hydrogen and oxygen to generate electricity with water as the only product. | | | |
| 8.5 | **Describe the advantages and disadvantages of using fuel cells in comparison with gasoline (petrol) engines in vehicles.** | | | |

# 8.1 Energy transfer in chemical reactions

**You need to:**

- Identify physical and chemical changes and understand the differences between them.
- Describe the meaning of the terms exothermic and endothermic.
- Describe the transfer of thermal energy in a reaction as an enthalpy change, $\Delta H$.
- Exothermic reactions have negative enthalpy changes and endothermic reactions have positive enthalpy changes.

An **exothermic reaction** releases thermal energy to the surroundings. The temperature of the surroundings increases.

An **endothermic reaction** absorbs thermal energy from the surroundings. The temperature of the surroundings decreases.

The **surroundings** are everything apart from the chemicals taking part in a reaction. Examples are the solution, the test tube and the air surrounding the test tube.

S **Enthalpy change, $\Delta H$**, is the thermal energy change which takes place during a chemical reaction.

**Worked example**

When magnesium is added to hydrochloric acid, the temperature of the surroundings increases.

State the meaning of the term surroundings and give two examples. [3]

Anything other than the chemical reaction itself. ✓ For example, the air ✓around the test tube and the test tube itself. ✓

Name the type of thermal energy change which happens when magnesium is added to hydrochloric acid. [1]

Exothermic ✓

When calcium carbonate is heated, thermal energy is absorbed. S

Give the symbol for enthalpy change. [1]

$\Delta H$ ✓

State the sign of the enthalpy change for this reaction. [1]

positive ✓

**Exam tip**

Make sure that you learn definitions such as 'endothermic' carefully. There may be more than one mark given.

**Recap**

S

- An exothermic reaction releases thermal energy to the surroundings. An endothermic reaction absorbs thermal energy from the surroundings.
- The enthalpy change is the exchange of thermal energy with the surroundings during a reaction.

## Apply

1. a. Copy and complete this sentence using words from the list.

decrease electrical surroundings reaction thermal

An endothermic reaction takes in .................... energy from the .................... leading to a .................... in the temperature of the surroundings.

b. Explain the meaning of the term exothermic.

S c. The reaction for the production of ammonia is shown:

$N_2 + 3H_2 \rightarrow 2NH_3 \qquad \Delta H = -92.4$ kJ/mol

State the type of thermal energy change taking place. Explain your answer.

# 8.2 Reaction pathway diagrams

**You need to:**

- Interpret reaction pathway diagrams for exothermic and endothermic reactions.
- **Define activation energy.**
- **Draw and label reaction pathway diagrams to include activation energy.**

**Recap**

- A reaction pathway diagram shows the relative energies of the reactants and products.
- In an exothermic reaction, the energy level of the products is lower. In an endothermic reaction, the energy level of the products is higher.

**Reaction pathway diagrams** show the energy level of the reactants and products on the vertical axis (*y* axis) and the reaction pathway on the horizontal axis (*x* axis).

In an *exothermic reaction pathway diagram*, the energy level of the reactants is higher than the energy level of the products.

In an *endothermic reaction pathway diagram*, the energy level of the reactants is lower than the energy level of the products.

**Worked example**

Complete the reaction pathway diagram for the endothermic reaction:

$$CaCO_3 \rightarrow CaO + CO_2$$

Include an arrow showing the direction of the energy change. [3]

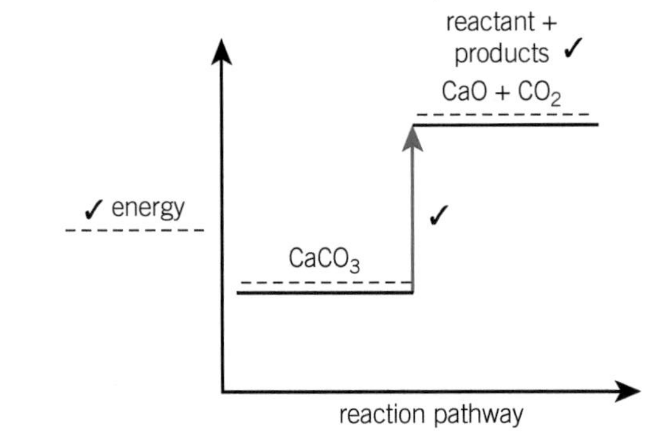


## Exam tip

**Watch out**

When drawing the arrow showing energy decrease or increase make sure that you get it the correct way round. Up for endothermic, down for exothermic.

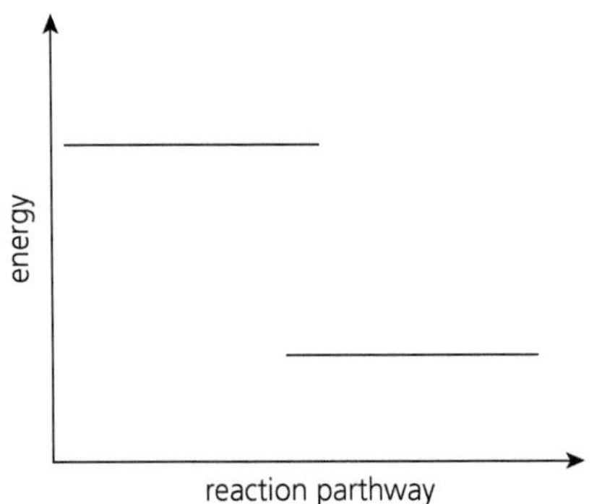


## Apply

2 a. Copy and complete the energy pathway diagram for this reaction:

$$N_2 + 3H_2 \rightarrow 2NH_3 \qquad \Delta H = -92.4 \text{ kJ/mol}$$

On your diagram include words 'reactants' and 'products' and an arrow showing the thermal energy change.

b. Explain how you know from the diagram that the reaction is exothermic.

S **Activation energy, $E_a$,** is the minimum energy that colliding particles must have in order to react.

*$E_a$ in reaction pathway diagrams* is drawn as an energy hump between reactants and products. The top of the activation energy hump is always higher than the energy levels of both the reactants and products.

**Worked example**

Draw and label a reaction pathway diagram for the exothermic reaction:

$$NaOH + HCl \rightarrow NaCl + H_2O$$

On your diagram show the activation energy for the reaction as well as the enthalpy change. [4]

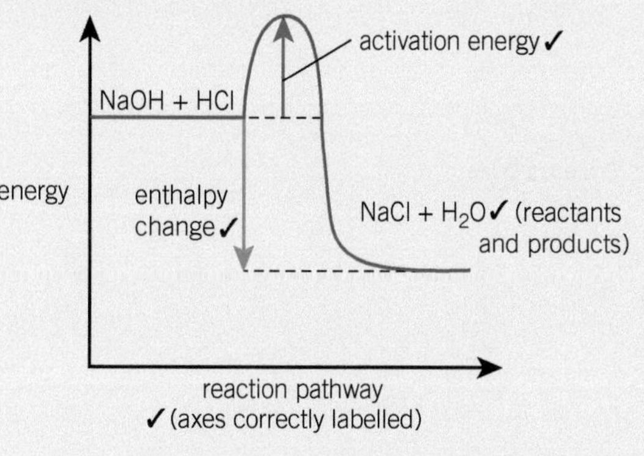


**Key skills**

You need to be able to draw and label reaction profile diagrams accurately as well as remembering scientific symbols such as $E_a$.

**Exam tip**

**Watch out**

When drawing the activation energy arrow, make sure that it goes from the reactants' energy level to the top of the energy 'hump'.

## Apply

3. Draw and label a reaction pathway diagram for the endothermic reaction:

$$2NaNO_3 \rightarrow 2NaNO_2 + O_2$$

On your diagram show the symbols for the activation energy and the enthalpy change.

# 8.3 Bond energy calculations

**You need to:**

- **Describe bond breaking as an endothermic process and bond making as an exothermic process.**
- **Calculate the overall energy change of a reaction using bond energies and determine if the reaction is exothermic or endothermic.**

*Bond breaking is endothermic* so energy is absorbed in breaking bonds.

*Bond making is exothermic* so energy is released in making bonds.

**Worked example**

Explain why the reaction $CaCO_3 \rightarrow CaO + CO_2$ is endothermic in terms of bond making and bond breaking. [2]

Energy absorbed in bond breaking and energy released in bond forming. ✓ Less energy released than absorbed. ✓

**Exam tip**

**Watch out**

When answering questions about bond breaking and bond making be careful NOT to write 'it needs more energy to break the bonds than to make them'. This common error suggests that energy is absorbed when making bonds. Energy is given out when bonds are formed.

## Apply

4. Explain why the reaction $CH_4 + 2O_2 \rightarrow CO_2 + 2H_2O$ is exothermic in terms of bond making and bond breaking.

Supplement

**Key skills**

You need to be able to set out bond energy calculations clearly in terms of bond making and bond breaking.

**Bond energy**, measured in kJ/mol, is the energy needed to break one mole of a particular bond.

*Bond energy calculations* show the difference between the energy of all the bonds in the reactants and all the bonds in the products.

The *value of the enthalpy change for an exothermic reaction* is given a negative sign.

The *value of the enthalpy change for an endothermic reaction* is given a positive sign.

### Exam tip

In the last step in bond energy calculations make sure that you take the sign of the enthalpy change into account. Bond breaking + and bond making –.

**Worked example**

Use the bond energy values given to calculate the enthalpy change of the reaction:

$$CH_4 + 2O_2 \rightarrow CO_2 + 2H_2O$$

(C–H = 435 kJ/mol; O=O = 498 kJ/mol; C=O = 805 kJ/mol; H–O = 464 kJ/mol) [3]

| bonds broken | bonds formed |
|---|---|
| $CH_4$ = 4 × 435 = 1740 | $CO_2$ = 2 × 805 = 1610 |
| $2O_2$ = 2 × 498 = 996 | $2H_2O$ = 4 × 464 = 1856 |
| Total 1740 + 996 = 2736 | Total 1610 + 1856 = 3466 |

–3466 + 2736 = –730 kJ/mol

multiplications for bonds broken correct ✓ multiplications for bonds formed correct ✓

difference in bonds –3466 + 2736 = –730 correct from calculated values ✓

Explain, using the results of your calculation, whether the reaction is exothermic or endothermic. [1]

Exothermic because the enthalpy change is negative. ✓

### Exam tip

**Watch out**

In bond energy calculations, you must take into account the number of bonds in a molecule. In $3CO_2$, there are three molecules with two bonds each O=C=O (six C=O bonds in all).

**Recap**

- Each type of bond needs a particular amount of energy to break it.
- The difference between the bond energies of the reactants and products gives us the enthalpy change of the reaction.
- An exothermic enthalpy change is given a negative sign and an endothermic change a positive sign.

## Apply

5. a. Use the bond energy values given to calculate the enthalpy change of the reaction:

$$N_2 + 3H_2 \rightarrow 2NH_3$$

(N≡N = 945 kJ/mol; H–H = 436 kJ/mol; N–H = 391 kJ/mol)

b. Use the bond energy values given to calculate the enthalpy change of the reaction:

$$2CO + O_2 \rightarrow 2CO_2$$

(C≡O in CO = 1077 kJ/mol; O=O = 498 kJ/mol; C=$O^2$ = 805 kJ/mol)

# 8.4 Fuels and energy production

**You need to:**

- Name the fossil fuels coal, natural gas and petroleum.
- Name methane as the main constituent of natural gas.
- Write word equations for the complete combustion of carbon-containing fuels.
- Describe the transfer of thermal energy by burning fuels.
- State that carbon monoxide is formed from the incomplete combustion of carbon-containing fuels.
- **Construct chemical equations for the complete combustion of carbon-containing fuels.**

**Fuels** are substances which produce energy when they are oxidised. Coal, natural gas (mainly methane) and petrol (and other hydrocarbons) are common fuels.

**Hydrocarbons** are compounds containing only hydrogen and carbon.

**Combustion** is an exothermic chemical reaction in which a fuel and oxidising agent (usually oxygen) react.

The **complete combustion** *of hydrocarbons* produces carbon dioxide and water.

**Incomplete combustion** occurs when oxygen is limiting.

The *incomplete combustion of carbon-containing compounds* produces carbon monoxide.

### Worked example

Butane is a fuel. The formula for butane is $C_4H_{10}$.

Name a fuel which is a solid at room temperature. [1]

Coal ✓

Explain why butane is a hydrocarbon. [2]

It is a compound which contains carbon and hydrogen ✓ and no other elements. ✓

Write a word equation for the complete combustion of butane. [2]

butane + oxygen → carbon dioxide + water

oxygen ✓ carbon dioxide and water ✓

State the meaning of the term incomplete combustion. [1]

Combustion where there is a limiting amount of oxygen ✓

Name a gas formed during the incomplete combustion of a hydrocarbon. [1]

carbon monoxide ✓

### Exam tip

When writing any equation involving the transfer of thermal energy, a common error is to include the word energy or heat on the left or right of the equation. Neither heat nor energy are substances!

### Recap

- Hydrocarbons are compounds of carbon and hydrogen only.
- The complete combustion of hydrocarbons produces carbon dioxide and water; incomplete combustion produces carbon monoxide and water.

**Exam tip**

You need to be able to apply your knowledge of different sections of the syllabus to any other particular section, e.g. considering practical aspects, writing equations.

## Apply

6. a. Pentane, $C_5H_{12}$, is a liquid at room temperature.
   (i) Name a fuel which is a gas at room temperature.
   (ii) Copy and complete the equation for the complete combustion of pentane.

   $C_5H_{12}$ + ............$O_2$ → ............$CO_2$ + ............$H_2O$

   b. Match the phrases **A** to **D** with the words or phrases **1** to **4**.

   **A** a solid fuel | **1** hydrocarbon
   **B** incomplete combustion | **2** carbon monoxide
   **C** formed in incomplete combustion | **3** burning when the fuel is in excess
   **D** contains only C and H | **4** coal

   c. 5 g of three different fuels are burned using the apparatus shown.

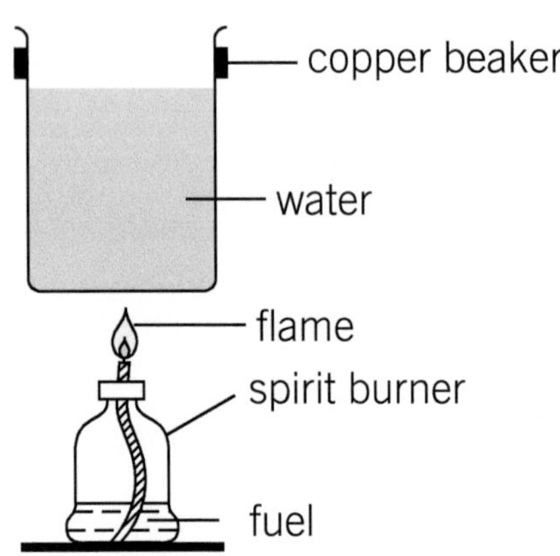


The table shows the results.

| Fuel | Initial temperature of the water / °C | Final temperature of the water / °C |
|---|---|---|
| A | 25 | 45 |
| B | 18 | 42 |
| C | 22 | 44 |

Which fuel produced the most energy per gram burned?

# 8.5 Fuel cells

**You need to:**

- State that a hydrogen-oxygen fuel cell uses hydrogen and oxygen to generate electricity with water as the only product.
- **Describe the advantages and disadvantages of using fuel cells in comparison with gasoline (petrol) engines in vehicles.**

A *hydrogen-oxygen* **fuel cell** can be used to generate electricity.

*Water is the only product* when a hydrogen-oxygen fuel cell is working. No **pollutants** are formed.

S *Advantages of a fuel cell compared to a petrol/diesel engine* include no polluting gases, more efficient energy transmission and more energy released per gram of fuel.

*Disadvantages of a fuel cell compared to a petrol/diesel engine* include hydrogen is not easily available and has to be stored safely and the platinum catalyst is expensive.

**Worked example**

A fuel cell produces water as the only product.

Name the two reactants in this fuel cell. [2]

hydrogen ✓and oxygen ✓

State the main advantage of running a car using a fuel cell rather than a petrol engine. [1]

Water is not a pollutant. ✓ The carbon dioxide produced in a petrol engine is a pollutant.

State one other advantage of a fuel cell compared with a petrol engine. S [1]

They produce more energy per gram than other fuels ✓

Give one disadvantage of a fuel cell. [1]

Hydrogen needs to be stored safely ✓

At the negative electrode in a fuel cell hydrogen loses electrons and forms hydrogen ions. Write an ionic half-equation for this reaction. [2]

$$H_2 \rightarrow 2H^+ + 2e^-$$

Correct reactants and products (including e-) ✓ Correct balance ✓

**Exam tip**

You do not need to remember details about the fuel cell but you should be prepared to write ionic half-equations for the reactions at the anode and cathode when given information.

**Recap**

- A fuel cell generates electricity, with water as the only product.
- Fuel cells have advantages over petrol engines (no polluting products/more efficient energy transmission) and disadvantages (unavailability of hydrogen/difficulties of storage). S

## Apply

7. a. Copy and complete these sentences about a fuel cell.

   A hydrogen–.................... fuel cell generates ....................
   The only product is ...................., whereas a petrol engine also produces .................... which is a pollutant.

S b. State one advantage and one disadvantage of a fuel cell compared with a petrol engine apart from pollution problems.

c. Write a chemical equation for the overall reaction in a hydrogen–oxygen fuel cell.

## Questions

**1.** State the meaning of these terms:

**a.** endothermic [2]

**b.** surroundings [1]

**c.** combustion [2]

2. A reaction pathway diagram is shown.

a. Complete the diagram by:

(i) writing the words 'reactants' and 'products' on the diagram [1]

(ii) labelling the axes [2]

b. Explain how this diagram shows that the reaction is endothermic. [1]

3. a. State the difference between the term complete combustion and the term incomplete combustion. [2]

b. Write the word equation for the complete combustion of hexane, $C_6H_{14}$. [2]

c. Name the compound which is the main constituent of natural gas. [1]

4. State the names of the reactants and product in a fuel cell. [2]

5. a. Give the meaning of the terms:

(i) activation energy [1]

(ii) enthalpy change [1]

b. Draw and label a reaction pathway diagram for an exothermic reaction. On your diagram label the enthalpy change and the activation energy with their correct symbols. [5]

6. Use the bond energy values given to calculate the enthalpy change of the reaction:

$$CH_4 + 4Cl_2 \rightarrow CCl_4 + 4HCl$$

S (C–H = 435 kJ/mol; Cl–Cl = 243 kJ/mol; C–Cl = 327 kJ/mol; H–Cl = 432 kJ/mol) [3]

7. At the positive electrode in a fuel cell, oxygen gains electrons and reacts with hydrogen ions to produce water. Write an ionic half-equation for this reaction. [2]

## Sample question

1. a. Combustion reactions are always exothermic.

(i) State the meaning of the term exothermic. [2]

(ii) Draw a reaction pathway diagram for an exothermic reaction. Label the reactants and products and draw an arrow to show the energy change in the reaction. [3]

b. (i) Copy and complete the equation for the complete combustion of ethane.

$$2C_2H_6 + \text{.........}O_2 \rightarrow \text{.........}CO_2 + \text{.........}H_2O$$ [2]

(ii) State the names of the products of the incomplete combustion of ethene. [2]

c. Describe how you can use the apparatus shown to compare the energy released when different fuels are burned.

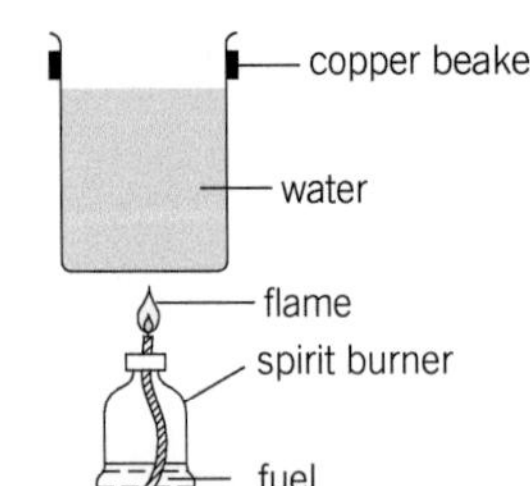


In your answer state what must be kept constant and what must be measured. [6]

S d. (i) Construct the symbol equation for the complete combustion of hexane, $C_6H_{14}$. [2]

(ii) Explain in terms of bond making and bond breaking why this reaction is exothermic. [2]

e. Use the bond energy values given to calculate the enthalpy change of the reaction:

$$2H_2S + 3O_2 \rightarrow 2SO_2 + 2H_2O$$

(H–S = 364 kJ/mol; O=O = 498 kJ/mol; S=O = 522 kJ/mol; H–O = 464 kJ/mol) [3]

f. (i) Fuel cells are non-polluting. Give two other advantages of using a fuel cell in a car instead of a petrol engine. [2]

(ii) An alkaline electrolyte is used in a fuel cell. At the negative electrode hydrogen reacts with hydroxide ions to produce water. Construct the half-equation for this reaction. [2]

# Rates of reaction

## Revision checklist

Tick these boxes to build a record of your revision. Columns 2 and 3 can be used if you want to make a record more than once.

| Core/**Supplement** syllabus content | | **1** | **2** | **3** |
|---|---|---|---|---|
| 9.1 | Describe practical methods for investigating rate of reaction when a gas is given off. | | | |
| 9.2 | Describe practical methods for investigating rate of reaction. | | | |
| 9.2 | Suggest advantages and disadvantages of experimental methods and apparatus. | | | |
| 9.2 | **Evaluate practical methods for investigating rate of reaction.** | | | |
| 9.3 | Interpret data including graphs from rate of reaction experiments. | | | |
| 9.4 | Describe the effect of surface area of solids and catalysts (including enzymes) on rate of reaction. | | | |
| 9.4 | **• Know that a catalyst lowers the activation energy so that a greater proportion of collisions are successful.**<br>**• Know that a catalyst is unchanged at the end of a reaction.**<br>**• Know that a catalyst lowers the activation energy so that a greater proportion of collisions are successful.**<br>**• Know that a catalyst is unchanged at the end of a reaction.** | | | |
| 9.5 | Describe the effect of concentration of solutions and pressure of gases on rate of reaction. | | | |
| 9.5 | **Explain using collision theory how increase in concentration of solution and increase in pressure increases the rate of reaction.** | | | |
| 9.6 | Describe the effect of temperature on the rate of reaction. | | | |
| 9.6 | **Explain using collision theory how increase in temperature increases rate of reaction.** | | | |

# 9.1 Investigating rates of reaction

**You need to:**

- Describe practical methods for investigating rate of reaction when a gas is given off.

The *progress of a reaction can be followed* by measuring how fast the reactants are used up or how fast the products are formed.

*In a reaction where a gas is produced* the reaction can be followed by measuring the loss of mass of the reaction mixture or increase in the volume of gas produced.

**Key skills**

You need to be able to draw clear labelled diagrams of apparatus used to measure the volume of gases.

**Exam tip**

**Watch out**

When drawing diagrams involving measurement of gas volumes, make sure that you draw the apparatus so that there are no gaps that let gas escape.

**Exam tip**

When labelling diagrams make sure that the full names are used. For example 'measuring cylinder' is better than 'cylinder'.

**Worked example**

Magnesium reacts with excess dilute hydrochloric acid.

$$Mg + 2HCl \rightarrow MgCl_2 + H_2$$

The volume of hydrogen gas is measured every 10 seconds until the reaction is finished.

Draw a labelled diagram to show the method used to collect the gas over water and measure its volume. [4]

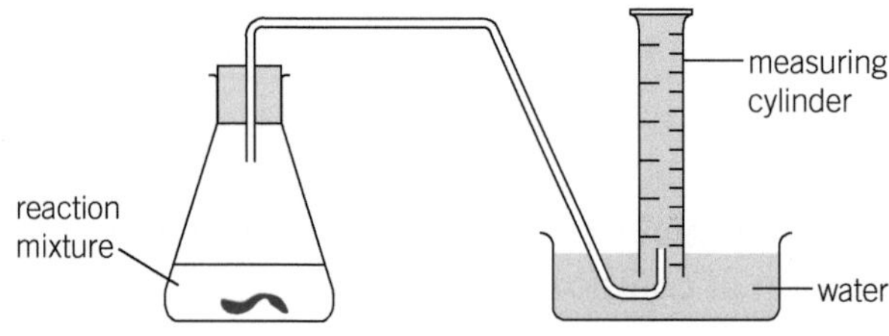


Measuring cylinder drawn full of water and dipping into water in a trough ✓

(Note: a burette is also acceptable)

Measuring cylinder labelled ✓

Rest of apparatus correct and airtight with no gaps ✓

Reaction mixture labelled ✓

Sketch a graph of the expected results. [2]

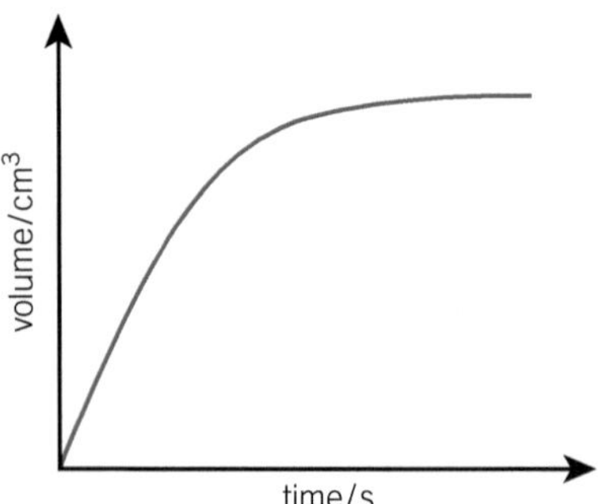


Axes correctly labelled ✓ graph as a curve which levels off ✓

## Apply

1. Zinc carbonate reacts with excess dilute acid.

$$ZnCO_3 + 2HNO_3 \rightarrow Zn(NO_3)_2 + H_2O + CO_2$$

The mass of the reaction mixture is measured every 20 seconds until the reaction is finished.

   a. Draw a labelled diagram to show the method used.

   b. Explain why the mass of the reaction mixture decreases with time.

   c. Sketch a graph of the expected results.

There are *advantages and disadvantages of experimental methods* involving weighing or collecting gases by different methods.

**Worked example**

Chlorine is a toxic gas which is moderately soluble in water. Chlorine is produced when manganese dioxide reacts with dilute hydrochloric acid. Explain the advantages and disadvantages of the following methods to show how the rate of reaction changes with time.

The mass of the reaction mixture is measured every 10 seconds. [3]

The poisonous gas will escape from the flask. ✓ The mass change is small compared with the mass of the flask and contents. ✓ It is a simple method. ✓

The volume of gas is measured using an upturned measuring cylinder full of water. [2]

The gas will dissolve in the water in the measuring cylinder. ✓ It is not easy to read the volume accurately. ✓

**Recap**

The progress of a reaction where a gas is produced can be followed by:

- measuring the volume of gas in a gas syringe or upturned measuring cylinder of water at different times
- measuring the decrease in mass of the reaction mixture at different times.

## Apply

2. Zinc reacts with hydrochloric acid to produce hydrogen. State which of these methods is likely to give more consistent results when conducting experiments to determine the rate of reaction. Give reasons for your answer by referring to both methods.

   a. measuring the decrease in mass of hydrogen with time

   b. measuring the increase in volume of hydrogen using a gas syringe

# 9.2 Evaluating experiments

**You need to:**

- Describe practical methods for investigating rate of reaction.
- Suggest advantages and disadvantages of experimental methods and apparatus.
- **Evaluate practical methods for investigating rate of reaction.**

*Methods for following the course of a reaction* include measuring changes in pH or electrical conductivity or timing how long it takes for a **precipitate** to form.

*When comparing the results of experiments*, you need to keep as many things constant as possible and change only the variable that you are interested in.

**Key skills**

You need to be able to discuss critically experimental apparatus and procedures.

**Exam tip**

Remember that change in mass is not suitable for investigating a reaction where hydrogen is produced. The change in the balance reading will be too small.

**Worked example**

Calcium carbonate reacts with hydrochloric acid.

$$CaCO_3(s) + 2HCl(aq) \rightarrow CaCl_2(aq) + H_2O(l) + CO_2(g)$$

Describe three different ways to follow the progress of this reaction with time. In each case describe the essential piece of equipment needed for the measurements other than a stopclock. Practical details are not required. [6]

Measure the volume of carbon dioxide ✓ produced using a gas syringe. ✓

Measure the decrease in mass of the reaction mixture ✓ using a top-pan balance. ✓

Use a pH meter ✓ to measure the decrease in acidity of the acid. ✓

For one of your examples, state what you need to keep constant in the experiment to make sure that the experiment can be repeated to get consistent results. [4]

Using a gas syringe: FTER SYRINGE, would keep the mass of calcium carbonate the same ✓ as well as the same size of the calcium carbonate pieces. ✓ The temperature needs to be kept the same ✓ as well as the same concentration and volume of acid. ✓

## Apply

3. Some carbonates decompose on heating:

$$CuCO_3(s) \rightarrow CuO(s) + CO_2(g)$$

Plan an experiment to compare the rate of decomposition of three different carbonates A, B and C. State what you need to keep constant in the experiment.

*When commenting on experiments*, you should think about the **accuracy** of the results and problems with the design of the experiment.

*Evaluation* means analysing the results carefully and commenting on what could be improved or why the results were good or bad. S

**Worked example**

Hydrogen peroxide can be decomposed by small amounts of manganese(IV) oxide, copper(I) oxide or lead(IV) oxide.

$$2H_2O_2(aq) \rightarrow 2H_2O(l) + O_2(g)$$

An experiment is done to compare the rate at which very small amounts of each of these compounds catalyse the decomposition of hydrogen peroxide using a gas syringe. You have access to a balance for weighing to one decimal place.

State what must be kept constant and what must be measured in the experiment. [5]

Measure the time ✓ taken to collect 20 $cm^3$ of oxygen ✓ in the gas syringe. The mass of each oxide should be the same ✓ and the temperature is kept constant ✓ as well as the size of the metal oxide particles ✓ and the volume and concentration ✓ of hydrogen peroxide.

(*Note*: the answer has scored more marking points than the 5 marks expected for the answer.)

The reaction is very fast. Explain any problems associated with this. [2]

It is hard to measure the volume accurately when the syringe plunger is moving. ✓ It is hard to read the stopclock and the volume at the same time. ✓

Suggest improvements that could be made to the experiment.  [2]

I would get someone else to read the volume ✓ and use a balance weighing to two decimal places. ✓

## Apply

4. A student does an experiment to show the effect of temperature on the reaction of zinc with hydrochloric acid using the apparatus shown.

$$Zn(s) + 2HCl(aq) \rightarrow ZnCl_2(aq) + H_2(g)$$

The student suggested measuring the loss in mass of the reaction mixture after 2 minutes at 20 °C. The student then suggested repeating the experiment at 30 °C, 40 °C and 50 °C.

a. Explain why the experiment is unlikely to be successful.

S b. The student repeated the experiment by measuring the volume of hydrogen released after 2 minutes using the apparatus shown, but placed the flask into a beaker of water heated by a Bunsen burner.

(i) Explain why it might be difficult to control the temperature using this apparatus.

(ii) Suggest a further improvement that you could make to the experiment.

**Recap**

When commenting on experiments think about:

- the suitability of the apparatus
- the accuracy of the measurements
- how easy it is to control the variables
- the consistency of the results in repeat experiments.

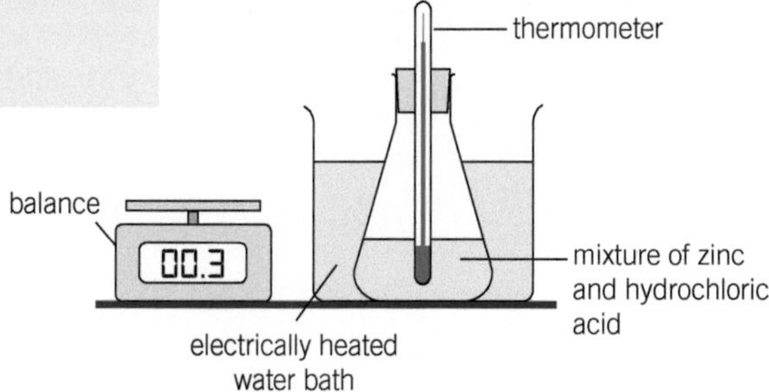

# 9.3 Interpreting data

**You need to:**

- Interpret data including graphs from rate of reaction experiments.

$$\textbf{Rate of reaction} = \frac{\text{change in amount (or concentration) of reactant or product}}{\text{time}}$$

The **rate of reaction** *decreases* as the reaction proceeds.

A *reaction stops* when the limiting reactant is used up.

When *interpreting graphs* of amount of substance or volume of gas plotted against time, the rate of reaction can be found from the slope of the graph at any particular point.

**Key skills**

You need to be able to interpret and draw graphs.

**Exam tip**

Remember that the rate of a reaction decreases as time increases.

**Exam tip**

If the rate of reaction seems proportional to the time at the beginning of a reaction, you can calculate the initial rate from the gradient of the graph. You will not be expected to calculate rates (other than average rates) from the curved part of the graph.

**Worked example**

The graph shows how the volume of oxygen released changes with time when hydrogen peroxide decomposes in the presence of a catalyst.

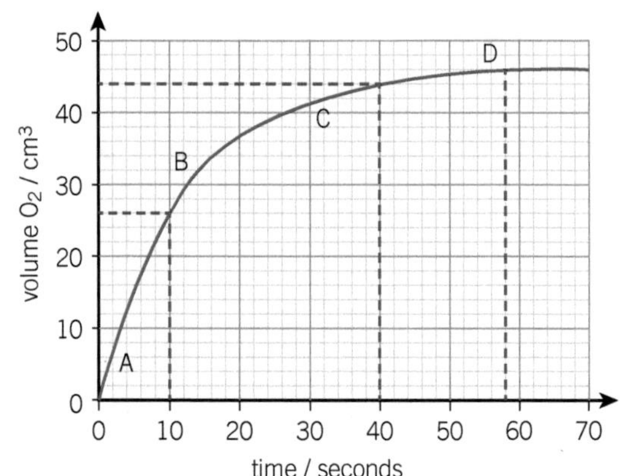


At what time has 44 $cm^3$ of gas been collected? [1]

40 seconds ✓

At what time is the reaction just complete? [1]

58 seconds ✓

On which part of the graph, **A**, **B**, **C** or **D**, is the rate of reaction fastest? Explain your answer. [2]

**A** ✓ because the gradient is steepest there. ✓

Calculate the rate of reaction in the first 10 seconds of the reaction. Show your working. [2]

$$\text{rate} = \frac{\text{volume}}{\text{time}} ✓ = \frac{26}{10} = 2.6 \text{ cm}^3/\text{s} ✓$$

Explain why the rate of reaction in the first 20 seconds of the reaction is an average rate of reaction. [1]

The gradient of the graph decreases with time ✓

## Apply

5. The graph shows how the mass of a flask + reaction mixture decreases with time in the reaction:

$$CaCO_3(s) + 2HCl(aq) \rightarrow CaCl_2(aq) + H_2O(l) + CO_2(g)$$

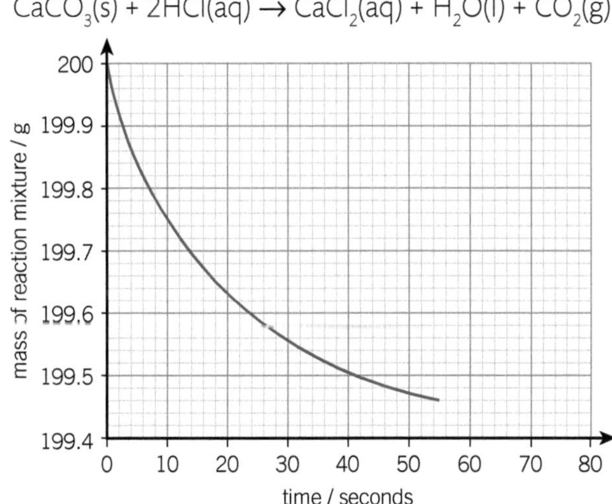


a. Explain why the mass of the flask + reaction mixture decreases.

b. Deduce the mass of the flask + reaction mixture after 20 seconds.

c. Deduce the mass loss 40 s from the beginning of the experiment.

d. Explain how the rate of reaction changes as the reaction proceeds.

e. After 140 s the reaction stops. Explain why it stops.

f. Extrapolate the curve to obtain a value for the mass of the flask + reaction mixture after 70 seconds.

**Recap**

- Rate of reaction is the change in concentration of reactant or product per unit time.
- The rate of reaction decreases as the reaction proceeds.

# 9.4 Surfaces and reaction rate

### You need to:

- Describe the effect of surface area of solids and catalysts (including enzymes) on rate of reaction.
- **Know that a catalyst lowers the activation energy so that a greater proportion of collisions are successful.**
- **Know that a catalyst is unchanged at the end of a reaction.**

The *total surface area* of small pieces of solid is larger than the total surface area of large pieces of solid of the same total mass.

*Increasing the surface area of a solid* increases its rate of reaction.

A **catalyst** is a substance which increases the rate of a chemical reaction but is not used up in the reaction.

**Exam tip**

**Watch out**

It is a common error to think that the total surface area of one large particle is greater than that of a number of small particles of the same total mass.

### Exam tip

Take care when defining a catalyst: 'A substance that changes the rate of a reaction' is too vague. The words 'increase rate' are essential.

### Worked example

Zinc reacts with hydrochloric acid. The reaction is catalysed by copper ions.

State the meaning of the term catalyst. [2]

> A substance which increases the rate of a chemical reaction ✓ and is not used up when the reaction has finished. ✓

The reaction is first done with large pieces of zinc and then with smaller pieces of zinc with the same mass. All other conditions stay the same. Describe and explain the difference in the rate of reaction using large and small pieces of zinc. [2]

> The reaction will be faster with smaller pieces ✓ of zinc because they have a larger total surface area. ✓

*Increasing the surface area of a solid* increases its rate of reaction because there are more particles available on the surface so that the frequency of collisions is increased.

*A catalyst speeds up a reaction* by lowering the activation energy of the reaction so that a greater proportion of collisions are successful.

### Worked example

Zinc reacts with hydrochloric acid. The rate of reaction is increased by adding copper ions.

The reaction is first done with large pieces of zinc and then with zinc powder of the same mass. All other conditions stay the same. Describe and explain, using **collision theory**, the difference in the rate of reaction using large pieces of zinc and zinc powder. [3]

> The zinc powder has a faster rate of reaction ✓ because it has a larger surface area ✓ so more particles are exposed for reaction and the collision frequency with acid molecules is greater. ✓

Explain why copper ions increase the rate of reaction by referring to activation energy. [3]

> Copper ions act as a catalyst. ✓ They lower the activation energy ✓ so that a greater proportion of the collisions are successful. ✓

### Recap

- The smaller the particle size, the faster the rate of reaction because the surface area is increased which increases the frequency of collisions.
- A catalyst speeds up a reaction (by lowering the activation energy of the reaction).

## Apply

6. Pieces of calcium carbonate of different sizes are reacted separately with hydrochloric acid. The sizes of the pieces are: large, medium and powder. The same mass of calcium carbonate is used in each experiment. The table shows the relative rate of the reaction.

| Size | Rate in $cm^3$ $CO_2$/s |
|---|---|
| | 0.8 |
| | 2.0 |
| | 0.5 |

   a. Link the size of the pieces to the rate of reaction.
   b. State two other things that should be kept constant in these experiments.

   c. Explain why finely powdered catalysts increase the rate of a chemical reaction faster than large pieces of catalyst of the same mass. Use ideas about colliding particles in your answer.

# 9.5 Concentration and rate of reaction

**You need to:**

- Describe the effect of concentration of solutions and pressure of gases on rate of reaction.
- **Explain using collision theory how increase in concentration of solution and increase in pressure increases the rate of reaction.**

*Increasing the concentration* of one or more reactants increases the rate of reaction.

*Increasing the pressure* of a reaction involving gases increases the rate of reaction.

**Exam tip**

When comparing reaction rates at different concentrations or different temperatures make sure that you use comparative phrases such as 'rate of reaction is greatER at highER concentrations'.

**Worked example**

Pieces of calcium carbonate of the same size and mass are reacted separately with hydrochloric acid of different concentrations. The concentrations of the acid are: 0.5 mol/dm$^3$, 1.0 mol/dm$^3$ and 2.0 mol/dm$^3$. All other conditions are kept the same. The table shows the relative rate of the reaction.

| Concentration in mol/dm$^3$ | Rate in cm$^3$ $CO_2$/s |
|---|---|
| | 0.8 |
| | 0.2 |
| | 1.6 |

Link the concentration of the acid to the rate of reaction. [2]

0.5 mol/dm$^3$ is 0.2 cm$^3$ $CO_2$/s and 2.0 mol/dm$^3$ is 1.6 cm$^3$ $CO_2$/s ✓ because the more concentrated the acid, the faster the rate of reaction. ✓

Deduce the rate of reaction using hydrochloric acid of concentration 4.0 mol/dm$^3$. Explain why you chose this value. [2]

About 3.2 cm$^3$ $CO_2$/s ✓ because as the concentration doubles the rate doubles. ✓

Hydrogen reacts with chlorine to produce hydrogen chloride.

$$H_2(g) + Cl_2(g) \rightarrow 2HCl(g)$$

Describe the effect of decreasing the pressure on the rate of this reaction. Explain your answer. [3]

Decreasing pressure decreases the rate ✓ because the particles are further apart ✓ and they collide less frequently ✓

S Increasing the concentration of one or more reactants increases the rate of reaction because:

- there are more reacting particles per unit volume
- the frequency of collisions increases.

**Worked example**

Hydrogen reacts with chlorine to produce hydrogen chloride.

$$H_2(g) + Cl_2(g) \rightarrow 2HCl(g)$$

Explain using the collision theory why increasing the pressure increases the rate of this reaction. [2]

Increasing the pressure pushes the particles closer together ✓ so the frequency of collisions between the $H_2$ and $Cl_2$ increases. ✓

**Exam tip**

When explaining the effect of concentration on reaction rate don't just refer to 'more particles' and 'more collisions'. It is 'more particles in a given volume' and 'more frequent collisions' that the examiners are looking for.

**Exam tip**

Increasing the concentration of a reactant has no effect on the force with which the particles hit each other.

Increasing the concentration of one or more reactants increases the rate of reaction (because the **collision frequency** increases).

Increasing the pressure of a reaction involving gases increases the rate of reaction.

## Apply

7. The graph shows the volume of hydrogen produced with time when excess magnesium reacts with hydrochloric acid of concentration 1.2 mol/dm³.

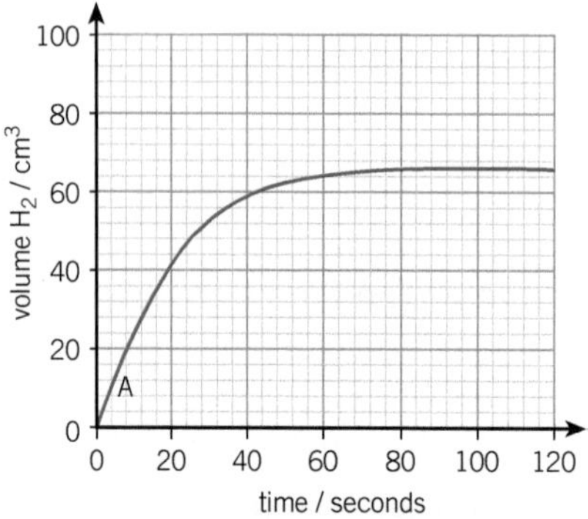


   a. On the graph, draw a line to show how the volume of hydrogen changes when hydrochloric acid of concentration 1.5 mol/dm³ is used. All other conditions stay the same.

   b. State how the line on the graph would differ if excess hydrochloric acid of concentration 1.2 mol/dm³ is used.

   S c. Explain the difference in the initial rate of reaction using 1.5 mol/dm³ acid and 1.2 mol/dm³ acid using the collision theory.

# 9.6 Temperature and rate of reaction

**You need to:**

- Describe the effect of temperature on the rate of reaction.
- **Explain using collision theory how increase in temperature increases rate of reaction.**

*Increasing the temperature* increases the rate of reaction.

**Worked example**

The table shows how the rate of reaction changes with temperature.

| Temperature/°C | 20 | 30 | 40 | 50 |
|---|---|---|---|---|
| Rate in $cm^3/s$ | 0.6 | 1.2 | 2.4 | 4.8 |

Plot a graph of rate of reaction against temperature using this information. [3]

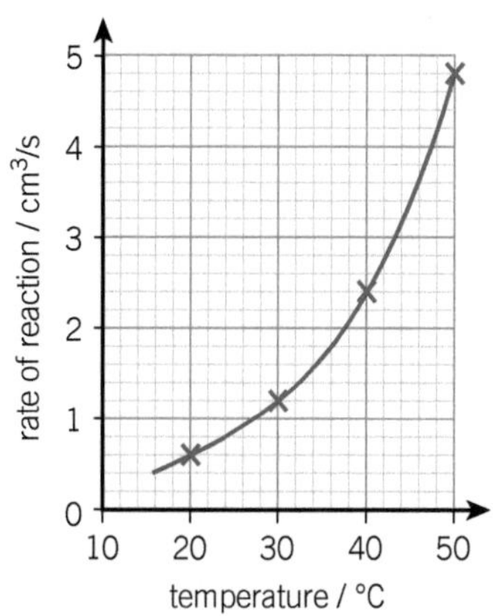


Axes correctly labelled. ✓ Points plotted correctly. ✓ Smooth line drawn through points. ✓

Describe how the rate of reaction changes as the temperature increases. [2]

The rate increases as the temperature increases. ✓ Rate increases faster and faster when temperature increases every 10 °C. ✓

*Increasing the temperature increases rate of reaction* because (1) the particles have more kinetic energy (2) so the frequency of collisions increases and (more importantly) more of the colliding particles have energy above the activation energy leading to more effective collisions.

**Worked example**

Calcium carbonate reacts with hydrochloric acid:

$$CaCO_3(s) + 2HCl(aq) \rightarrow CaCl_2(aq) + H_2O(l) + CO_2(g)$$

The time taken for 20 $cm^3$ of carbon dioxide to be produced is measured at different temperatures.

The table shows the results.

| Temperature/°C | 30 | 40 | 50 | 60 |
|---|---|---|---|---|
| Time for 20 $cm^3$ $CO_2$ to be collected/s | 75 | 37 | 19 | 9 |

Calculate the rate of reaction, in $cm^3/s$ at 30 °C. [1]

$\frac{20}{75} = 0.267\ cm^3/s$ ✓

Describe how the rate of this reaction changes as the temperature decreases. Explain your answer using the collision theory. [3]

Rate decreases as temperature decreases ✓ because the frequency of collisions decreases with decrease in temperature ✓and there are fewer particles with energy above the activation energy at lower temperatures. ✓

**Key skills**

You need to be able to plot graphs and draw lines of best fit.

### Exam tip

**Watch out**

It is a common error to muddle rate with the time taken to produce a certain volume of gas. The longer the time taken, the slower the rate.

### Exam tip

When plotting graphs (1) use a sensible scale (2) use as much of the graph paper as possible (3) use x for the points (4) draw the line of best fit if there is a trend (not straight lines).

### Exam tip

The better explanation of the effect of temperature on reaction rate is 'more particles with energy above the activation energy'. Although the frequency of collisions does increase with temperature, this effect is very small. It does no harm to put both reasons down in an exam.

Increasing the temperature increases the rate of reaction (because there are more particles with energy above the activation energy).

## Apply

8. a. Copy and complete the sentence using the words below:

finish longer rate shorter start time

The .................... the time taken for a reaction to .................... the faster is the .................... of reaction.

b. A student determined the time it took for pieces of zinc to react completely with hydrochloric acid at four different temperatures.

(i) State three things that should be kept constant in this experiment.

(ii) Sketch a graph to show how the time taken for the zinc to react completely depends on the temperature.

c. Explain, using the collision theory, why the rate of reaction of zinc with hydrochloric acid increases when the temperature increases. 

## Questions

**1.** Magnesium carbonate reacts with sulfuric acid:

$$MgCO_3(s) + H_2SO_4(aq) \rightarrow MgSO_4(aq) + H_2O(l) + CO_2(g)$$

**a.** Describe how the rate of this reaction over the first 20 seconds can be measured using a gas collection method. [3]

**b.** Describe the effect of the following on the rate of this reaction:

**(i)** increasing the temperature

**(ii)** using large pieces of magnesium carbonate instead of magnesium carbonate powder

**(iii)** adding water to the sulfuric acid [3]

**c.** The table shows how the volume of carbon dioxide changes with time.

| Volume/cm³ | 28 | 50 | 52 | 62 | 62 | 67 | 70 | 72 | 72 |
|---|---|---|---|---|---|---|---|---|---|
| Time/s | 10 | 20 | 30 | 40 | 50 | 60 | 70 | 80 | 90 |

**(i)** Plot these points on a piece of graph paper and label the axes of the graph. [3]

**(ii)** Draw a curved line that shows the relationship between the volume and time. [1]

**(iii)** Using your graph, state the volume of gas produced 35 s from the start of the experiment. [1]

S **2.** The equation shows the reaction of sulfur dioxide with oxygen.

$$2SO_2(g) + O_2(g) \rightarrow 2SO_3(g)$$

**a.** Describe and explain, using the collision theory, how the rate of the reaction of sulfur dioxide with sulfur trioxide changes when:

**(i)** the pressure decreases [3]

**(ii)** the temperature increases [4]

**3.** Link the words **A** to **D** with the phrases **1** to **4**.

**A** kinetic energy

**B** frequency of collisions

**C** effective collisions

**D** activation energy

**1** the number of collisions per second

**2** the minimum energy particles must have to react when they collide

**3** the energy of moving particles

**4** collisions which result in a reaction taking place [2]

## Sample question

1. **a.** The graph shows how the volume of carbon dioxide produced changes when hydrochloric acid of three different concentrations reacts with large pieces of calcium carbonate.

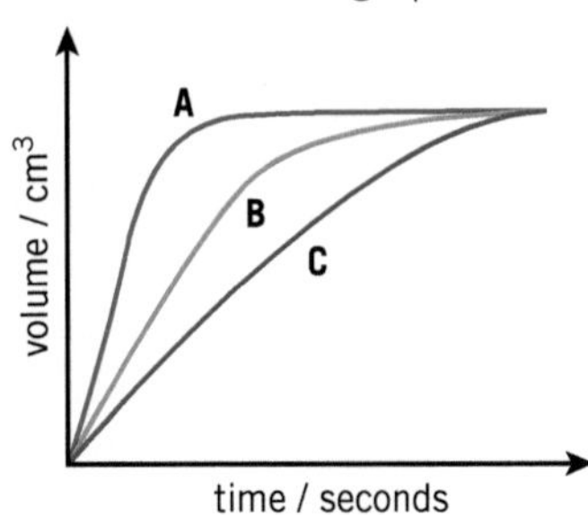


**(i)** Which line, **A**, **B** or **C**, represents the most concentrated acid? Explain your answer. [2]

**(ii)** Is the calcium carbonate or hydrochloric acid in excess? Explain your answer. [2]

**(iii)** Suggest two other ways of increasing the rate of this reaction. [2]

**(iv)** Draw a labelled diagram of the apparatus you can use to obtain these results. [3]

**b.** A student reacted large pieces of zinc with 1.0 mol/dm$^3$ hydrochloric acid. The experiment was repeated with zinc powder. Describe and explain any differences in the rates of reaction. [2]

**S** A student investigated the reaction of calcium carbonate with hydrochloric acid by measuring the loss in mass of the reaction mixture.

Describe, referring to the shape of the graph expected, and explain using ideas about colliding particles how the rate of reaction changes as the reaction proceeds. [6]

**d.** In another experiment, the student investigated how long it takes for 1 g of calcium carbonate to react completely in excess acid at four different temperatures. The results are shown in the table.

| Temperature/°C | 30 | 40 | 50 | 60 |
|---|---|---|---|---|
| Time/seconds | 192 | 96 | 48 | 24 |

**(i)** Estimate the time taken for the 1 g of calcium carbonate to react completely at a temperature of 70°C. Give a reason for your answer. [2]

**(ii)** Explain the results in the table using ideas about rate of reaction and colliding particles. [4]

**(iii)** Explain why the experiment will not work if the hydrochloric acid is the limiting reactant. [2]

**e.** Catalysts speed up the rate of reaction. Explain how they do this. [2]

# Chemical reactions

## Revision checklist

Tick these boxes to build a record of your revision. Columns 2 and 3 can be used if you want to make a record more than once.

| Core/**Supplement** syllabus content | | 1 | 2 | 3 |
|---|---|---|---|---|
| 10.1 | Know that some chemical reactions are reversible. | | | |
| 10.1 | Describe the reversible reactions between anhydrous and hydrated salts. | | | |
| 10.1 | **State the meaning of equilibrium in terms of rates of forward and backward reactions and concentrations of reactants and products.** | | | |
| 10.2 | **Predict and explain how the position of equilibrium is affected by changing concentration, pressure or temperature.** | | | |
| 10.2 | **Know that catalysts do not affect the position of equilibrium.** | | | |
| 10.3 | Use a Roman numeral to indicate the oxidation number of a particular element in a compound. | | | |
| 10.3 | Define oxidation and reduction in terms of oxygen gain and loss. | | | |
| 10.3 | Identify redox reactions in terms of gain and loss of oxygen. | | | |
| 10.3 | **Define redox reactions in terms of loss and gain of electrons.** | | | |
| 10.4 | **Identify oxidation and reduction in terms of electron gain and loss.** | | | |
| 10.4 | **Define redox reactions in terms of change in oxidation numbers.** | | | |
| 10.5 | **Identify redox reactions by colour changes using potassium manganate(VII) or potassium iodide.** | | | |
| 10.5 | **Define the terms oxidising agent and reducing agent.** | | | |
| 10.5 | **Identify oxidising agents and reducing agents in redox equations.** | | | |

# 10.1 Reversible reactions

**You need to:**

- Know that some chemical reactions are reversible; describe the reversible reactions between anhydrous and hydrated salts.
- **State the meaning of equilibrium in terms of rates of forward and backward reactions and concentrations of reactants and products.**

In **reversible reactions** (symbol $\rightleftharpoons$) the products can react to form the original reactants.

*Anhydrous copper(II) sulfate* (white) can be converted to hydrated copper(II) sulfate (blue) in a reversible reaction by adding water.

*Anhydrous cobalt(II) chloride* (blue) can be converted to hydrated cobalt(II) chloride (pink) in a reversible reaction by adding water.

### Exam tip

You may be asked about other anhydrous and hydrated salts in the exam when given suitable information.

### Worked example

The equation shows the addition of water to anhydrous copper(II) sulfate.

$$CuSO_4(s) + 5H_2O(l) \rightleftharpoons CuSO_4{\cdot}5H_2O(s)$$

State the colour of $CuSO_4(s)$. [1]

White ✓

State the meaning of the symbol $\rightleftharpoons$. [1]

Reversible reaction ✓

$CuSO_4(s)$ is described as anhydrous copper(II) sulfate. State how $CuSO_4{\cdot}5H_2O(s)$ is described. [1]

Hydrated copper(II) sulfate ✓

Describe how you can change $CuSO_4{\cdot}5H_2O(s)$ back to $CuSO_4(s)$. [1]

Heat it ✓

### Recap

- In reversible reactions the products can react to form the original reactants.
- Anhydrous copper(II) sulfate and anhydrous cobalt(II) chloride can be converted to hydrated copper(II) sulfate and cobalt(II) chloride by adding water.

## Apply

1. The equation shows the removal of water from hydrated nickel(II) bromide.

$$\underset{\text{yellow-green}}{NiBr_2{\cdot}3H_2O(s)} \rightleftharpoons \underset{\text{yellow-brown}}{NiBr_2(s)} + 3H_2O(l)$$

   a. $NiBr_2{\cdot}3H_2O(s)$ is described as hydrated nickel(II) bromide. State how $NiBr_2(s)$ is described.

   b. State the name given to the water bonded to $NiBr_2$ in $NiBr_2{\cdot}3H_2O(s)$.

   c. Describe how you can change yellow-brown nickel(II) bromide to yellow-green nickel(II) bromide.

   d. Describe the colour change when water is added to cobalt(II) chloride which has no water bonded to it.

Supplement

An **equilibrium reaction** is one where the reactants are converted to the products at the same rate as the products are converted back to reactants.

The *concentration of reactants and products in an equilibrium reaction* are constant at constant temperature and pressure.

An *equilibrium reaction only takes place* in a closed system.

A **closed system** is one where there is not loss or gain of matter; for example, a sealed tube.

**Position of equilibrium** indicates how far the reaction goes in favour of either the reactants or products.

**Recap**

An equilibrium reaction is one where the reactants are converted to the products at the same rate as the products are converted back to reactants. This can only take place in a closed system.

**Exam tip**

It is important to realise that at equilibrium the rate of the forward reaction is equal to the rate of the reverse reaction.

**Worked example**

Calcium carbonate decomposes as shown: $CaCO_3(s) \rightleftharpoons CaO(s) + CO_2(g)$

Explain why this reaction needs to be carried out in a closed system. [2]

> Carbon dioxide is a gas. ✓ If the system is not closed, gas will escape from the container ✓ causing more calcium carbonate to decompose.

Give an example of a closed system. [1]

> a sealed glass tube ✓

At 300 °C there is very little calcium oxide in the equilibrium mixture compared with the amount of calcium carbonate. What does this tell you about the position of equilibrium? [1]

> The position of equilibrium is in favour of the reactants ✓ – it is over to the left of the reaction.

Explain why the concentrations of calcium carbonate, calcium oxide and carbon dioxide remain constant at 300 °C. [1]

> Products are being converted to reactants at the same rate as the reactants are being converted to products. ✓

## Apply

2. Complete these sentences about this reaction using words from the list.

$$Ag_2CO_3(s) \rightleftharpoons Ag_2O(s) + CO_2(g)$$

changes closed concentrations decreases
equals equilibrium increases open pressure
rate saturation temperature

a. Silver carbonate is heated to 400 °C in a .................... system at constant pressure. The concentration of silver oxide and carbon dioxide .................... until the .................... of the backward reaction .................... the rate of the forward reaction. At this point the reaction has reached .................... and the .................... of the reactants and products stay the same. The amount of carbon dioxide present at equilibrium depends on both the temperature and ....................

b. Define the term closed system.

# 10.2 Shifting the equilibrium

**You need to:**

- **Predict and explain how the position of equilibrium is affected by changing concentration, pressure or temperature.**
- **Know that catalysts do not affect the position of equilibrium.**

*Increasing the concentration* of one or more reactants at equilibrium moves the position of equilibrium in the direction of more products. Increasing concentration of products moves the position of equilibrium to form more reactants.

*Increasing the pressure* moves the position of equilibrium in the direction of a lower number of moles of gas molecules in the chemical equation.

*For an endothermic reaction*, increase in temperature moves the position of equilibrium in the direction of the formation of more products.

*For an exothermic reaction*, increase in temperature moves the position of equilibrium in the direction of the formation of more reactants.

**Catalysts** have no effect on the position of equilibrium.

**Key skills**

You need to be able to use all the information in a chemical equation including state symbols and enthalpy changes when answering questions about equilibrium.

**Worked example**

The equation shows a reaction at equilibrium.

$$2SO_2(g) + O_2(g) \rightleftharpoons 2SO_3(g) \qquad \Delta H = -197 \text{ kJ/mol}$$

Describe and explain the effect on the position of equilibrium when:

The pressure is decreased. [3]

> Position of equilibrium moves to the left. ✓ It goes in the direction of more moles of gas ✓ (3 moles of gas on the left and only 2 on the right). It does this to oppose the reduction in pressure. ✓

The temperature is increased. [3]

> Position of equilibrium moves to the left ✓ because the forward reaction is exothermic. ✓ Thermal energy is given out in an exothermic reaction, so it has to move in the direction of absorbing thermal energy. ✓

A catalyst is added. [2]

> There is no effect on the equilibrium ✓ because the catalyst just increases the rate of the backward and forward reaction equally. ✓

The concentration of oxygen is increased. [2]

> The reaction moves in the direction so that more $SO_3$ is formed. ✓ It goes in this direction to try and decrease the concentration of the oxygen. ✓

## Exam tip

**Watch out**

When explaining the effect of temperature on the position of equilibrium it is essential to refer to the forward or backward reaction. Statements such as 'because the reaction is exothermic' are not sufficient.

## Exam tip

Remember that if equilibrium conditions are changed, the reaction always tries to act to oppose the change; for example, if you increase the concentration of reactant, the reaction tries to decrease the concentration.

Supplement

In an equilibrium reaction:

- Increasing concentration of reactants moves the position of equilibrium in the direction of more products.
- Increasing the pressure moves the position of equilibrium in the direction of a lower number of moles of gas molecules.
- For an endothermic reaction, increase in temperature moves the position of equilibrium in the direction of the formation of more products.

## Apply

3. The equation shows a reaction at equilibrium.

$$H_2(g) + I_2(g) \rightleftharpoons 2HI(g) \qquad \Delta H = -9.6\ \text{kJ/mol}$$

The reaction is done in a closed glass tube.

a. Explain the meaning of the term equilibrium.

b. Explain why the reaction is done in a closed glass tube.

c. Describe and explain the effect on the position of equilibrium if any when:

(i) the pressure is increased

(ii) the temperature is decreased

(iii) a hole is made in the glass tube

(iv) the concentration of hydrogen iodide is increased

### Exam tip

**Watch out**

Remember that the effect of pressure on equilibrium only applies to reactions where gases appear in the equation and there are different volumes of gases on each side of the equation.

### Exam tip

Remember that catalysts have no effect on the position of equilibrium.

# 10.3 Redox reactions

**You need to:**

- Use a Roman numeral to indicate the oxidation number of a particular element in a compound.
- Define oxidation and reduction in terms of oxygen gain and loss.
- Identify redox reactions in terms of gain and loss of oxygen.
- **Define redox reactions in terms of loss and gain of electrons.**

**Oxidation** is gain of oxygen by a substance.

**Reduction** is loss of oxygen from a compound.

**Redox reactions** are those where oxidation and reduction take place at the same time.

**Oxidation numbers** give information about the degree of oxidation or reduction of a compound.

*Roman numerals* are used to show the oxidation number of particular elements in a compound.

**Worked example**

The equation shows a redox reaction.

$$CuO(s) + H_2(g) \rightleftharpoons Cu(s) + H_2O(l)$$

State the meaning of the term redox. [2]

Oxidation and reduction occurring ✓ in the same equation. ✓

Deduce which compound or element in the equation has been reduced. Explain your answer. [2]

CuO has been reduced ✓ because it has lost oxygen. ✓

CuO(s) is copper(II) oxide. State the name given to the number such as (II) that is shown in some formulae. [1]

Oxidation number ✓

Explain, in terms of oxidation or reduction, the difference between copper(I) oxide and copper(II) oxide. [2]

The copper in copper(II) oxide is more oxidised than copper(I) oxide ✓ because it has a higher oxidation number. ✓

## Apply

4. a. Define reduction in terms of oxygen.

   b. Deduce which reactants in each of these equations is oxidised and which is reduced.

   (i) $PbO + C \rightarrow Pb + CO$

   (ii) $2H_2 + O_2 \rightarrow 2H_2O$

   (iii) $Ag_2O + H_2 \rightarrow 2Ag + H_2O$

   (iv) $CH_4 + 2O_2 \rightarrow CO_2 + 2H_2O$

   c. Put these compounds in order of increasing oxidation states of the metal.

   manganese(IV) oxide
   potassium manganate(VII)
   potassium manganate(VI)

**Recap**

- Oxidation is gain of oxygen and reduction is loss of oxygen.
- Oxidation numbers give information about the degree of oxidation or reduction of a compound.

**Supplement**

**Oxidation** is loss of electrons.

**Reduction** is gain of electrons.

**Worked example**

Complete these ionic half-equations and state if oxidation or reduction has taken place. In each case explain your answer.

$Na \rightarrow Na^+$ [3]

$Na \rightarrow Na^+ + e^-$ ✓ oxidation of sodium ✓ because sodium has lost electrons ✓

$Mg^{2+} \rightarrow Mg$ [3]

$Mg^{2+} + 2e^- \rightarrow Mg$ ✓ reduction of magnesium ions ✓ because $Mg^{2+}$ ions have gained electrons ✓

State which ion or element has been reduced and which has been oxidised in this reaction. Explain your answers in terms of electron transfer.

$Cl_2 + 2I^- \rightarrow 2Cl^- + I_2$ [4]

Each chlorine atom in $Cl_2$ has been reduced ✓ because each atom has gained an electron. ✓
Iodide ions have been oxidised ✓ because they have lost electrons ✓ when iodine is formed.

### Exam tip

Remember OIL RIG: Oxidation Is Loss of electrons and Reduction Is Gain of electrons.

### Exam tip

**Watch out**

When identifying the atoms or ions which are being oxidised or reduced, make sure that you write with precision. In the equation $Mg + Zn^{2+} \rightarrow Zn + Mg^{2+}$, it is the zinc **ions** that are being reduced.

## Apply

5. a. Complete these sentences about redox reactions.

   Redox reactions involve .................... and .................... happening at the same .................... a reaction. In terms of electron transfer oxidation is .................... of .................... and reduction is .................... of ....................

   b. Identify the element or ion which has been oxidised and which has been reduced in these equations. Explain your answer in terms of electron transfer.

   (i) $2Ag^{+} + Ca \rightarrow 2Ag + Ca^{2+}$

   (ii) $2K + Br_2 \rightarrow 2K^{+}Br^{-}$

   (iii) $Zn + Cu^{2+} \rightarrow Zn^{2+} + Cu$

Supplement

# 10.4 More about redox reactions

**You need to:**

- **Identify oxidation and reduction in terms of electron gain and loss.**
- **Define redox reactions in terms of change in oxidation numbers.**

*Oxidation and reduction of* **species** *(atoms or ions) in an equation* can be identified by comparing the charges on each reactant and product.

### Worked example

Complete these ionic half-equations and state if oxidation or reduction has taken place. In each case explain your answer.

$Ca \rightarrow Ca^{2+}$ [3]

$Ca \rightarrow Ca^{2+} + 2e^{-}$ ✓ oxidation of calcium ✓ because calcium has lost electrons ✓

$Al^{3+} \rightarrow Al$ [3]

$Al^{3+} + 3e^{-} \rightarrow Al$ ✓ reduction of aluminium ions ✓ because $Al^{3+}$ ions have gained electrons ✓

Identify the element or ion which has been reduced in this equation. Explain your answer in terms of electron transfer.

$Mg + ZnCl_2 \rightarrow MgCl_2 + Zn$ [2]

Zinc ions in zinc chloride have been reduced ✓ because zinc ions have gained electrons ✓ from magnesium

Identify the element or ion which has been is oxidised in this equation. Explain your answer in terms of electron transfer.

$2Br^{-} + Cl_2 \rightarrow 2Cl^{-} + Br_2$ [2]

Bromide ions have been oxidised ✓ because they have lost electrons ✓ in forming bromine

## Apply

6. a. Identify the element or ion which has been oxidised in these equations. Explain your answer in terms of electron transfer.

   (i) $Br_2 + 2I^- \rightarrow 2Br^- + I_2$

   (ii) $2Na + Cl_2 \rightarrow 2NaCl$

   (iii) $Zn + Cu(NO_3)_2 \rightarrow Zn(NO_3)_2 + Cu$

   b. Identify the element, compound or ion which has been reduced in these equations. Explain your answer in terms of electron transfer.

   (i) $Na + H_2O \rightarrow NaOH + H_2$

   (ii) $Ni + Cu^{2+} \rightarrow Cu + Ni^{2+}$

   (iii) $I_2 + 2At^- \rightarrow 2I^- + At_2$

**Oxidation** is increase in oxidation number.

**Reduction** is decrease in oxidation number.

Oxidation number rules are used to deduce oxidation numbers of ions or elements in compounds.

1. The oxidation number of an element is 0.
2. The oxidation number of a simple ion = the charge on the ion.
3. The total oxidation number of all the elements in a compound is 0.
4. The total oxidation number of ions such as $SO_4^{2-}$ = the charge on the ion.

**Key skills**

You need to be able to apply oxidation number rules in order to calculate oxidation numbers of particular atoms or ions.

**Worked example**

Use oxidation number rules to work out the oxidation numbers, OxNo. Explain your working.

Cr in $CrCl_3$ [2]

OxNo Cl in a simple compound is −1 ✓ (Rule 2)

So Cr is +3 to balance 3(−1) for 3Cl ✓ (Rule 3)

Fe in $FeSO_4$ [2]

OxNo of $SO_4^{2-}$ is −2 ✓ (Rule 4)

So Fe is +2 to balance −2 ✓ (Rule 3)

Use oxidation number (OxNo) changes to show which atoms have been oxidised and which have been reduced in these reactions. Explain your answer by referring to oxidation numbers.

$PbO + H_2 \rightarrow Pb + H_2O$ [4]

OxNo of Pb in PbO = +2 OxNo of Pb = 0 ✓; reduction of Pb because decrease in OxNo ✓ of Pb

OxNo of H in $H_2$ = 0 OxNo of H in $H_2O$ = +1 ✓; oxidation of H because increase in OxNo ✓ of H

$Fe_2O_3 + 3CO \rightarrow 2Fe + 3CO_2$ [4]

OxNo of Fe in $Fe_2O_3$ = +3 (2Fe balances 3(−2)O so Fe = +3) OxNo of Fe = 0 ✓; reduction of Fe because decrease in OxNo of Fe ✓

OxNo of C in CO = +2 OxNo of C in $CO_2$ = +4 ✓; oxidation of C in CO because increase in OxNo of C ✓

### Exam tip

You need to know the oxidation number rules in order to work out if a substance has been oxidised or reduced. You need to use these in equations where no ions appear.

Supplement

**Recap**

- Oxidation is loss of electrons or increase in oxidation number.
- Reduction is gain of electrons or decrease in oxidation number.

## Apply

7. a. Use oxidation number rules to work out the oxidation numbers, OxNo. Explain your working.

   (i) Cu in CuO (ii) Mn in $MnO_2$ (iii) Cl in $Cl_2O_7$

   (iv) S in $S_2Cl_2$ (v) Ni in $Ni(OH)_2$

   b. Use oxidation number (OxNo) changes to show which atoms or ions have been oxidised and which have been reduced in these reactions. Explain your answer by referring to oxidation numbers.

   (i) $Ca + 2H_2O \rightarrow Ca(OH)_2 + H_2$ (ii) $Mg + CuCl_2 \rightarrow Cu + MgCl_2$

   (iii) $Fe_2O_3 + 3C \rightarrow 2Fe + 3CO$ (iv) $Br_2 + 2I^- \rightarrow 2Br^- + I_2$

# 10.5 Oxidising agents and reducing agents

**You need to:**

- **Identify redox reactions by colour changes using potassium manganate(VII) or potassium iodide.**
- **Define the terms oxidising agent and reducing agent.**
- **Identify oxidising agents and reducing agents in redox equations.**

**Exam tip**

**Watch out**

Make sure that you don't confuse oxidising agents and reducing agents with the compounds that are being oxidised or reduced.

**Exam tip**

Remember that oxidising agents get reduced when they react and reducing agents get oxidised when they react.

An **oxidising agent** oxidises another substance and is itself reduced in the process.

*Acidified aqueous potassium manganate(VII)* is an oxidising agent which changes in colour from purple to colourless when it oxidises another substance and is not in excess.

A **reducing agent** reduces another substance and is itself oxidised in the process.

*Aqueous potassium iodide* is a reducing agent which changes in colour from colourless to brown when it reduces other substances.

**Worked example**

Magnesium reacts with aqueous zinc ions.

$$Mg(s) + Zn^{2+}(aq) \rightarrow Zn(s) + Mg^{2+}(aq)$$

Identify the oxidising agent in this reaction. Give a reason for your answer in terms of electron transfer. [2]

Zinc ions act as the oxidising agent ✓ because they oxidise magnesium by removing electrons from the magnesium atoms. ✓

Aluminium reacts with iron(III) oxide when heated.

$$2Al(s) + Fe_2O_3(s) \rightarrow Al_2O_3(s) + 2Fe(s)$$

Identify the reducing agent in this reaction. Give a reason for your answer in terms of change in oxidation number. [2]

Aluminium atoms act as the reducing agent ✓ because they reduce the iron in the iron oxide by decreasing the oxidation number of iron ✓ from + 3 to 0.

Potassium iodide, KI, can be used to test for oxidising agents.

Describe the colour change when potassium iodide reacts with a colourless oxidising agent. [2]

From colourless ✓ to brown. ✓

Identify the atoms or ions responsible for this colour change and explain this colour change in terms of electron transfer. [3]

The colourless iodide ions ✓ get oxidised to iodine which is brown. ✓ The iodide ions lose electrons during this reaction. ✓

- An oxidising agent oxidises another substance and is itself reduced in the process.
- A reducing agent reduces another substance and is itself oxidised in the process.

## Apply

8. a. Define the term oxidising agent.

   b. Identify the oxidising and reducing agents in these reactions. Explain your answers in terms of both electron transfer and oxidation number change.

      (i) $2Br^- + Cl_2 \rightarrow 2Cl^- + Br_2$

      (ii) $Mg + Pb^{2+} \rightarrow Pb + Mg^{2+}$

      (iii) $2Fe^{2+} + H_2O_2 + 2H^+ \rightarrow 2Fe^{3+} + 2H_2O$ (O in $H_2O_2$ has an oxidation number of –1)

   c. Potassium manganate(VII), $KMnO_4$, is run from a burette into a flask containing a colourless reducing agent.

      (i) Describe the colour change in the flask, if any, when the aqueous potassium manganate(VII) is not in excess. Explain your answer.

      (ii) Describe the colour change in the flask, if any, when the aqueous potassium manganate(VII) is in excess. Explain your answer.

      (iii) $Mn^{2+}$ ions are one of the products of the reaction. Explain what happens to the potassium manganate(VII) during this reaction in terms of the oxidation number of the manganese atoms or ions.

## Questions

1. The equation shows the action of water on cobalt(II) chloride.

$$CoCl_2(s) + 6H_2O(l) \rightleftharpoons CoCl_2{\cdot}6H_2O(s)$$

   a. State the meaning of symbol $\rightleftharpoons$. [1]

   b. Describe the colour change in this reaction. [2]

   c. Give the full name of $CoCl_2{\cdot}6H_2O$. [1]

2. a. Identify the atoms which are reduced and which are oxidised in this equation. Explain your answer in terms of oxygen loss or gain.

$$CuO(s) + CO(g) \rightarrow Cu(s) + CO_2(g)$$ [4]

   b. Identify the atoms which are oxidised and which are reduced in this equation. Explain your answer in terms of oxygen loss or gain.

$$PbO(s) + H_2(g) \rightarrow Pb(s) + H_2O(g)$$ [4]

   c. Potassium manganate(VII) is an .................................. agent. When excess potassium manganate(VII) reacts with a reducing agent the final colour of the reaction mixture is .................................. [2]

S c. Identify the atoms or ions which are oxidised and which are reduced in this equation. Explain your answer in terms of transfer of electrons.

$$2Ce(s) + 3Fe^{2+}(aq) \rightarrow 2Ce^{3+}(aq) + 3Fe(s)$$ [4]

   d. Identify the atoms or ions which are oxidised and which are reduced in this equation. Explain your answer in terms of change in oxidation numbers.

$$H_2S(g) + Br_2(g) \rightarrow S(s) + 2HBr$$ [4]

3. Link the words or phrases **A** to **E** with the phrases **1** to **5**.

| | |
|---|---|
| **A** Redox reaction | **1** This happens when an atom loses one or more electrons |
| **B** Oxidising agent | **2** The simultaneous oxidation and reduction in the same equation |
| **C** Reduction | **3** This happens when an atom gains one or more electrons |
| **D** Reducing agent | **4** A substance that removes electrons from another substance |
| **E** Oxidation | **5** A substance that gives electrons to another substance |

4. Complete these sentences about oxidising agents.

   a. An oxidising agent brings about .................................. by removing .................................. from another atom or .................................. [3]

   b. Potassium .................................. is a reducing agent. When reducing a colourless substance, the colour of the reaction mixture changes from .................................. to .................................. [3]

5. The equation for the reaction of bismuth trichloride with water is shown.

$$BiCl_3(aq) + H_2O(l) \rightleftharpoons BiOCl(s) + 2HCl(aq)$$

Describe and explain the effect on the position of equilibrium if any when:

   a. the pressure is decreased [2]

   b. water is added to the reaction mixture [2]

   c. the concentration of acid is increased [2]

6. The reaction between hydrogen and carbon dioxide is shown.

$$H_2(g) + CO_2(g) \rightleftharpoons H_2O(g) + CO(g) \qquad \Delta H = +41\ kJ/mol$$

   a. Explain why increase in pressure has no effect on the position of equilibrium. [1]

   b. Describe and explain the effect on the position of equilibrium when the temperature is increased. [3]

## Sample question

**1. a.** The equation shows the effect of heating hydrated nickel(II)chloride.

$$NiCl_2{\cdot}6H_2O(s) \rightleftharpoons NiCl_2(s) + 6H_2O(l)$$

green nickel chloride    yellow nickel chloride

**(i)** Describe how to change yellow nickel chloride back to green nickel chloride. [1]

**(ii)** State the name of a reaction like this one in which the reactants can be converted back to the products. [1]

**b.** The equation shows a redox reaction.

$$ZnO(s) + C(s) \rightarrow Zn(s) + CO(g)$$

**(i)** Deduce which compound or element in the equation has been reduced. Explain your answer. [2]

**(ii)** Define the term oxidation. [1]

**S c.** Iron reacts with steam:

$$3Fe(s) + 4H_2O(g) \rightarrow Fe_3O_4(s) + 4H_2(g)$$

**(i)** Identify the atom which has been oxidised in this reaction. Explain your answer by referring to oxidation numbers. [2]

**(ii)** Magnesium reacts with the ionic compound lead(II) nitrate:

$$Mg(s) + Pb(NO_3)_2(aq) \rightarrow Pb(s) + Mg(NO_3)_2(aq)$$

Identify the atom or ion which has been reduced in this reaction. Explain your answer by referring to transfer of electrons. [3]

**d. (i)** Define the term reducing agent. [2]

**(ii)** Iron(II) sulfate is light green in colour. Potassium manganate(VII), $KMnO_4$, reacts with iron(II) sulfate. Iron(III) sulfate is produced.

$$KMnO_4(aq) + 5Fe^{2+} + 8H^+ \rightarrow Mn^{2+} + 5Fe^{3+} + 4H_2O$$

Describe the colour change in the reaction mixture when aqueous potassium manganate(VII) reacts with excess iron(II) sulfate. [1]

**(iii)** Identify the atoms or ions responsible for this colour change and explain this colour change in terms of electron transfer. [3]

**e.** The equation describes the synthesis of methanol.

$$2H_2(g) + CO(g) \rightleftharpoons CH_3OH(g) \qquad \Delta H = -91 \text{ kJ/mol}$$

**(i)** The reaction is carried out in a closed system. Explain the meaning of closed system. [1]

**(ii)** Describe and explain the effect on the position of equilibrium if any when:

**(i)** the pressure is decreased [3]

**(ii)** the temperature is increased [3]

**(iii)** methanol is removed from the reaction mixture [2]

**(iv)** the reaction is done in the presence of a catalyst [2]

# Acids and bases

## Revision checklist

Tick these boxes to build a record of your revision. Columns 2 and 3 can be used if you want to make a record more than once.

| Core/**Supplement** syllabus content | | 1 | 2 | 3 |
|---|---|---|---|---|
| 11.1 | Know that aqueous solutions of acids contain $H^+$ ions and aqueous solutions of alkalis contain $OH^-$ ions. | | | |
| 11.1 | Describe acidity and alkalinity in terms of the pH scale. | | | |
| 11.1 | Describe the use of universal indicator to find pH (and therefore the concentration of $H^+$ ions). | | | |
| 11.2 | Describe how acids react with metals, metal oxides, metal hydroxides and carbonates. | | | |
| 11.2 | Describe acids in terms of their effect on litmus. | | | |
| 11.3 | Know that metal oxides and hydroxides are bases. | | | |
| 11.3 | Know that alkalis are soluble bases. | | | |
| 11.3 | Describe the characteristic properties of bases as reactions with acids and with ammonium salts and effect on litmus. | | | |
| 11.3 | Know that a neutralisation reaction occurs between an acid and a base. | | | |
| 11.4 | Describe neutralisation as $H^+(aq) + OH^-(aq) \rightarrow H_2O(l)$. | | | |
| 11.4 | **Define acids and bases in terms of proton transfer.** | | | |
| 11.4 | **Understand the difference between strong and weak acids and bases.** | | | |
| 11.4 | **Write ionic equations for acid–base reactions.** | | | |
| 11.5 | Describe how to do an acid–base titration. | | | |
| 11.5 | Describe how to identify the end point of a titration. | | | |
| 11.5 | Describe the effect of acids and alkalis on litmus, thymolphthalein and methyl orange. | | | |
| 11.6 | Classify oxides as acidic or basic related to non-metallic or metallic character. | | | |
| 11.6 | **Know that zinc oxide and aluminium oxide are amphoteric.** | | | |

# 11.1 How acidic?

**You need to:**

- Know that aqueous solutions of acids contain $H^+$ ions and aqueous solutions of alkalis contain $OH^-$ ions.
- Describe acidity and alkalinity in terms of the pH scale.
- Describe the use of universal indicator to find pH (and therefore the concentration of $H^+$ ions).

**Acids** *contain $H^+$ ions* in aqueous solution.

**Alkalis** *contain $OH^-$ ions* in aqueous solution.

The **pH scale** (from 0 to 14) is used to show how acidic or alkaline a substance is.

*A solution of pH 7 is* **neutral**. Solutions below pH 7 are acidic. Solutions above pH 7 are alkaline.

**Worked example**

A sample of orange juice is slightly acidic. Hydrochloric acid is strongly acidic.

Give the name and formula of the ion responsible for acidity. [2]

Hydrogen ion, ✓ $H^+$ ✓

Suggest the pH values of orange juice and concentrated hydrochloric acid. [2]

Orange juice pH 5 ✓ hydrochloric acid pH 1 ✓

(Comment: pH above 4 but below 7 is acceptable for orange juice and pH from 0 to 2 for hydrochloric acid)

Complete this sentence by giving the missing words **A** and **B**.

A solution of pH 7 is said to be **A**. Solutions above pH 7 are said to be **B**. [2]

A: neutral ✓ B: alkaline ✓

**Exam tip**

**Watch out**

Remember that a high acidity gives a low pH and a low acidity gives a high pH.

**Exam tip**

Remember that in organic acids, not all the hydrogen can form ions. In ethanoic acid, $CH_3COOH$, only the H of the COOH group ionises.

*Universal indicator* is a mixture of indicators which is used to determine pH of a solution by comparing its colour to the colours on a pH colour chart.

**Worked example**

Describe how universal indicator is used to find the pH of a of solution. [3]

Dip the universal indicator paper into the solution ✓ and observe the colour of the indicator paper. ✓ Compare the colour with the colour chart for the universal indicator. ✓ The matching colour on the colour chart gives the pH.

**Exam tip**

Remember that when using universal indicator to find the pH, always compare the colour with a colour chart. The colours may vary slightly according to the mixture of indicators present in the universal indicator.

**Recap**

- In aqueous solutions acids contain $H^+$ ions and alkalis contain $OH^-$ ions.
- pH 7 is neutral. Acids have pH values below 7 and alkalis have pH values above pH 7.

## Apply

1. a. A student dissolves solid **G** in water. Drops of universal indicator solution are added separately to both the water and a solution of **G**. Solution **G** is highly alkaline.

   (i) Suggest the colour of the universal indicator in water and in a solution of **G**.

   (ii) Name and give the formula of the ion responsible for alkalinity.

   b. A list of pH values is shown: pH 1 pH 6 pH 7 pH 8 pH 14

   State which of these pH values represents:

   (i) a concentrated alkali

   (ii) distilled water

   (iii) a solution of a very weak acid

# 11.2 Properties of acids

**You need to:**

- Describe how acids react with metals, metal oxides, metal hydroxides and carbonates.
- Describe acids in terms of their effect on litmus.

**Key skills**

You need to be able to write word equations and symbol equations.

*Most acids react with reactive metals* to produce a salt and hydrogen.

*Acids react with metal oxides or metal hydroxides* to produce a salt and water.

*Acids react with carbonates* to produce a salt, water and carbon dioxide.

*Acids turn blue* **litmus** paper red.

**Exam tip**

Remember that when acids react with carbonates there are three products: a salt, water and carbon dioxide.

**Exam tip**

Remember that salts are formed when acids react with oxides, hydroxides or metals. Salts are compounds formed when the hydrogen in an acid is replaced by a metal or an ammonium group.

**Worked example**

Describe how you can use damp litmus paper to test whether a gas is acidic. [2]

Place the damp blue litmus paper ✓ in the gas. If it turns red ✓ the gas is acidic.

Name the products formed in these reactions.

nitric acid + sodium hydroxide → .................... + .................... [2]

sodium nitrate ✓ + water ✓

hydrochloric acid + zinc → .................... + .................... [2]

zinc chloride ✓ + hydrogen ✓

lithium oxide + sulfuric acid → .................... + .................... [2]

lithium sulfate ✓ + water ✓

An acid reacts with a green powder. Copper(II) sulfate, carbon dioxide and one other product are formed.

Name the other product. [1]

water ✓

Suggest the name of the green powder and the acid that reacted with it. State how you made this conclusion. [4]

copper(II) carbonate ✓ and sulfuric acid. ✓ A carbonate reacts with an acid to produce a salt, water and carbon dioxide. ✓ Sulfates are formed from sulfuric acid. ✓

Copy and complete the symbol equation for the reaction of calcium with hydrochloric acid.

$Ca + \text{.........}HCl \rightarrow CaCl_2 + \text{.........}$ [2]

$Ca + 2HCl$ ✓ $\rightarrow CaCl_2 + H_2$ ✓

**Exam tip**

You will be expected to be able to write symbol equations for the reactions of acids if you are studying the supplement. For the core you will be given some or all of the formulae.

## Apply

2. a. Copy and complete these word equations for the reactions of acids.
   (i) sodium carbonate + hydrochloric acid → .......... + .......... + ..........
   (ii) .......... + magnesium oxide → magnesium nitrate + ..........
   (iii) .......... + potassium hydroxide → potassium sulfate + ..........
   (iv) hydrochloric acid + iron → .......... + ..........
   b. Copy and complete these symbol equations:
   (i) $\text{.........}Li + H_2SO_4 \rightarrow Li_2SO_4 + \text{.........}$
   (ii) $CaCO_3 + \text{.........}HCl \rightarrow CaCl_2 + \text{.........} + \text{.........}$
   S c. Construct symbol equations for these reactions:
   (i) The reaction of sulfuric acid, $H_2SO_4$, with magnesium carbonate, $MgCO_3$.
   (ii) The reaction of nitric acid, $HNO_3$, with barium hydroxide, $Ba(OH)_2$.
   (iii) The reaction of hydrochloric acid with zinc.

Acids react with:

- reactive metals to produce a salt and hydrogen
- metal oxides or metal hydroxides to produce a salt and water
- carbonates to produce a salt, water and carbon dioxide.

# 11.3 Bases

**You need to:**

- Know that metal oxides and hydroxides are bases.
- Know that alkalis are soluble bases.
- Describe the characteristic properties of bases as reactions with acids and with ammonium salts and effect on litmus.
- Know that a neutralisation reaction occurs between an acid and a base.

**Bases** are substances which react with acids to produce a salt and water.

*Metal oxides and metal hydroxides* are bases.

*Alkalis* are bases which are soluble in water.

### Exam tip

**Watch out**

When writing equations for the reaction of ammonia with an acid remember that water does not appear as a product.

### Exam tip

For the core paper you are expected to know the word equations and simple symbol equations (when given information) for the reactions of bases.

### Exam tip

Remember that ammonia is an alkali because it produces $OH^-$ ions in aqueous solution.

### Worked example

State the meaning of the term alkali. [1]

An alkali is a soluble base ✓

Describe how you can use damp litmus paper to test if a gas is alkaline. [2]

Place the damp red litmus paper ✓ in the gas. If it turns blue ✓ the gas is alkaline.

A dental mouthwash is slightly alkaline. Concentrated sodium hydroxide is strongly alkaline.

Give the name and formula of the ion responsible for alkalinity. [2]

Hydroxide ion, ✓ $OH^-$ ✓

Suggest pH values for the dental mouthwash and concentrated sodium hydroxide. [2]

Mouthwash pH 8 ✓ sodium hydroxide pH 13 ✓

(Comment: pH below 11 but above 7 acceptable for mouthwash and pH 12 to 14 for sodium hydroxide)

Complete this general word equation by naming the products.

acid + base → .................... + .................... [2]

salt ✓ and water ✓

Name and give the formula of the product formed in this equation for **neutralisation**. Include the correct state symbol.

$H^+(aq) + OH^-(aq) \rightarrow$ .................... [2]

$H_2O$ ✓ (l) ✓

*Alkalis react with ammonium salts* to produce a salt, water and ammonia.

**Worked example**

Ammonium chloride reacts with sodium hydroxide.

State the name of the salt formed in this reaction. [1]

sodium chloride ✓

Ammonia is a base. State the meaning of the term base. [1]

A substance which reacts with an acid to form a salt and water. ✓

Aqueous ammonia reacts with sulfuric acid. Copy and complete the equation for this reaction.

..........$NH_3(aq) + H_2SO_4(aq) \rightarrow (NH_4)_2SO_4(aq)$ [1]

$2NH_3(aq)$ ✓ $+ H_2SO_4(aq) \rightarrow (NH_4)_2SO_4(aq)$

Bases neutralise acids to produce a salt and water.

Name the salt formed when calcium hydroxide reacts with nitric acid. [1]

calcium nitrate ✓

### Exam tip

**Watch out**

It is a common error to name ammonium salts incorrectly. Remember that ammonia changes to ammonium in salts such as ammonium chloride.

**Recap**

Bases react with acids to produce a salt and water.

## Apply

3. a. Choose from the list the two compounds which are bases.

   $CaO$ $CuCO_3$ $HCl$ $KNO_3$ $Mg(OH)_2$ $NaCl$ $SO_2$

   b. Copy and complete these word equations for the reactions of bases.

   (i) sodium hydroxide + sulfuric acid → .......... + ..........

   (ii) ammonia + hydrochloric acid → ..........

   (iii) lithium oxide + nitric acid → .......... + ..........

   (iv) sodium hydroxide + ammonium chloride → .......... + .......... + ..........

   c. Copy and complete this equation for the formation of water from the ions present in an acid and an alkali.

   .......... + .......... $\rightarrow H_2O$

   d. Copy and complete these equations for the reactions of bases.

   (i) ..........$NaOH + H_2SO_4 \rightarrow Na_2SO_4 +$ ..........

   (ii) $NH_4Cl + NaOH \rightarrow NaCl +$ .......... + ..........

   (iii) $MgO +$ ..........$HCl \rightarrow MgCl_2 +$ ..........

   S e. Construct symbol equations for these reactions:

   (i) the reaction of calcium hydroxide, $Ca(OH)_2$, with hydrochloric acid

   (ii) the reaction of sodium hydroxide with ammonium sulphate, $(NH_4)_2SO_4$ to produce a salt, ammonia and water

# 11.4 More about acids and bases

**You need to:**

- Describe neutralisation as $H^+(aq) + OH^-(aq) \rightarrow H_2O(l)$.
- **Define acids and bases in terms of proton transfer.**
- **Understand the difference between strong and weak acids and bases.**
- **Write ionic equations for acid-base reactions.**

**Acids** are proton ($H^+$) donors.

**Bases** are proton ($H^+$) acceptors.

**Neutralisation** is the reaction $H^+(aq) + OH^-(aq) \rightarrow H_2O(l)$.

**Key skills**

S You need to be able to analyse symbol equations to see where ions are accepted or donated.

**Exam tip**

Remember that acids contain $H^+$ ions in aqueous solution and alkalis contain $OH^-$ ions.

**Exam tip** S

Take care not to use the words 'strong' or 'weak' referring to the concentration of acids or alkalis. These words refer to the degree of dissociation. For concentration use the words dilute or concentrated.

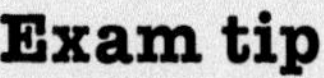

**Worked example**

An equation for neutralisation is:

$$HCl(aq) + NaOH(aq) \rightarrow NaCl(aq) + H_2O(l)$$

Give the formulae of the ions present in the products. [2]

Na+ ✓ and $Cl^-$ ✓

Construct the ionic equation for this reaction. [1]

$H^+ + OH^- \rightarrow H_2O$ ✓

S Describe this equation in terms of proton transfer of acids and bases. Give reasons for your answers. [2]

HCl is an acid because the proton $H^+$ is donated to the $OH^-$ ion in NaOH ✓ to form water.

NaOH is a base because the $OH^-$ ion accepts a proton from HCl ✓ to form water.

Ammonia reacts with water to form an equilibrium:

$$NH_3(g) + H_2O(l) \rightleftharpoons NH_4^+(aq) + OH^-(aq)$$

Describe $NH_3(g)$ and $H_2O(l)$ as acids or bases in terms of proton transfer. [2]

$NH_3$ is a base because it accepts a proton from water ✓ to become $NH_4^+$. Water is acting as an acid because it donates a proton to the $NH_3$ molecule. ✓

S **Strong acids and strong bases** are completely **dissociated** (ionised) in aqueous solution.

**Weak acids and weak bases** are partially dissociated (ionised) in aqueous solution.

**Worked example**

Ethanoic acid, $CH_3COOH$, is a weak acid.

Write an equation to show the ionisation of ethanoic acid. [2]

$CH_3COOH \rightleftharpoons CH_3COO^- + H^+$

(equation correct ✓ equilibrium sign ✓)

At a concentration of 0.1 mol/dm$^3$ ethanoic acid reacts slowly with magnesium but 0.1 mol/dm$^3$ hydrochloric acid reacts rapidly with magnesium. All conditions remain the same. Explain why the rates of reaction are different in terms of ionisation and collisions. [4]

Ethanoic acid is a weak acid and hydrochloric acid is a strong acid. ✓ Weak acids are incompletely dissociated but strong acids are completely dissociated ✓ in aqueous solution. There is a greater concentration of hydrogen ions in the hydrochloric acid ✓ so the rate of reaction is faster for hydrochloric acid. The collision frequency of the $H^+$ ions with magnesium is greater for hydrochloric acid. ✓

**Recap**

- Acids are **proton ($H^+$) donors** and bases are **proton acceptors**.
- Strong acids and strong bases are completely dissociated in aqueous solution.
- Weak acids and weak bases are partially dissociated in aqueous solution.

## Apply

4. Ammonia is a weak base.
   a. State the meaning of the term *weak* as applied to bases.
   b. Ammonia reacts with hydrochloric acid.

   $$NH_3(aq) + HCl(aq) \rightarrow NH_4Cl(aq)$$

   (i) Explain this reaction in terms of proton transfer.

   (ii) Write an equation to show the ionisation of hydrogen chloride, HCl(g), when it dissolves in water to form hydrochloric acid.

   c. A solution of 0.1 mol/dm$^3$ ammonia in water has a pH of about 11. A solution of 0.1 mol/dm$^3$ sodium hydroxide in water has a pH of 13.

   (i) Explain this difference in pH values.

   (ii) When ammonia dissolves in water the following equilibrium is set up.

   $$NH_3(g) + H_2O(l) \rightleftharpoons NH_4^+(aq) + OH^-(aq)$$

   Describe and explain whether $NH_4^+$ and $OH^-$ are acids or bases in terms of proton transfer.

# 11.5 Acid-base titrations and indicators

**You need to:**

- Describe how to do an acid-base titration.
- Describe how to identify the end point of a titration.
- Describe the effect of acids and alkalis on litmus, thymolphthalein and methyl orange.

**Exam tip**

You should be prepared to answer questions about titrations in the theory paper as well as in the practical papers.

An *acid-base titration* requires the correct use of a volumetric pipette and a burette.

The **end point** of a titration is the point at which an **indicator** changes colour to show that an acid has completely reacted with an alkali.

The ***titre*** in a titration is the final burette volume minus the initial burette volume.

An *acid-base indicator* is a substance that changes colour at the end point of a titration.

*Methyl orange indicator* is red in acid and yellow in alkali.

*Thymolphthalein indicator* is colourless in acid and blue in alkali.

**Worked example**

The concentration of an alkali can be found by means of an acid-base titration.

Name a piece of equipment, other than a burette, which can be used to put exactly 25.0 $cm^3$ of an alkali into a titration flask. [1]

Volumetric pipette ✓

A few drops of thymolphthalein indicator are then added to the flask.

State the purpose of adding the indicator. [1]

To determine when the acid has exactly neutralised the alkali. ✓

State the colour of thymolphthalein in the flask at the start of the experiment and when the acid is in excess. [2]

At the start it is blue ✓ and when acid is in excess it is colourless. ✓

The acid is placed in the burette and the initial burette reading taken. Which letter on the diagram below shows the best position to read the burette from. [1]

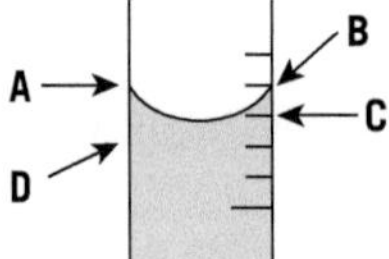


C ✓

Describe how to do the titration to get consistent results. [4]

Add acid from the burette, keeping the flask shaken ✓ until the indicator changes colour ✓ at the end point. This is the rough titre. Repeat the titration ✓ but near the end point add the acid slowly drop by drop until the end point is just reached. ✓ Repeat until the results are consistent.

Acid–base indicators such as litmus, methyl orange and thymolphthalein change colour at the end point of a titration.

## Apply

5. The concentration of dilute hydrochloric acid in a flask can be found by adding dilute sodium hydroxide of known concentration drop by drop to the acid.
   a. Name the most suitable piece of equipment used to add the alkali to the acid.
   b. State how you know when the sodium hydroxide has neutralised the acid exactly.
   c. A flask contains a solution of sodium hydroxide to which a few drops of methyl orange have been added.
      (i) State the colour change observed in the flask when sodium hydroxide is added until it is in excess.
      (ii) Name the piece of equipment used to put a few drops of indicator into the flask.

**Exam tip**

Make sure that you know the colours of litmus, methyl orange and thymolphthalein in acidic and alkaline solutions.

You need to be able to analyse the results of titrations and select results which are consistent (see question 4 at the end of this chapter).

# 11.6 Oxides

**You need to:**

- Classify oxides as acidic or basic related to non-metallic or metallic character.
- **Know that zinc oxide and aluminium oxide are amphoteric.**

**Basic oxides** react with acids. They are oxides of metals.

**Acidic oxides** react with bases. They are oxides of non-metals.

S **Amphoteric oxides** such as aluminium and zinc oxides react with acids as well as with bases.

**Exam tip**

For the core paper you are expected to know the word equations and simple symbol equations (when given information) for the reactions of oxides.

**Worked example**

There are several types of oxide. What type of oxide is sulfur dioxide? Give a reason for your answer. [2]

It's an acidic oxide ✓ because sulfur is a non-metal ✓ and non-metallic oxides are acidic.

Name the products of the reaction of copper(II) oxide with sulfuric acid. [2]

Copper(II) sulfate ✓ and water. ✓

Carbon dioxide reacts with sodium hydroxide.

Complete the symbol equation for this reaction.

$CO_2$ + ............NaOH → $Na_2CO_3$ + .......................... [2]

$CO_2$ + 2✓NaOH → $Na_2CO_3$ + $H_2O$✓

In which part of the Periodic Table are elements which form basic oxides found? [1]

On the left-hand side, mainly in Groups I to III ✓

Aluminium oxide is an amphoteric oxide. S

State the meaning of the term amphoteric oxide. [1]

Oxides which react with both acids and alkalis ✓

Write a symbol equation for the reaction of zinc oxide, ZnO, with hydrochloric acid. [2]

ZnO + 2HCl → $ZnCl_2$ + $H_2O$

(correct symbols ✓ correct balance ✓)

**Recap**

- Basic oxides react with acids and acidic oxides react with bases.
- Amphoteric oxides react with acids as well as with bases. 

## Apply

6. a. What type of oxide is magnesium oxide. Give a reason for your answer.

   b. Name the products of this reaction: Calcium oxide + nitric acid

   c. Some oxides react with water to produce acids or alkalis. Suggest the names of the acids formed when:

      (i) lithium oxide reacts with water

      (ii) sulfur dioxide reacts with water

   d. Balance these equations:

      (i) MgO + ............HCl → .......................... + $H_2O$

      (ii) .......................... + 2NaOH → $Na_2CO_3$ + ..........................

   e. (i) State the name for an oxide, such as zinc oxide, which reacts with both acids and bases.

      (ii) The equation for the reaction of zinc oxide with sodium hydroxide to form sodium zincate is: S
      ZnO(s) + 2NaOH(aq) → $Na_2ZnO_2$(aq) + $H_2O$(l)

      Construct the ionic equation for this reaction.

## Questions

1. **a.** Which one of these pH values represents a neutral solution?

   pH 0 pH 4 pH 7 pH 9 pH 14 [1]

   **b.** Describe how you can use universal indicator solution to determine if a solution is neutral. [3]

   **c.** **(i)** State the colour of methyl orange in alkaline solution. [1]

   **(ii)** State the colour of thymolphthalein in acidic solution. [1]

2. Write word equations for these reactions:

   **a.** sodium carbonate with nitric acid [2]

   **b.** zinc with sulfuric acid [2]

   **c.** ammonia with sulfuric acid [1]

3. **a.** Write a symbol equation for the reaction of barium oxide, BaO, with hydrochloric acid to produce barium chloride, $BaCl_2$, and one other product. [2]

   **b.** What type of oxide is barium oxide? Give a reason for your answer. [2]

4. A student titrated sodium hydroxide in a flask with sulfuric acid from a burette.

   The initial and final burette readings for a number of repeat experiments are shown.

| | 1st accurate titration | 2nd accurate titration | 3rd accurate titration | 4th accurate titration |
|---|---|---|---|---|
| final reading / $cm^3$ | 47.20 | 23.90 | 48.35 | 47.40 |
| initial reading / $cm^3$ | 24.00 | 0.30 | 24.80 | 23.90 |
| titre / $cm^3$ | **A** | **B** | **C** | **D** |

   **a.** Deduce the value of each titre **A**, **B**, **C** and **D**. [2]

   **b.** State which titre was not consistent with the others. [1]

   **c.** Calculate the average of the consistent titres to the nearest 0.05 $cm^3$. [1]

   **d.** A rough titration is never included in the results. Suggest why the rough titration is likely to be inconsistent with the other results. [1]

5. **a.** Define the term *strong* in the phrase 'strong acid'. [1]

   S **b.** Explain why 1.0 mol/$dm^3$ nitric acid reacts with magnesium oxide much faster than 1.0 mol/$dm^3$ ethanoic acid. [3]

   **c.** Construct the symbol equation for the reaction of magnesium oxide with hydrochloric acid. [2]

   **d.** An equation is shown: $CH_3COOH + NH_3 \rightarrow CH_3COO^- + NH_4^+$

   Explain which is the acid and base in this reaction in terms of proton transfer. [3]

## Sample question

1. Hydrochloric acid and ethanoic acid are acids. Ammonia and sodium hydroxide are alkalis.

   **a.** Define the term alkali. [1]

   **b.** Write the simplest equation for the neutralisation of any alkali by any acid. [2]

   **c.** Describe how you can use litmus paper to distinguish between hydrochloric acid and aqueous ammonia. [2]

   **d.** Write a symbol equation for the reaction of hydrochloric acid with zinc to produce zinc chloride, $ZnCl_2$, and a gas. [3]

   **e.** Suggest the pH of a concentrated solution of aqueous sodium hydroxide. [1]

   **f.** Sodium hydroxide reacts with chlorine dioxide. What type of oxide is chlorine dioxide? Explain your answer. [2]

   S **g.** Construct a symbol equation for the reaction of sodium hydroxide with ammonium sulfate, $(NH_4)_2SO_4$. [2]

   **h.** **(i)** Describe and explain how you can tell the difference between 0.5 mol/dm³ aqueous ethanoic acid and 0.5 mol/dm³ hydrochloric acid using zinc carbonate. [5]

   **(ii)** The equation shows an acid-base reaction.

   $$CH_3COOH + HNO_3 \rightleftharpoons CH_3COOH_2^+ + NO_3^-$$

   Describe which is the acid and which is the base. Explain your answer in terms of proton transfer. [3]

   **i.** Aluminium oxide is an amphoteric oxide.

   **(i)** Explain the meaning of the term amphoteric. [1]

   **(ii)** Construct a symbol equation for the reaction of aluminium oxide, $Al_2O_3$, with sodium hydroxide to form $NaAlO_2$ and one other product. [2]

# Making and identifying salts

## Revision checklist

Tick these boxes to build a record of your revision. Columns 2 and 3 can be used if you want to make a record more than once.

| Core/**Supplement** syllabus content | | 1 | 2 | 3 |
|---|---|---|---|---|
| 12.1 | Describe the preparation, separation and purification of soluble salts from metals, insoluble bases or insoluble carbonates. | | | |
| 12.2 | Describe preparation, separation and purification of soluble salts by a titration method. | | | |
| 12.3 | Describe the general solubility rules for salts. | | | |
| 12.3 | **Describe the preparation of insoluble salts by precipitation.** | | | |
| 12.4 | Describe tests for ammonia, carbon dioxide, chlorine, hydrogen, oxygen and sulfur dioxide. | | | |
| 12.5 | Describe tests for these ions in aqueous solution: $Al^{3+}$, $Ca^{2+}$, $Cr^{3+}$, $Cu^{2+}$, $Fe^{2+}$, $Fe^{3+}$, $NH_4^+$ and $Zn^{2+}$. | | | |
| 12.5 | Describe flame tests for $Li^+$, $Na^+$, $K^+$, $Ca^{2+}$, $Ba^{2+}$ and $Cu^{2+}$. | | | |
| 12.6 | Describe tests for halide ions. | | | |
| 12.6 | Describe tests for carbonates, nitrates and sulfates and sulfites. | | | |

# 12.1 Making salts from metals, bases or carbonates

**You need to:**

- Describe the preparation, separation and purification of soluble salts from metals, insoluble bases or insoluble carbonates.

**Key skills**

You should be able to write a practical procedure in the correct sequence using scientific terms.

**Exam tip**

When making a salt from a metal or metal oxide, remember:

- The solid is in excess so that the acid is the limiting reactant.
- The excess solid is filtered off before crystallising.

**Exam tip**

A common error is to suggest that you heat the crystals in an oven or put them in a desiccator to dry them. You will remove the water of crystallisation if you do this.

A **salt** is a compound formed when a metal or ammonium group replaces the hydrogen in an acid.

*Soluble salts* can be made by adding excess metal oxide or metal carbonate to an acid.

*Soluble salts of a metal above hydrogen in the reactivity series* can be made by adding excess metal to an acid.

**Worked example**

Suggest how you can make pure dry crystals of copper(II) sulfate from copper(II) oxide and sulfuric acid. [6]

Step 1: Add copper(II) oxide to the sulfuric acid until the copper(II) oxide is in excess ✓ then warm.

Step 2: Remove the excess solid copper(II) oxide from the mixture by filtration. ✓ The filtrate is a solution of copper(II) sulfate.

Step 3: Heat the solution of copper(II) sulfate in an evaporating basin until it is saturated so that you see crystals starting to form. ✓

Step 4: Leave the mixture to form crystals on cooling. ✓

Step 5: Filter off the crystals. ✓

Step 6: Dry the crystals between filter papers. ✓

**Recap**

Soluble salts are made by:

1. Adding excess metal, metal oxide or metal carbonate to an acid.
2. Warming to the crystallisation point then cooling.
3. Filtering off the crystals and drying them on filter paper.

**Exam tip**

**Watch out**

When crystallising a substance it is a common error to suggest that a solution is heated to dryness.

## Apply

1. a. Suggest how you can make a solution of magnesium chloride by using magnesium and a named acid.

   b. Suggest how you can make pure dry crystals of zinc nitrate from a solution of zinc nitrate.

   c. Explain why you should **not** heat crystals of copper(II) sulfate in an oven to dry them.

# 12.2 Making salts by titration

**You need to:**

- Describe preparation, separation and purification of soluble salts by a titration method.

The *titration method for making salts* is used when an acid is added to an alkali. The titration is carried out first with an indicator then without an indicator.

**Worked example**

Suggest how you can make pure dry crystals of potassium sulfate from potassium hydroxide and sulfuric acid using a titration method. [7]

Step 1: Put potassium hydroxide of known concentration and volume into a flask with an indicator. ✓

Step 2: Add sulfuric acid from a burette until the indicator changes colour and record the volume of acid. ✓

Step 3: Repeat the experiment without the indicator using the same volume and concentration of potassium hydroxide. ✓ (The solution in the flask is aqueous potassium sulfate.)

Step 4: Heat the solution of potassium sulfate in an evaporating basin until it is saturated so that you see crystals starting to form. ✓

Step 5: Leave the mixture to form crystals on cooling. ✓

Step 6: Filter off the crystals. ✓

Step 7: Dry the crystals between filter papers. ✓

## Apply

2. a. Suggest suitable acids and alkalis to make these salts.
   (i) sodium nitrate
   (ii) barium chloride
   (iii) lithium sulfate

   b. Suggest how you can make a colourless aqueous solution of sodium chloride from sodium hydroxide and hydrochloric acid using a titration method.

   c. A student makes crystals of potassium sulfate using the titration method with potassium hydroxide in the flask.
   (i) Explain why the titration has to be done a second time without the indicator.
   (ii) Explain why the volume and concentration of potassium hydroxide in the flask should be the same in each titration.

**Key skills**

You should be able to select an appropriate practical procedure based on the reactants given.

**Exam tip**

Remember that the titration method for making salts is only used for acid + alkali.

**Recap**

Soluble salts are made from an acid and alkali by:

1. Titrating the alkali with the acid using an indicator.
2. Repeating the titration without the indicator using the volume of acid found from the first titration.
3. Crystallising, filtering and drying the crystals.

**Exam tip**

Remember the alkali usually goes in the titration flask and the acid in the burette.

# 12.3 Making salts by precipitation

**You need to:**

- Describe the general solubility rules for salts.
- **Describe the preparation of insoluble salts by precipitation.**

*Soluble salts* include salts of Group I elements and ammonium salts, all nitrates and most chlorides, bromides, iodides and sulfates.

*Insoluble salts* include halides of silver and lead and sulfates of calcium, barium and lead.

*Group I hydroxides* and carbonates are soluble. Most other hydroxides and carbonates are insoluble.

### Worked example

Explain using solubility rules if the salts formed by these reactions are soluble or insoluble in water.

Aqueous sodium hydroxide is added to dilute sulfuric acid. [2]

Sodium sulfate ✓ and water are formed. All salts of Group I elements are soluble. ✓ So, sodium sulfate is soluble in water.

Aqueous silver nitrate is added to dilute hydrochloric acid. [2]

Silver chloride ✓ and dilute nitric acid are formed. Halides of silver are insoluble in water. ✓ Chlorides are halides, so silver chloride is insoluble.

## Apply

3. Predict whether these compounds are soluble or insoluble in water. Explain your answers using the solubility rules.
   a. potassium chloride
   b. barium sulfate
   c. iron(III) hydroxide
   d. ammonium sulfate
   e. silver nitrate
   f. potassium carbonate

### Exam tip

Halides are salts containing the ions $F^-$, $Cl^-$, $Br^-$ or $I^-$.

### Key skills

You should be able to use a set of rules to determine if a substance is soluble or insoluble.

### Exam tip

In questions about salt preparation, you may be given information about the solubility of the reactants and products. This can be an equation with state symbols.

### Recap

- Salts of Group I elements and ammonium salts, all nitrates and most chlorides, bromides, iodides and sulfates are soluble in water.
- Halides of silver and lead, sulfates of calcium, barium and lead and hydroxides (except Group I hydroxides) are insoluble in water.

*Insoluble salts are made* by mixing two soluble salts.

**Worked example**

Describe how to prepare a pure dry sample of silver iodide from aqueous silver nitrate and a named soluble salt. [5]

Step 1: A suitable soluble salt is potassium iodide ✓ because all Group I halides are soluble.

Step 2: Add aqueous silver nitrate to aqueous potassium iodide until no more precipitate forms. ✓

Step 3: Filter off the precipitate of silver iodide. ✓ Silver iodide is the residue.

Step 4: Wash the silver iodide residue with distilled water ✓ to remove any excess potassium or nitrate ions.

Step 5: Dry the silver iodide with filter paper ✓ or in a low temperature oven.

Convert this symbol equation into an ionic equation by showing the ions present in the aqueous reactants and products, cancelling the spectator ions and writing the ionic equation. [4]

$$Pb(NO_3)_2(aq) + 2NaCl(aq) \rightarrow PbCl_2(s) + 2NaNO_3(aq)$$

$$Pb^{2+}(aq) + 2NO_3^-(aq) + 2Na^+(aq) + 2Cl^-(aq) \rightarrow PbCl_2(s) + 2Na^+(aq) + 2NO_3^-(aq)$$

ions in reactants ✓ ions in products ✓

$$Pb^{2+}(aq) + \cancel{2NO_3^-(aq)} + \cancel{2Na^+(aq)} + 2Cl^-(aq) \rightarrow PbCl_2(s) + \cancel{2Na^+(aq)} + \cancel{2NO_3^-(aq)}$$ ✓

$$Pb^{2+}(aq) + 2Cl^-(aq) \rightarrow PbCl_2(s)$$ ✓

**Key skills**

You should be able to select an appropriate practical procedure based on the reactants given.

**Exam tip**

Make sure that you know the types of compound that are insoluble. Without this knowledge you cannot select precipitation as the correct way to make a particular salt.

**Recap**

Insoluble salts are made by:

1. adding two soluble salts together to produce a precipitate of the insoluble salt
2. filtering off the precipitate then washing and drying the crystals

## Apply

4. a. Describe how to prepare a pure dry sample of barium sulfate from aqueous barium chloride and a named soluble salt.

   b. Convert these symbol equations into ionic equations.

   (i) $AgNO_3(aq) + NaBr(aq) \rightarrow AgBr(s) + NaNO_3(aq)$

   (ii) $CuCl_2(aq) + 2NaOH(aq) \rightarrow Cu(OH)_2(s) + 2NaCl(aq)$

# 12.4 What's that gas?

**You need to:**

- **Describe tests for ammonia, carbon dioxide, chlorine, hydrogen, oxygen and sulfur dioxide.**

*Ammonia* turns damp red litmus paper blue.

*Carbon dioxide* turns limewater milky.

*Chlorine* bleaches damp litmus paper.

*Hydrogen* gives a squeaky pop with a lighted splint.

*Oxygen* relights a glowing splint.

*Sulfur dioxide* turns acidified aqueous potassium manganate(VII) colourless.

**Exam tip**

Remember that gases less dense than air, such as hydrogen or ammonia, are collected with the tube or gas jar upside down (downward displacement of air).

### Exam tip

**Watch out**

You cannot collect a gas over water if the gas is very soluble in water!

### Recap

- Ammonia turns damp red litmus paper blue and chlorine bleaches damp litmus paper.
- Carbon dioxide turns limewater milky.
- Hydrogen gives a squeaky pop with a lighted splint but oxygen relights a glowing splint.
- Sulfur dioxide turns acidified aqueous potassium manganate(VII) colourless.

### Exam tip

**Watch out**

It is a common error to mix up the tests for hydrogen and oxygen. Remember that the test for oxygen uses a glowing splint and the test for hydrogen uses a lighted splint.

### Worked example

Three different methods of collecting gases are shown.

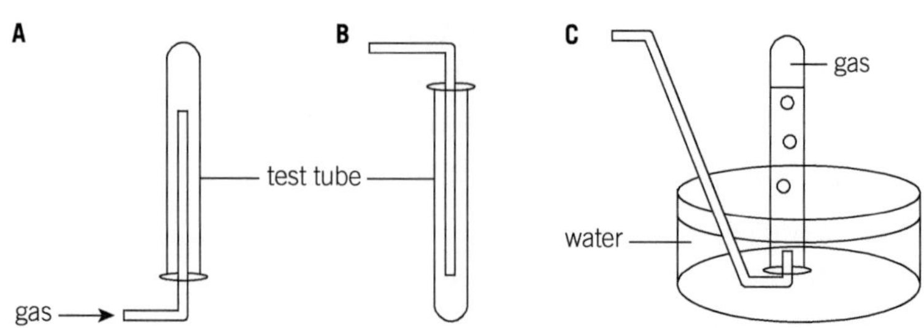


The relative molecular masses of some gases are:

ammonia 15, chlorine 71, nitrogen 28, oxygen 32

Suggest which method is best used for collecting **a** chlorine and **b** ammonia. In each case explain your answer by referring to each method. [8]

**a** Method **B** ✓ because chlorine has a higher molecular mass than the oxygen and nitrogen in the air. ✓

In method **A** chlorine would not displace the air in the tube and come out the bottom of the tube. ✓

In method **C** some chlorine dissolves in the water. ✓

**b** Method **A** ✓ because ammonia has a lower molecular mass than the oxygen and nitrogen in the air. ✓

In method **B** the ammonia would float above the air in the tube and come out of the top. ✓

In method **C** most of the ammonia dissolves in the water. ✓

Suggest why method **C** is not suitable for collecting sulfur dioxide. [1]

Sulfur dioxide dissolves in water. ✓

Give a test for sulfur dioxide and the colour change expected if sulfur dioxide is present. [3]

Add a few drops of acidified potassium manganate(VII) ✓ to a test tube containing sulfur dioxide gas. The potassium manganate(VII) turns from purple ✓ to colourless. ✓

## Apply

5. a. Give a test for chlorine and the expected result if chlorine is present.

   b. You are given three test tubes of the same colourless gas. Describe how you could identify whether the gas is hydrogen, oxygen or carbon dioxide.

   c. A gas turns damp red litmus paper blue. Identify this gas and suggest why it turns the litmus paper blue.

# 12.5 Testing for cations

**You need to:**

- Describe tests for these ions in aqueous solution: $Al^{3+}$, $Ca^{2+}$, $Cr^{3+}$, $Cu^{2+}$, $Fe^{2+}$, $Fe^{3+}$, $NH_4^+$ and $Zn^{2+}$; describe flame tests for $Li^+$, $Na^+$, $K^+$, $Ca^{2+}$, $Ba^{2+}$ and $Cu^{2+}$.

*Ammonium ions* are present if, on warming with sodium hydroxide, damp red litmus paper turns blue.

*Ions of copper(II), chromium(III), iron(II) and iron(III)* give coloured precipitates with sodium hydroxide or ammonia. Only the copper(II) ions dissolve in excess ammonia.

*Ions of aluminium, calcium and zinc* give white precipitates with sodium hydroxide.

*Zinc ions dissolve* in excess aqueous ammonia but aluminium ions do not.

**Key skills**

You need to be able to find suitable methods to help you memorise information related to the **qualitative analysis** of **cations**. This could be making lists in columns and testing yourself or making spider diagrams.

**Worked example**

When a few drops of aqueous sodium hydroxide are added to solution **T**, a white precipitate is observed. Describe how you could use aqueous ammonia to tell if solution **T** contains aluminium, calcium or zinc ions. [6]

Add a few drops of aqueous ammonia to solution **T** and then excess aqueous ammonia. ✓

If calcium ions are present there will be no precipitate or a very slight white precipitate. ✓

If aluminium ions are present there will be a white precipitate ✓ which does not dissolve in excess ammonia. ✓

If zinc ions are present, there will be a white precipitate ✓ which dissolves in excess ammonia ✓ to form a colourless solution.

**Exam tip**

You do not have to know the equations for copper ions dissolving in excess ammonia or chromium ions dissolving in excess hydroxide. Those aiming for higher grades may be asked to write ionic equations for some of these reactions when given relevant information.

**Exam tip**

When conducting the test for iron(II) ions, make sure that you observe the colour straight away. The surface of the precipitate soon oxidises and becomes brown.

**Exam tip**

**Watch out**

It is a common error to muddle the results of tests for $Fe^{2+}$ and $Fe^{3+}$ ions.

## Apply

6. a. A sample of compound **S** is warmed with a few drops of sodium hydroxide solution. A gas is produced which turns damp red litmus paper blue. Identify the gas and state the name of the positive ion present in compound **S** which produces this gas.
   b. Another sample of compound **S** is dissolved in water and a few drops of aqueous sodium hydroxide added. A red-brown precipitate is observed. Identify another positive ion present in compound **S**.
   c. Describe the effect of aqueous ammonia on a solution of compound **S**.
   d. A solution contains $Cr^{3+}$ ions. Describe the effect of adding a few drops of sodium hydroxide to the solution and then excess sodium hydroxide.

   e. Write an ionic equation for the reaction of $Cr^{3+}$ ions with a few drops of aqueous sodium hydroxide.

**Exam tip**

**Watch out**

Salts of ammonia are called ammon<u>ium</u> salts. It is a common error to write ammonia ✗ chloride instead of ammon<u>ium</u> ✓ chloride.

A *flame test* can be used to identify some metal cations.

**Worked example**

Describe how to carry out a flame test to identify potassium ions in a compound and state the results. [3]

Put a small sample of the compound on the end of a platinum wire. ✓ Put the end of the wire at the edge of a blue Bunsen flame ✓ and observe the colour of the flame. If potassium is present the flame will be coloured lilac. ✓

**Exam tip**

When testing for metal ions think about: (i) whether there is a precipitate (ii) the colour of the precipitate (iii) does the precipitate dissolve in excess aqueous sodium hydroxide or aqueous ammonia?

## Apply

7. Match the flame colours **A** to **D** with the ions **1** to **4**.

| | |
|---|---|
| **A** blue-green | **1** $Na^+$ |
| **B** yellow | **2** $Li^+$ |
| **C** red | **3** $Ba^{2+}$ |
| **D** light green | **4** $Cu^{2+}$ |

**Recap**

- Ammonia is formed on warming ammonium salts with sodium hydroxide.
- Ions of $Cu^{2+}$, $Cr^{3+}$, $Fe^{2+}$ and $Fe^{3+}$ give coloured precipitates with sodium hydroxide or ammonia.
- Ions of $Al^{3+}$, $Ca^{2+}$ and $Zn^{2+}$ give white precipitates with sodium hydroxide.
- $Cu^{2+}$ and $Zn^{2+}$ ions dissolve in excess aqueous ammonia.

# 12.6 Testing for anions

**You need to:**

- Describe tests for halide ions; describe tests for carbonates, nitrates and sulfates and sulfites.

**Exam tip**

**Watch out**

When testing for sulfates, the barium chloride is acidified with *nitric* acid. Take care not to use sulfuric acid – it contains sulfate ions!

*Aqueous silver nitrate* is used to test for halides. Chlorides give a white precipitate, bromides give a cream precipitate and iodides give a yellow precipitate.

*Carbonates* produce carbon dioxide on addition of an acid.

*Nitrates* release ammonia when heated with sodium hydroxide and aluminium foil.

*Sulfates* produce a white precipitate on addition of acidified barium chloride.

*Sulfites* release sulfur dioxide when heated with hydrochloric acid.

**Worked example**

A sample of compound **R** is heated with aluminium foil and concentrated sodium hydroxide. A gas is produced which turns damp red litmus paper blue. Identify the gas and state the name and give the formula of the negative ion present in compound **R** which produces this gas. [3]

The gas is ammonia ✓ and the ion is nitrate, ✓ $NO_3^-$. ✓

Describe and explain the test for carbonate ions and give the result if carbonate ions are present. [4]

Add hydrochloric acid to the sample ✓ then test the gas by bubbling through limewater. ✓ If the limewater goes milky ✓ carbon dioxide is present. Carbon dioxide is produced when an acid reacts with a carbonate. ✓

**Recap**

- Aqueous silver nitrate is used to test for halides.
- Nitrates release ammonia when heated with sodium hydroxide and aluminium foil.
- Sulfates give a white precipitate with barium chloride.
- Sulfites release sulfur dioxide when heated with an acid.

## Apply

8. a. A sample of compound **S** is warmed gently with dilute hydrochloric acid. The gas produced is tested. A gas is produced that turns acidified aqueous potassium manganate(VII) colourless.

   (i) State the colour of aqueous potassium manganate(VII).

   (ii) Identify the gas and state the name and give the formula of the negative ion present in compound **S** which produces this gas.

   b. The labels have fallen off two bottles of white solids. The solids are either potassium bromide or potassium chloride. Describe a test for halide ions to help you deduce which solid is which. Give the results of a positive test for each.

   S c. Write an ionic equation for the reaction of $Br^-$ ions with a few drops of aqueous silver nitrate.

### Exam tip

**Watch out**

Remember that you add *nitric* acid and silver nitrate in the test for halide ions. If you add hydrochloric acid, you will be adding chloride ions!

### Exam tip

A solution that loses its colour is 'colourless'. It is incorrect to describe it as 'clear'.

## Questions

1. Match the formula of the ions **A** to **E** with the colour of the precipitate formed (**1** to **5**) when aqueous sodium hydroxide is added to solutions of compounds containing these ions.

| | |
|---|---|
| **A** $Fe^{2+}$ | **1** red-brown |
| **B** $Cu^{2+}$ | **2** grey-green |
| **C** $Cr^{3+}$ | **3** white |
| **D** $Zn^{2+}$ | **4** green turning brown on the surface |
| **E** $Fe^{3+}$ | **5** light blue |

[2]

2. Describe the observations when a few drops of aqueous ammonia are added to a solution containing $Cu^{2+}$ ions and then when excess aqueous ammonia is added. [2]

3. Describe how to produce pure dry crystals of nickel(II) chloride from a dilute solution of nickel(II) chloride. [4]

4. Describe how to produce crystals of zinc sulfate using zinc and a named acid. [6]

5. A student wants to prepare crystals of barium chloride using an acid and an alkali.

   **a.** Name a suitable acid and alkali which the student could use. [2]

   **b.** Describe how the student can make a concentrated solution of barium chloride from this acid and alkali. [5]

6. State whether these compounds are soluble or insoluble in water. In each case give a reason for your answer using the solubility rules.

   **a.** lithium hydroxide [2]

   **b.** silver nitrate [2]

   **c.** magnesium carbonate [2]

   **d.** ammonium sulfate [2]

7. Match the formula of the ions **Q** to **T** with the tests for these ions, **1** to **4**.

| | |
|---|---|
| **Q** $SO_4^{2-}$ | **1** warm with acid and test the gas with acidified potassium manganate(VII) |
| **R** $I^-$ | **2** add nitric acid and aqueous barium chloride |
| **S** $NO_3^-$ | **3** add acidified silver nitrate |
| **T** $SO_3^{2-}$ | **4** add Al foil and sodium hydroxide then warm and test the gas |

[2]

S 8. Write an ionic equation for the reaction of aqueous sulfate ions with a few drops of aqueous barium chloride, $BaCl_2$. [1]

## Sample question

1. a. A student prepares ammonia by heating calcium hydroxide with ammonium chloride. The student suggested using the apparatus shown.

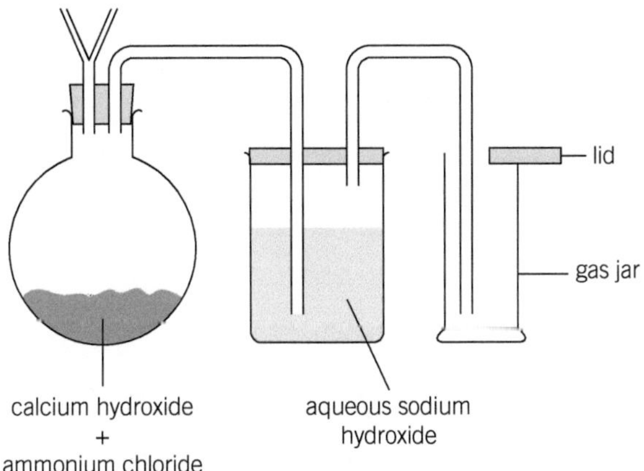


(i) Where should the apparatus be heated? [1]

(ii) Suggest three errors in the way the apparatus is set up. For each error give a reason. [6]

(iii) Ammonium chloride is a white solid. Describe how you could show that the white solid contains ammonium ions and sulfate ions. [5]

b. Crystals of ammonium chloride can be prepared by neutralising aqueous ammonia with dilute hydrochloric acid.

(i) Explain why a titration method should be used. [2]

(ii) Describe how to prepare pure dry crystals of ammonium chloride using the titration method. [7]

c. Two solutions, **X** and **Y**, both form a green precipitate when a few drops of sodium hydroxide are added.

(i) When an excess of sodium hydroxide is added to **X**, the precipitate dissolves. When an excess of sodium hydroxide is added to **Y**, the precipitate does not dissolve.

Identify the cations present in **X** and **Y**. [2]

(ii) Describe the effect of adding a few drops of aqueous ammonia to **X** and **Y** and then adding excess aqueous ammonia. [3]

S (iii) The green precipitate from **Y** is left in the air for 5 minutes. The precipitate starts to turn brown. Suggest why it starts to turn brown and write an ionic equation for this reaction. [3]

d. Lead iodide is an insoluble salt.

(i) Suggest a method of preparing dry crystals of lead iodide from aqueous lead nitrate, $Pb(NO_3)_2$. [5]

(ii) Write an ionic equation for the reaction of aqueous iodide ions with a few drops of aqueous lead nitrate. Include state symbols. [3]

# The Periodic Table

## Revision checklist

Tick these boxes to build a record of your revision. Columns 2 and 3 can be used if you want to make a record more than once.

| Core/**Supplement** syllabus content | | 1 | 2 | 3 |
|---|---|---|---|---|
| 13.1 | Describe the arrangement of the elements in the Periodic Table. | | | |
| 13.1 | Describe the change from metallic to non-metallic character across a period. | | | |
| 13.1 | Describe the relationship between the group number and ionic charge of an element. | | | |
| 13.1 | Explain similarity in chemical properties in the same group in terms of electronic configuration. | | | |
| 13.2 | Know that the Group I metals (the alkali metals) are relatively soft. | | | |
| 13.2 | Describe the trends in the properties of the Group I metals. | | | |
| 13.2 | Predict the properties of other Group I elements given data. | | | |
| 13.3 | Know that Group VII (the halogens) are diatomic non-metals. | | | |
| 13.3 | Describe the appearance of the halogens and the trend in their density and reactivity. | | | |
| 13.3 | Describe the reactions of halogens with halide ions. | | | |
| 13.3 | Predict the properties of other halogens given data. | | | |
| 13.4 | Describe the noble gases as being unreactive, monatomic gases and explain this in terms of electronic structure. | | | |
| 13.4 | Explain how the position of an element in the Periodic Table can be used to predict its properties. | | | |
| 13.4 | **Identify trends in groups given suitable information.** | | | |
| 13.5 | Describe transition elements as metals having high densities, high melting points, forming coloured compounds and acting (as elements and compounds) as catalysts. | | | |
| 13.5 | **Know that transition elements have variable oxidation states.** | | | |

# 13.1 The Periodic Table

**You need to:**

- Describe the arrangement of the elements in the Periodic Table.
- Describe the change from metallic to non-metallic character across a period.
- Describe the relationship between the group number and ionic charge of an element.
- Explain similarity in chemical properties in the same group in terms of electronic configuration.

*Elements in the same* **group** of the Periodic Table often have similar chemical properties because their atoms have the same number of electrons in their outer shell.

*Metallic character* decreases across a period.

In *Groups I, II and III* the ionic charge is positive and the value of the charge is the same as the group number.

In *Groups V, VI and VII* the ionic charge is negative and the value of the charge is 8 – group number.

**Worked example**

Some elements in the Periodic Table are shown.

| Na | Mg | Al | Si | P | S | Cl | Ar |
|---|---|---|---|---|---|---|---|

State which period these elements belong to. Give a reason in terms of electronic configuration. [2]

Period 3 ✓ because all the outer electrons are in the third electron shell. ✓

Describe how the proton number changes across the period. Each successive element has one more proton ✓ ✓ BUT increases across period (alone) ✓. [2]

Which elements are most likely to form positive ions? Explain your answer. [2]

Na, Mg and Al ✓ because they are metals and metals lose electrons when they form compounds. ✓

Suggest the formula for a sulfide ion. [1]

$S^{2-}$ ✓

Use the Periodic Table to identify one other element that has similar chemical properties to magnesium. Give a reason for your answer in terms of electronic configuration. [2]

Calcium ✓ because it has the same number of electrons as magnesium in its outer shell. ✓

Describe how the metallic character changes across this period. [1]

It decreases from left to right. ✓

**Exam tip**

You need to know where the metals and non-metals appear in the Periodic Table but you do not have to remember exactly where the dividing line between the two in Groups III to VI.

**Exam tip**

Don't forget to refer to the Periodic Table at the back of the exam paper to find the position of elements and their atomic numbers.

**Exam tip**

Remember that the first period contains only two elements H and He.

**Recap**

- Elements in the same group have similar chemical properties because their atoms have the same number of electrons in their outer shell.
- Metallic character decreases across a period.
- Typical ionic charges: Group I +1, Group II +2, Group III +3, Group VI −2, Group VII −1.

## Apply

1. Some elements in the Periodic Table are shown.

| Li | Be | B | C | N | O | F | Ne |
|---|---|---|---|---|---|---|---|
| Na | Mg | Al | Si | P | S | Cl | Ar |

a. State which two elements are in Group IV.

b. The proton number of aluminium is 13. Explain by reference to the position in the Periodic Table why the proton number of argon is 18.

c. Which elements are most likely to form negative ions? Explain your answer.

d. Suggest the formula for (i) a beryllium ion (ii) a nitride ion.

e. Explain in terms of electronic configuration why lithium and sodium have similar chemical properties.

f. (i) State which period the elements C, N and O belong to. Give a reason in terms of electronic configuration.

(ii) Describe how non-metallic character changes in this period.

# 13.2 Group I metals

**You need to:**

- Know that the Group I metals (the alkali metals) are relatively soft.
- Describe the trends in the properties of the Group I metals.
- Predict the properties of other Group I elements given data.

**Key skills**

You need to be able to interpret data about elements from tables and graphs and identify trends.

*Boiling point, melting point and hardness* of the alkali metals decrease down the group.

The *trend in density* of the alkali metals is towards higher densities going down the group.

**Alkali metals** *react with water* to form hydrogen and a solution of metal hydroxide.

*The reactivity of the alkali metals* increases down the group.

## Worked example

The table shows some properties of the Group I metals.

| Metal | Density in g/cm³ | Melting point/°C |
|---|---|---|
| lithium | 0.53 | 181 |
| sodium | 0.97 | 98 |
| potassium | 0.86 | |
| rubidium | 1.53 | 39 |

Describe the general trend in density down the group. [1]

Density generally increases down the group. ✓

Suggest a value for the melting point of potassium. Explain how you reached your conclusion. [2]

60 °C ✓ because the trend is downwards and 60 is about halfway between 98 and 39 °C. ✓

When sodium reacts with water, it floats on the surface and produces a steady stream of bubbles. Describe the observation when lithium reacts with water. Give a reason for your answer. [2]

Bubbles form slowly ✓ because the reactivity of the Group I metals increases down the group so it decreases up the group. ✓

Copy and complete the equation for the reaction of sodium with water.

2Na(s) + ..........$H_2O$(l) → 2NaOH(aq) + .................... (g) [2]

2Na(s) + 2$H_2O$(l) → 2NaOH(aq) ✓ + $H_2$(g) ✓

Name the compound with the formula NaOH. [1]

sodium hydroxide ✓

Suggest a pH value for the solution formed when the reaction is complete. Explain your answer. [2]

pH 13 ✓ because sodium hydroxide is an alkali and contains $OH^-$ ions. ✓

### Exam tip

When asked for observations, make sure that you write about what you see (or hear, smell or feel). 'Gas given off' is *not* an observation.

### Exam tip

When deducing values for physical properties such as melting points from tables of data, make sure the values that you choose follow the trend of the data. If you want to deduce a value between two others, it is acceptable to choose one which is halfway between. For the trend 100 °C → **X** → 50 °C → 30 °C, a suitable value for **X** is 75 °C.

### Recap

- In Group I, boiling point, melting point and hardness decrease down the group but density and reactivity increase.
- Alkali metals react with water to form hydrogen and aqueous metal hydroxide.

## Apply

2. The table shows some properties of the Group I metals.

| Metal | Relative hardness | Boiling point/°C |
|---|---|---|
| lithium | 12 | 1342 |
| sodium | 10 | 883 |
| potassium | 8 | 760 |
| rubidium | 7 | |

a. Describe the general trend in hardness down the group.

b. Suggest a value for the boiling point of rubidium.

c. State the general trend in density from lithium to rubidium.

### Exam tip

Note that Group I elements have 'similar properties' **not** 'the same properties'.

d. (i) Describe two observations when potassium reacts with water.
(ii) Write an equation to show the formation of a potassium ion from a potassium atom.
(iii) Write a word equation for the reaction of potassium with water.
(iv) Describe the reactivity of the other Group I metals with water compared with potassium.

# 13.3 Group VII elements

**You need to:**

- Know that Group VII (the halogens) are diatomic non-metals.
- Describe the appearance of the halogens and the trend in their density and reactivity.
- Describe the reactions of halogens with halide ions; predict the properties of other halogens given data.

The *Group VII* elements (**halogens**) have diatomic molecules.

*At r.t.p.* chlorine is a yellow-green gas, bromine is a red-brown liquid and iodine is a grey-black solid.

*Melting and boiling points of the halogens* increase down the group.

The *reactivity of the halogens* decreases down the group.

**Worked example**

The table shows some properties of the halogens.

| Element | Density of the liquid at the melting point in g/cm³ | Melting point/°C |
|---|---|---|
| fluorine | 1.51 | |
| chlorine | 1.56 | −101 |
| bromine | 3.12 | − 7 |
| iodine | 4.93 | +114 |

Describe the general trend in density down the group. [1]

Density increases down the group. ✓

Deduce the melting point of fluorine. [1]

−200 °C ✓

The halogens are diatomic. Give the meaning of the term diatomic. [1]

The molecule contains two atoms. ✓

**Exam tip**

**Watch out**

Take care with negative values. A temperature of −100 °C is lower than −80 °C but higher than −120 °C.

**Exam tip**

Make sure that you know the difference between the colour of iodine solid and solution. The solid is grey-black and the aqueous solution is brown. The vapour is purple but you do not need to know this for the exam.

**Exam tip**

When extrapolating values for physical properties such as boiling points make the values that you choose follow the trend of the data. For the trend **B** → 360 °C → 200 °C → 120 °C, a suitable value for **B** is 400–800 °C but **not** 2000 °C which is too high.

State the colour of bromine at room temperature. [1]

red-brown ✓

The melting point of bromine is −7 °C. The boiling point of bromine is +59 °C. Deduce the physical state of bromine at 20 °C. Give a reason for your answer. [2]

Liquid ✓ because 20 °C is above the melting point but below the boiling point. ✓

**Halides** are salts of the halogens or compounds containing halogen atoms. Group I and Group II halides are colourless.

A **displacement reaction** is where one atom or group of atoms replaces another.

A *more reactive halogen displaces a less reactive halogen* from a solution of its halide.

**Worked example**

Aqueous chlorine reacts with aqueous potassium bromide in a displacement reaction.

Construct the word equation for this reaction. [2]

chlorine + potassium bromide → bromine ✓ + potassium chloride ✓

Describe the colour change in the reaction. [2]

Very light green ✓ (chlorine) turns to red-brown ✓ (bromine).

The unbalanced equation for another displacement reaction is shown.

Copy and complete this equation.

$Cl_2$ + ..........NaI → .................... + ..........NaCl [2]

$Cl_2$ + 2NaI → $I_2$ ✓ + 2NaCl ✓

Suggest why aqueous iodine does not react with aqueous sodium chloride. [1]

Chlorine is more reactive than iodine. ✓

## Apply

3. The table shows some properties of the halogens.

| Element | State at r.t.p. | Boiling point/°C |
|---|---|---|
| fluorine | gas | −188 |
| chlorine | gas | −35 |
| bromine | liquid | |
| iodine | solid | +184 |

a. Deduce the general trend in density down the group. Give a reason for your answer.

b. Deduce the boiling point of bromine.

c. State the colour of chlorine at room temperature.

d. The melting point of chlorine is −101 °C. Deduce the physical state of chlorine at −90 °C. Give a reason for your answer.

### Exam tip

**Watch out**

When answering questions about the lack of reaction of halogens with halides it is a common error to compare the reactivity of the halide with the halogen, e.g. 'chlorine is more reactive than bromide' ✗. The correct answer is 'chlorine is more reactive than bromine'. ✓

### Exam tip

Make sure that you can tell the difference between halogens (elements) and halides (compounds of halogens). It is a common error to write chlorine ✗ ions instead of chloride ✓ ions.

### Exam tip

Although dilute aqueous solutions of chlorine used in schools appear colourless, you should give the colour of chlorine as yellow-green in exams.

### Recap

- Halogens (Group VII) have diatomic molecules. Halides are compounds containing halogen atoms.
- The melting and boiling points of the halogens increases down the group but their reactivity decreases down the group.
- A more reactive halogen displaces a less reactive halogen from a solution of its halide.

### Exam tip

Remember that halogens are diatomic molecules but halides are ions with a single negative charge, e.g. $Cl^-$.

e. Aqueous bromine reacts with aqueous potassium iodide in a displacement reaction.

(i) Copy and complete the equation for this reaction.

$Br_2$ + ............KI → ........................ + ............KBr

(ii) Suggest why aqueous iodine does not react with aqueous potassium bromide.

# 13.4 Noble gases and periodic trends

**You need to:**

- Describe the noble gases as being unreactive, monatomic gases and explain this in terms of electronic structure.
- Explain how the position of an element in the Periodic Table can be used to predict its properties.
- **Identify trends in groups given suitable information.**

The **noble gases** *(Group 0 or VIII)* are **monatomic** (only contain single atoms).

The *noble gases are inert* because they have a full outer shell of electrons which is a stable electronic configuration.

*The melting points, boiling points and densities of the noble gases* increase down the group.

### Exam tip

Don't make the mistake of writing that 'all ✗ noble gases have eight electrons in their outer shell'. Remember that helium has an outer shell of two electrons. It is better to refer to a 'complete outer shell of electrons'.

### Worked example

The noble gases are monatomic elements of increasing relative atomic mass.

State the meaning of the term monatomic. [1]

Elements made up of single atoms ✓

Suggest how the boiling points of the noble gases vary with their position in the group. Give a reason for your answer. [2]

The boiling points increase down the group ✓ because the **forces of attraction** between the atoms are greater, the greater the relative atomic mass. ✓

Explain why the noble gases are unreactive. [2]

They have a full outer shell of electrons ✓ which is a stable electronic configuration. ✓

## Apply

4. Argon is a noble gas. Its melting point is −189 °C and its boiling point is −186 °C.
   a. Deduce the state of argon at −199 °C. Give a reason for your answer.
   b. (i) Complete this sentence about argon by writing the missing words **A**, **B** and **C**.

      Argon does not **A** directly with other elements because it cannot **B**, lose or share **C**.

      (ii) Give the electronic configuration of argon.
   c. Suggest the trend in density down Group VIII elements. Give a reason for your answer.

The *position of an element in the Periodic Table* in terms of its group and period can be used to predict its properties.

*Trends in each group* can be recognised using physical and chemical data provided. 

**Key skills**

You need to be able to predict properties of elements using prior knowledge and further information provided.

### Exam tip

Be prepared to answer questions about trends in periods as well as trends in groups when given information about elements. Look out for the direction of the trend in properties in order to predict the properties of elements.

**Worked example**

Some properties of some elements in Period 3 of the Periodic Table are shown.

| **Element** | magnesium | aluminium | silicon | phosphorus | sulfur |
|---|---|---|---|---|---|
| **Relative electrical conductivity** | 20 0000 | 40 0000 | 0.0001 | 0.000000001 | |
| **Bonding** | metallic | metallic | covalent | | covalent |
| **Atomic radius/nm** | 0.136 | | 0.117 | 0.110 | 0.104 |

Suggest values for

the relative electrical conductivity of sulfur [1]

less than phosphorus – 0.00000000001 ✓

the atomic radius of aluminium [1]

0.125 nm ✓

Deduce the type of bonding present in phosphorus. Give a reason for your answer. [2]

Covalent ✓ because it is between silicon and sulfur which are both covalent. ✓

Some properties of the Group IV elements and compounds are shown. 

| Element | Melting point/°C | Type of oxide, $XO_2$ | Electrical conductivity |
|---|---|---|---|
| carbon (diamond) | 3550 | acidic | poor conductor |
| silicon | 1410 | weakly acidic | semi-conductor |
| germanium | | | |
| tin | 232 | amphoteric | conductor |

Deduce the melting point of germanium. [1]

800 °C ✓

Suggest what type of oxide germanium forms. Give a reason for your answer.  [2]

Either amphoteric or less acidic than silicon. ✓ The trend is from acidic to amphoteric *oxides*. ✓

Germanium has some characteristics of metals and some characteristics of non-metals. How can you deduce this from the information about the other elements in Group IV? [2]

It is partly non-metal since its oxide is very weakly acidic or amphoteric ✓ and it is between a metal and non-metal in electrical conduction. ✓

**Recap**

- Noble gases are monatomic and are inert because they have a full outer shell of electrons which is a stable electronic configuration.
- The position of an element in the Periodic Table can be used to predict its properties.

## Apply

5. Some properties of some elements in Period 3 of the Periodic Table are shown.

| **Element** | magnesium | aluminium | silicon | phosphorus | sulfur |
|---|---|---|---|---|---|
| **Boiling point/°C** | 1107 | | 2355 | 280 | 455 |
| **Electrical conduction** | good | good | conducts slightly | poor | |
| **Formula of hydride** | $MgH_2$ | $AlH_3$ | $SiH_4$ | | $H_2S$ |
| **Type of oxide formed** | basic | basic | acidic | | acidic |

a. Suggest a value for the boiling point of aluminium. Give a reason for your answer.

b. State how well sulfur conducts electricity. Give a reason for your answer.

c. Deduce the formula for the hydride of phosphorus. Give a reason for your answer.

d. Deduce the type of oxide formed by phosphorus.

e. Explain from the information in the table why phosphorus is a non-metal.

 6. Some properties of the Group IV elements and compounds are shown.

| **Element** | **Bond energy in kJ/mol** | **Boiling point of tetrahalide, $XCl_4$/°C** | **Reaction of $XCl_4$ with water** |
|---|---|---|---|
| carbon (diamond) | 350 | 76 | none |
| silicon | | 57 | reacts slowly |
| germanium | 188 | | |
| tin | 187 | 114 | very fast |

a. Deduce the bond energy of silicon.

b. Explain why it is difficult to deduce the boiling point of germanium tetrachloride.

c. Suggest the rate of reaction of germanium tetrachloride with water. Explain your answer.

# 13.5 Transition elements

**You need to:**

- Describe transition elements as metals having high densities, high melting points, forming coloured compounds and acting (as elements and compounds) as catalysts.
- **Know that transition elements have variable oxidation states.**

The **transition elements** are metals with high melting and boiling points and high densities.

*Compounds of the transition elements* are coloured.

S The *ions in different transition element compounds* have a range of oxidation states.

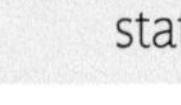

**Worked example**

Sodium is a metal in Group I of the Periodic Table. Nickel is a transition element.

Describe three differences in the physical properties of sodium and nickel. [3]

Sodium is soft but nickel is hard. ✓ Nickel has a higher density than sodium. ✓ Sodium has a lower melting point than nickel. ✓

Describe two differences in the chemical properties of sodium and nickel. [2]

Sodium reacts rapidly with cold water but nickel does not. ✓ Nickel is a catalyst but sodium is not. ✓

## Apply

7. a. Which of these statements refers to a transition element?

   **A** density 1.20 g/cm$^3$

   **B** forms a chloride which is green in colour

   **C** is not a catalyst

   **D** density 5.96 g/cm$^3$

   **E** melting point 63 °C

   **F** forms a colourless chloride

   **G** is a good catalyst

   **H** melting point is 1890 °C

S b. Give two other properties of transition elements or their compounds not mentioned above.

**Recap**

Transition elements are metals with high melting and boiling points, high densities, catalytic activity and have coloured compounds which have variable oxidation numbers.

### Exam tip

When comparing properties of transition elements with other metals do **not** refer to conductivity or make vague statements such as 'Group I metals are malleable'. You need a comparison such as 'Group I metals are less malleable'. It is better to stick to the examples of properties given in the syllabus.

### Exam tip

**Watch out**

- A common error is to suggest that transition elements are coloured. It is their *compounds* which are coloured.
- Make sure that you know the difference between chemical and physical properties. Do not write about chemical reactions (including colour and catalysis) if physical properties are asked for.

### Exam tip

- Remember that oxidation number does not always refer to the charge on the ions. For example in $MnO_4^-$ the oxidation number of Mn is +7 but the charge on the ion is −1.
- Note that Sc and Zn are not transition elements. They do not form coloured compounds and only have one type of ion.

## Questions

1. Complete these sentences about the Periodic Table.
   a. The elements in the Periodic Table are arranged in order of .................................. [1]
   b. Elements in the same group of the Periodic Table have similar chemical properties because .................................. [1]
   c. Metallic character .................................. across a .................................. [1]
2. Write the formula for **(i)** an oxide ion **(ii)** an aluminium ion **(iii)** a chloride ion. [3]
3. a. State the colour and physical state of bromine at r.t.p. [2]
   b. **(i)** Copy and complete the equation for the reaction of aqueous bromine with aqueous magnesium iodide. $Br_2 + MgI_2 \rightarrow$ .................... + .................... [2]
   **(ii)** State the colour change in the reaction. [2]
   **(iii)** Write a word equation for the reaction of chlorine with potassium bromide. [2]
4. a. State two trends in physical properties of the Group I elements. [2]
   b. State one trend in the chemical properties of the Group I elements. [1]
   c. **(i)** Copy and complete the equation for the reaction of sodium with water. Include state symbols.
   ..........Na(..........) + ..........$H_2O$(..........) → ..........NaOH(..........) + .......... (..........) [3]
   **(ii)** Describe how you can show that the solution formed is alkaline. [2]
   **(iii)** Describe one observation when lithium reacts with water. [1]
5. State three properties of transition elements which are not shown by Group I elements. [3]
6. Where in the Periodic Table are elements having basic oxides found? [1]
7. Neon, argon and xenon are in Group VIII of the Periodic Table.
   a. State the name given to this group of elements. [1]
   b. Explain why these elements cannot react directly with the halogens. [2]
   c. Describe the structure and physical state of these elements. [2]

## Sample question

This question is about the Periodic Table.

**1. a.** Potassium is in Group I of the Periodic Table. Iron is a transition element.

**(i)** Give two properties of transition element compounds which are not shown by compounds of Group I elements. [2]

**(ii)** Write a balanced equation for the reaction of potassium with water to produce potassium hydroxide, KOH, and a gas which pops with a lighted splint. Include state symbols. [3]

**(iii)** Describe two observations when potassium reacts with water. [2]

**b.** The table shows some properties of some Group I elements.

| Element | Melting point/°C | Reaction with oxygen when heated | Density in g/cm³ |
|---|---|---|---|
| lithium | 180 | burns slowly | 0.53 |
| sodium | 98 | | 0.97 |
| potassium | 64 | burns very quickly | 0.86 |
| rubidium | | explodes | |

**(i)** Deduce a value for the melting point of rubidium. [1]

**(ii)** Describe the reaction of sodium with oxygen. [1]

**(iii)** Suggest a value for the density of rubidium and suggest why it is more difficult to predict this than to predict the melting point. [2]

**(iv)** Explain why the Group I elements have similar chemical reactions. [1]

**c. (i)** Iodine is a halogen. State the colour of iodine at r.t.p. [1]

**(ii)** Explain why an iodide ion has a single negative charge. [1]

**d.** Astatine, At, is a halogen which is below iodine in Group VII. It forms salts called astatides.

**(i)** Construct the chemical equation for the displacement reaction of aqueous iodine with aqueous potassium astatide, KAt. [2]

**(ii)** Explain why aqueous potassium iodide does not react with astatine. [1]

**(iii)** Define the term *displacement reaction*. [1]

S **e.** The first four elements in Group VI are oxygen, sulfur, selenium and tellurium.

The melting points of the Group VI elements oxygen, sulfur and tellurium are:

O = −218 °C, S = 113 °C, Te = 450 °C

Predict some physical properties of selenium from this information and the position of selenium in the Periodic Table. Give reasons for your predictions. [6]

# Metals and reactivity

## Revision checklist

Tick these boxes to build a record of your revision. Columns 2 and 3 can be used if you want to make a record more than once.

| Core/**Supplement** syllabus content | | 1 | 2 | 3 |
|---|---|---|---|---|
| 14.1 | State the order of selected metals in the reactivity series. | | | |
| 14.1 | Describe the chemical properties of metals with dilute acids and water. | | | |
| 14.1 | Explain selected reactions of metals with cold water, steam and hydrochloric acid in terms of the position of the metals and hydrogen in the reactivity series. | | | |
| 14.1 | Deduce an order of reactivity from experimental results. | | | |
| 14.2 | Describe the reaction of metals with oxygen. | | | |
| 14.2 | **Explain the apparent unreactivity of aluminium in terms of its oxide layer.** | | | |
| 14.3 | Describe bauxite as an ore of aluminium and why aluminium is extracted by electrolysis. | | | |
| 14.3 | Describe the ease of obtaining metals from their ores based on the reactivity of metals. | | | |
| 14.4 | **Describe the reactivity of metals in terms of how easy it is to form positive ions in displacement reactions.** | | | |

# 14.1 The metal reactivity series

**You need to:**

- State the order of selected metals in the reactivity series.
- Describe the chemical properties of metals with dilute acids and water.
- Explain selected reactions of metals with cold water, steam and hydrochloric acid in terms of the position of the metals and hydrogen in the reactivity series.
- Deduce an order of reactivity from experimental results.

The **reactivity series** shows the relative reactivity of the metals with water, steam or dilute hydrochloric acid.

The *order of reactivity of metals* starting from the most reactive is: K, Na, Ca, Mg, Al, Zn, Fe, (H), Cu, Ag, Au.

*Metals high in the reactivity series react with water* to produce a metal hydroxide and hydrogen.

*Metals above hydrogen in the reactivity series react with steam* ***to*** produce a metal oxide and hydrogen.

*Metals above hydrogen in the reactivity series react with dilute hydrochloric acid* to produce a metal chloride and hydrogen.

**Key skills**

You need to be able to interpret information in tables of data.

**Exam tip**

Remember that metals that react with cold water produce aqueous metal hydroxides but metals reacting with steam produce the solid oxide. In both cases hydrogen is formed as well.

**Exam tip**

Be prepared to deduce an order of reactivity of unfamiliar metals from experimental results.

**Worked example**

Calcium, copper, iron, magnesium and silver are metals.

State the order of these metals in the reactivity series. Put the most reactive first. [2]

calcium, magnesium, iron, copper, silver. ✓✓

(allow 1 mark for one pair of metals reversed or all reversed)

Which of these metals do not react with water or steam? Give a reason for your answer. [2]

Copper and silver ✓ because they are below hydrogen in the reactivity series. ✓

The table shows the observations when some metals react with the same concentration of hydrochloric acid.

| Metal | Observations |
|---|---|
| cerium | bubbles produced very rapidly |
| lead | no bubbles produced |
| nickel | a few bubbles produced slowly |
| sodium | explosive reaction |
| zinc | bubbles produced rapidly |

Deduce the order of reactivity of these metals. Put the most reactive first. [2]

sodium, cerium, zinc, nickel, lead ✓✓

(allow 1 mark for one pair of metals reversed or all reversed)

**Recap**

- Metals high in the reactivity series react with water to produce a metal hydroxide and hydrogen.
- Metals above hydrogen in the reactivity series react with steam to produce a metal oxide and hydrogen and with hydrochloric acid to produce a metal chloride and hydrogen.

Write a word equation for the reaction of zinc with dilute hydrochloric acid. [2]

zinc + hydrochloric acid → zinc chloride ✓ + hydrogen ✓

Write a word equation for the reaction of magnesium with steam. [2]

magnesium + steam → magnesium oxide ✓ + hydrogen ✓

Copy and complete the symbol equation for the reaction of calcium with cold water.

$Ca + \ldots\ldots H_2O \rightarrow Ca(OH)_2 + \ldots\ldots$ [2]

$Ca + 2H_2O$ ✓ $\rightarrow Ca(OH)_2 + H_2$ ✓

**Exam tip**

You will be expected to write word and symbol equations for the reactions related to the reactivity series.

**Exam tip**

You are expected to know the order of reactivity of the metals stated in the reactivity series in the syllabus.

**Exam tip**

**Watch out**

Remember that the state symbol for steam is (g). Don't write the state symbol for liquid water!

## Apply

1. Copy and complete these sentences about metal reactivity using words from the list.

   below high hydrogen hydroxide magnesium oxide rapidly slowly

   When a metal .................. in the reactivity series reacts with cold water a metal .................. and hydrogen are formed. Metals such as .................. and iron react very .................. with cold water. They react .................. with steam to form the metal .................. and .................. Metals .................. hydrogen in the reactivity series do not react with steam.

2. The table shows some observations when five different metals react with water.

| Metal | Observations |
|---|---|
| calcium | rapid bubbling with cold water |
| iron | reacts only when heated in steam |
| magnesium | produces a few bubbles with hot water |
| silver | no reaction with steam |

   a. Put calcium, magnesium, iron and silver in order of their reactivity. Put the most reactive first.

   b. Barium is more reactive than calcium. Suggest the observations when barium reacts with cold water.

3. Write word equations for:

   a. the reaction of zinc with steam

   b. the reaction of potassium with cold water

4. Suggest why gold does not react with steam.

5. Copy and complete these symbol equations. Include state symbols.

   a. $\ldots\ldots K(s) + \ldots\ldots H_2O(l) \rightarrow \ldots\ldots KOH(\ldots\ldots) + \ldots\ldots(\ldots\ldots)$

   b. $\ldots\ldots Fe(\ldots\ldots) + \ldots\ldots(g) \rightarrow Fe_3O_4(s) + \ldots\ldots(\ldots\ldots)$

# 14.2 Metal oxides and their reduction

**You need to:**

- Describe the reaction of metals with oxygen.
- **Explain the apparent unreactivity of aluminium in terms of its oxide layer.**

*Most metals react with oxygen* to form metal oxides.

*Metal oxides below carbon in the reactivity series* are reduced by carbon when heated.

*When a more reactive metal is heated with the oxide of a less reactive metal* the more reactive metal acts as a reducing agent.

*Aluminium appears unreactive* because it forms a layer of unreactive aluminium oxide on its surface which does not flake off easily.

**Key skills**

You need to be able to relate different sections of the syllabus. For example, metal extraction involves redox reactions.

**Worked example**

The table shows some observations when metals are put in a Bunsen flame.

| Metal | Observations |
|---|---|
| copper | surface turns black but does not burn |
| iron | iron wire burns steadily |
| gold | surface remains golden |
| magnesium | thin ribbon burns rapidly |

Deduce the order of reactivity of these metals with oxygen. Put the most reactive first. [2]

Magnesium, iron, copper, gold ✓✓

(allow 1 mark for one pair of metals reversed or all reversed)

Copper(II) oxide can be reduced by heating with carbon. One of the products is carbon dioxide. Copy and complete the equation for this reaction.

..............CuO + C → ...................................... + ...................................... [2]

$2CuO + C \rightarrow 2Cu + CO_2$ ✓✓

(1 mark for correct formulae, 1 mark for correct balance)

Which of these metal oxides can be easily reduced by carbon? Give a reason for your answer.

calcium oxide    iron(III) oxide    lead(II) oxide
magnesium oxide    zinc oxide

Zinc oxide, iron(III) oxide, lead(II) oxide ✓ because they are below carbon in the reactivity series. ✓

Aluminium reacts with iron(III) oxide when heated: $2Al + Fe_2O_3 \rightarrow 2Fe + Al_2O_3$

Describe how this equation shows that iron(III) oxide has been reduced. [1]

Oxygen has been removed from $Fe_2O_3$. ✓

Suggest why aluminium can reduce iron(III) oxide but copper cannot. [2]

Aluminium is more reactive than iron ✓ but copper is less reactive than iron. ✓

Identify the reducing agent in this reaction. Give a reason for your answer. [2]

The reducing agent is aluminium ✓ because it is removing oxygen from iron oxide ✓ and is itself oxidised.

Aluminium does not react with acids as rapidly as expected from its position in the reactivity series. Explain why aluminium appears relatively unreactive. S [2]

There is a layer of aluminium oxide on the surface of the aluminium ✓ which is relatively unreactive. ✓

## Apply

6. a. The table shows some observations when metals are heated in air.

| Metal oxide | Observations |
|---|---|
| mercury | surface turns slightly red only when very hot |
| nickel | surface turns black very slowly |
| sodium | surface turns white very quickly and sodium burns |
| zinc | surface turns white slowly |

Deduce the order of reactivity of these metals with oxygen. Put the most reactive first.

b. Zinc oxide, ZnO, can be reduced by heating with carbon. One of the products is carbon monoxide. Construct the symbol equation for this reaction.

c. Magnesium reacts with lead oxide when heated:
$Mg + PbO \rightarrow Pb + MgO$

(i) Describe how this equation shows that lead oxide has been reduced.

(ii) Suggest why hydrogen can also reduce lead oxide.

(iii) Write a symbol equation for the reaction of lead oxide with hydrogen.

d. Manganese is extracted by reduction of manganese oxide, $Mn_3O_4$, with hot aluminium.

Write a word equation for this reaction.

S e. Copy and complete these sentences about aluminium using words from the list.

high layer oxide oxygen sticks surface

Aluminium is .................... in the reactivity series but does not seem to react with water or acids. When it is freshly made, aluminium reacts with .................... in the air. A thin .................... of aluminium .................... is formed on the .................... of the metal. This layer is unreactive. The layer .................... to the surface of the aluminium and does not flake off easily.

### Recap

- Metal oxides below carbon in the reactivity series are reduced by carbon when heated.
- Aluminium appears unreactive because it forms a layer of unreactive aluminium oxide on its surface. S

### Exam tip

Take care with writing the order of reactivity. Look carefully at the question to see if the examiner wants the order to be increasing or decreasing.

# 14.3 From metal compounds to metals

**You need to:**

- Describe bauxite as an ore of aluminium and why aluminium is extracted by electrolysis.
- Describe the ease of obtaining metals from their ores based on the reactivity of metals.

An **ore** is a rock containing a compound from which a metal is extracted.

**Bauxite** is an ore of aluminium which contains aluminium oxide.

**Hematite** is an ore of iron which contains iron(III) oxide.

*Metal oxides below carbon in the reactivity series* can be extracted by reduction with carbon or carbon monoxide when heated.

*Metal oxides above carbon in the reactivity series* are extracted by electrolysis.

**Key skills**

You need to be able to construct chemical (symbol) equations.

### Exam tip

When deducing the order of reactivity of metals from information about the reduction of metal oxides, remember that the oxide of the *more reactive* metal is *more difficult to reduce*.

### Exam tip

When deducing the order of reactivity of metals from information about the reduction of metal oxides remember to write the name of the metal not the metal oxide!

**Worked example**

Name the main ore of iron and state the name of the compound in the ore from which iron is extracted. [2]

Hematite ✓ ore contains iron(III) oxide. ✓

The table shows the effect of heating different metal oxides with carbon.

| Metal oxide | Observations |
|---|---|
| aluminium oxide | not reduced at 1000 °C |
| copper(II) oxide | reduced below 400 °C |
| iron(III) oxide | reduced at 700 °C |
| tin(IV) oxide | reduced at 400 °C |

Explain why aluminium is not easily reduced by carbon by referring to the reactivity series. [1]

Aluminium is above carbon in the reactivity series. ✓

Deduce the order of reactivity of the metals. Put the least reactive metal first. [2]

copper, tin, iron, aluminium ✓✓

(allow 1 mark for one pair of metals reversed or all reversed)

Carbon monoxide, CO, can be used to reduce metal oxides. A gas which turns limewater milky is one of the products.

Write a symbol equation for the reduction of lead oxide, PbO, by carbon monoxide. [1]

$PbO + CO \rightarrow Pb + CO_2$ ✓

Copy and complete the symbol equation for the reduction of iron(III) oxide by carbon monoxide.

$Fe_2O_3$ + .................. .................. → ..................Fe + 3.................. [2]

**Recap**

- Bauxite is an ore of aluminium and hematite is an ore of iron.
- Metal oxides below carbon in the reactivity series can be extracted by reduction with carbon. Metal oxides above carbon in the reactivity series are extracted by electrolysis.

**Exam tip**

You are expected to know the formulae of simple compounds mentioned in the syllabus such as CO, $CO_2$ and $H_2O$.

$Fe_2O_3 + 3CO \rightarrow 2Fe + 3CO_2$

Correct formulae ✓ correct balance ✓

State which of these metals are extracted by electrolysis. Give a reason for your answer.

calcium copper iron magnesium potassium silver [2]

Calcium, magnesium and potassium ✓ are extracted by electrolysis because they are above carbon in the reactivity series. ✓

## Apply

7. a. Name the main ore of aluminium and state the name of the compound in the ore from which aluminium is extracted.

   b. The table shows the effect of heating different metal oxides with carbon monoxide.

| Metal oxide | Observations |
|---|---|
| copper(II) oxide | reduced below 400 °C but not below 200 °C |
| magnesium oxide | not reduced at 1200 °C |
| silver oxide | reduced below 200 °C |
| zinc oxide | reduced at 500 °C |

   (i) Explain why magnesium is not easily reduced by carbon monoxide.

   (ii) Deduce the order of reactivity of the metals. Put the most reactive metal first.

   c. State which of these metals are extracted by electrolysis. Give a reason for your answer.

   (lead is between iron and copper in the reactivity series)

   aluminium copper gold lead sodium

   d. (i) Write a symbol equation for the reduction of lead oxide, PbO, by carbon monoxide.

   (ii) Write the word equation for the reduction of copper(II) oxide by carbon monoxide.

# 14.4 More about metal reactivity

**You need to:**

- **Describe the reactivity of metals in terms of how easy it is to form positive ions in displacement reactions.**

**Supplement**

*A more reactive metal displaces a less reactive metal* from a solution of the salt of the less reactive metal.

*A more reactive metal forms positive ions and loses electrons* more easily than a less reactive metal.

### Worked example

Magnesium is more reactive than aqueous zinc but silver is less reactive than zinc.

Write a word equation for the reaction of zinc sulfate with magnesium. Describe and explain the type of reaction that is occurring. [3]

zinc sulfate + magnesium → magnesium sulfate + zinc ✓

The reaction is a displacement ✓ because the more reactive metal (magnesium) is replacing the less reactive metal (zinc) from zinc sulfate. ✓

Write an ionic equation for the reaction of aqueous silver nitrate, $AgNO_3$, with zinc to form silver and aqueous zinc nitrate, $Zn(NO_3)_2$. Use these steps:

Deduce the charge on a silver ion and a zinc ion. [1]

$NO_3^-$ has −1 charge so Ag ion is $Ag^+$ to balance and charge on zinc ion is $Zn^{2+}$ to balance two $NO_3^-$ ions. ✓

Write the ionic equation. [1]

$2Ag^+ + Zn \rightarrow Zn^{2+} + 2Ag$ ✓

S Explain why magnesium reacts with aqueous copper(II) sulfate but silver does not react with aqueous copper(II) sulfate. In your answer refer to the ease with which metals form ions. [4]

Magnesium is higher than copper in the reactivity series ✓ because magnesium forms positive ions more easily than copper. ✓ Silver is lower than copper in the reactivity series ✓ so forms positive ions less easily than copper. ✓

### Exam tip

When answering questions about the reaction of metals with metal ions, remember to make it clear that you are referring to the ions. For example, magnesium reduces copper is incorrect. Magnesium reduces copper ions IS correct.

### Recap

A more reactive metal displaces a less reactive metal from a solution of the salt of the less reactive metal. The more reactive metal forms positive ions more easily.

## Apply

8. a. Copy and complete these sentences using the words in the list.

aqueous displaces ions metal positive reactive salt

A more ........ metal ........ a less reactive metal from an ........ solution of its ........ This is because the more reactive metal forms ........ more easily than the less reactive ........

9. a. Zinc reacts with aqueous tin(II) chloride, $SnCl_2$, but tin(II) chloride does not react with copper.

   Explain why tin(II) chloride does not react with copper but zinc reacts with aqueous tin(II) chloride.

   b. Write a word equation for the reaction of zinc with aqueous tin(II) chloride. Describe and explain the type of reaction that is occurring.

   c. Write an ionic equation for the reaction of aqueous copper(II) chloride, $CuCl_2$, with tin.

10. The table shows the results of adding some metals to solutions containing aqueous metal ions.

| Aqueous metal ion | Cerium | Copper | Lead |
|---|---|---|---|
| $Ce^{3+}$ | no reaction | no reaction | no reaction |
| $Cu^{2+}$ | reacts | no reaction | reacts |
| $Pb^{2+}$ | reacts | no reaction | no reaction |

Put the three metals in order of increasing reactivity.

## Questions

1. Put these metals in order of decreasing reactivity.

   calcium copper gold iron sodium zinc [2]

2. The table shows some observations when five different metals react with water.

| Metal | Observations |
|---|---|
| sodium | very rapid bubbling with cold water |
| tin | reacts slowly only when heated in steam |
| iron | reacts rapidly only when heated in steam |
| cerium | rapid bubbling with cold water |

   Put the metals in order of their reactivity. Put the most reactive first. [2]

3. Write word equations and symbol equations for:
   a. the reaction of iron with steam to form $Fe_3O_4$ as one of the products [4]
   b. the reaction of calcium with cold water [2]
4. Suggest why silver does not react with steam. [1]
5. Copy and compete these sentences.

   The main ore of iron is ........................ The iron(III) oxide in this ore is extracted by heating with ........................ The main ore of aluminium is ........................ Aluminium is extracted from the aluminium ........................ in this ore by ........................ [5]

6. Carbon or carbon monoxide can be used to reduce metal oxides.
   a. Write a symbol equation for the reduction of tin oxide, SnO, by carbon monoxide. [2]
   b. Copy and complete the symbol equation for the reduction of iron(III) oxide by carbon to form carbon monoxide as one of the products.

   $Fe_2O_3$ + ........................ ........................ → ........................Fe + 3........................ [2]

7. The table shows the ease of reduction of some metal oxides.

| Metal oxide | Observations |
|---|---|
| chromium(III) oxide | reduced by carbon at 1200 °C |
| copper(II) oxide | reduced by carbon below 400 °C |
| manganese(II) oxide | reduced by carbon at 1400 °C |
| tin(IV) oxide | reduced by carbon at 400 °C |

   Deduce the order of reactivity of the metals. Put the most reactive metal first. [2]

8. The table shows the results of adding some metals to solutions containing aqueous metal ions.

S

| Aqueous metal ion | Copper | Iron | Nickel |
|---|---|---|---|
| $Cu^{2+}$ | no reaction | reacts | reacts |
| $Fe^{2+}$ | no reaction | no reaction | no reaction |
| $Ni^{2+}$ | no reaction | reacts | no reaction |

   a. Put the three metals in order of increasing reactivity. [1]
   b. Write an ionic equation for the reaction of aqueous $Cu^{2+}$ ions with nickel. Include state symbols. [2]

## Sample question

1. **a.** Calcium, copper, iron, magnesium and zinc are all metals.

**(i)** State which two of these metals are most likely to be extracted from their oxides by electrolysis rather than by heating with carbon. Give a reason for your answer in terms of both the reactivity series and strength of bonding in the oxide. [3]

**(ii)** Zinc can be extracted either by electrolysis or by reduction with carbon. Suggest why zinc can be extracted by both methods. [1]

**b.** Zinc reacts with steam.

**(i)** Write a word equation for this reaction. [2]

**(ii)** Construct the symbol equation for this reaction. Include state symbols. [2]

**c.** S Identify the reducing agents in each of these reactions. In **(i)** explain your answer in terms of oxidation number changes. In **(ii)** explain your answer in terms of electron loss or gain.

**(i)** $Fe_2O_3 + 3Mg \rightarrow 2Fe + 3MgO$ [2]

**(ii)** $V + Cu^{2+} \rightarrow Cu + V^{2+}$ [2]

**d.** Aluminium is more reactive than iron.

**(i)** Describe how you can use aluminium to extract iron from iron(III) oxide, $Fe_2O_3$. [2]

**(ii)** Construct the chemical equation for this reaction. [2]

**(iii)** Explain why aluminium does not appear to react with water. [2]

**e.** Magnesium reacts with an aqueous solution of zinc chloride but silver does not.

Explain why magnesium reacts but silver does not. In your answer refer to the ease with which metals form ions and the transfer of electrons. [6]

**f.** **(i)** Write an ionic equation for the reaction of magnesium with aqueous silver nitrate. [2]

**(ii)** Explain in terms of electron transfer which is the reducing agent and which is the oxidising agent. [2]

# More about metals

## Revision checklist

Tick these boxes to build a record of your revision. Columns 2 and 3 can be used if you want to make a record more than once.

| Core/**Supplement** syllabus content | | 1 | 2 | 3 |
|---|---|---|---|---|
| 15.1 | Describe the essential reactions in the blast furnace for the production of iron from hematite including word equations. | | | |
| 15.1 | **State the chemical equations for the extraction of iron from hematite.** | | | |
| 15.2 | State the conditions required for rusting. | | | |
| 15.2 | Describe and explain barrier methods for preventing rusting. | | | |
| 15.2 | **Describe the use of zinc in galvanising (barrier method and sacrificial protection).** | | | |
| 15.2 | **Explain sacrificial protection in terms of metal reactivity and electron transfer.** | | | |
| 15.3 | Know that alloys can be harder, stronger and more resistant to corrosion than pure metals. | | | |
| 15.3 | Identify representations of alloys from diagrams of their structure. | | | |
| 15.3 | **Explain why alloys can be harder and stronger than pure metals.** | | | |
| 15.4 | Describe the uses of aluminium and copper in terms of their physical properties. | | | |
| 15.4 | Know that brass is a mixture of copper and zinc and that stainless steel is a mixture of iron and other elements. | | | |
| 15.4 | State that alloys are often more useful than the pure metals. | | | |
| 15.4 | Describe the uses of stainless steel. | | | |

# 15.1 Extracting iron

**You need to:**

- Describe the essential reactions in the blast furnace for the production of iron from hematite including word equations.
- **State the chemical equations for the extraction of iron from hematite.**

The *raw materials for the extraction of iron* in the **blast furnace** are hematite ore, limestone and air.

*Carbon monoxide is formed* in the blast furnace by the reaction of **coke** (carbon) with carbon dioxide.

*Carbon monoxide reduces iron(III) oxide* in the blast furnace to iron.

**Key skills**

You need to know how to balance chemical equations.

**Worked example**

Air is one of the raw materials added to the blast furnace in the extraction of iron.

Name one other raw material added to the blast furnace. [1]

hematite ✓

State two reasons why carbon is added to the blast furnace. [2]

To burn in air to produce heat ✓ and to form carbon monoxide ✓ which reduces the iron oxide.

In the blast furnace, carbon monoxide reacts with iron(III) oxide.

Write a word equation for this reaction. [2]

iron(III) oxide + carbon monoxide → iron ✓ + carbon dioxide ✓

Write a symbol equation for this reaction. S [2]

$Fe_2O_3 + 3CO \rightarrow 2Fe + 3CO_2$

(correct formulae ✓ correct balance ✓)

## Exam tip

Remember that coke is not a raw material because it is coal which has been treated to remove gases.

## Exam tip

**Watch out**

It is a common error to suggest that calcium carbonate reacts directly with silicon(IV) oxide in the blast furnace. Remember that it has got to be decomposed first.

**Thermal decomposition** is the breakdown of a substance by heating strongly.

The *thermal decomposition of limestone (calcium carbonate)* in the blast furnace produces calcium oxide and carbon dioxide.

*Calcium oxide reacts with impurities in the iron ore* such as silicon(IV) oxide to form slag.

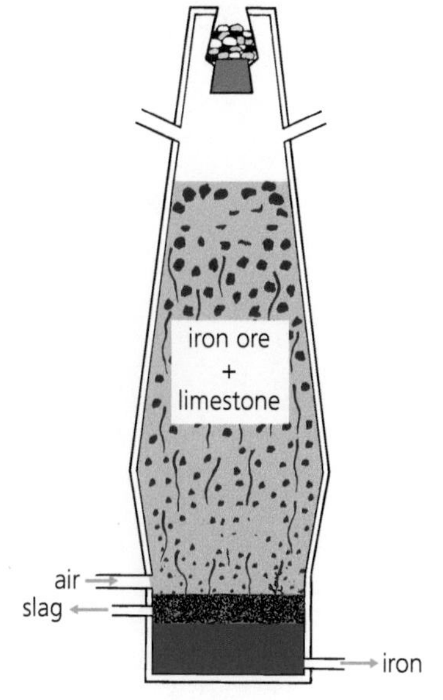


▲ A blast furnace

**Exam tip**

For higher grades, you must be able to write symbol equations for the reactions in the blast furnace. For the core paper you can still be asked to balance equations when given the formulae.

**Worked example**

Explain the purpose of adding calcium carbonate to the blast furnace by describing relevant chemical reactions. [3]

The calcium carbonate decomposes in the high temperature to form calcium oxide. ✓ The calcium oxide then reacts with the silicon oxide(IV) impurity ✓ in the iron ore to form slag. ✓

**Recap**

In the blast furnace:

1. Carbon monoxide is formed by the reaction of coke with carbon dioxide.
2. Carbon monoxide reduces iron(III) oxide to iron.
3. Thermal decomposition of limestone forms calcium oxide and carbon dioxide.
4. Calcium oxide reacts with silicon(IV) oxide to form slag.

**Exam tip**

You should be prepared to answer questions related to a diagram of the blast furnace.

**Exam tip**

Remember that there are two parts to the definition of thermal decomposition:
(i) breaking down
(ii) by heating.

## Apply

1. a. Carbon monoxide produced in the blast furnace reduces iron(III) oxide.
   (i) Write a word equation for the formation of carbon dioxide in the blast furnace.
   (ii) Carbon dioxide is converted to carbon monoxide in the blast furnace.

$$CO_2 + C \rightarrow 2CO$$

   Explain how you know that carbon dioxide is reduced in this reaction.

   b. (i) Copy and complete this symbol equation for the reaction of iron(III) oxide with carbon monoxide.

$$Fe_2O_3 + \text{..........}CO \rightarrow 2Fe + 3\text{..........}$$

   (ii) What type of chemical reaction is this?

   c. The limestone added to the blast furnace breaks down:

$$CaCO_3 \rightarrow CaO + CO_2$$

   (i) State the name given to this type of chemical reaction.
   (ii) Write a word equation for this reaction.

   S d. Write a symbol equation for the reaction of CaO with silicon dioxide and explain why this reaction is important.

# 15.2 The rusting of iron

**You need to:**

- State the conditions required for rusting.
- Describe and explain barrier methods for preventing rusting.
- **Describe the use of zinc in galvanising (barrier method and sacrificial protection).**
- **Explain sacrificial protection in terms of metal reactivity and electron transfer.**

**Rust** is hydrated iron(III) oxide.

*Oxygen and water* are needed for rusting to take place.

*Rusting can be prevented by barrier methods* such as coating the iron with paint, plastic, metal or grease.

**Key skills**

You need to be able to interpret information from diagrams.

**Worked example**

Iron nails are placed under different conditions in three test tubes. The tubes were left for 2 weeks. The results are shown.

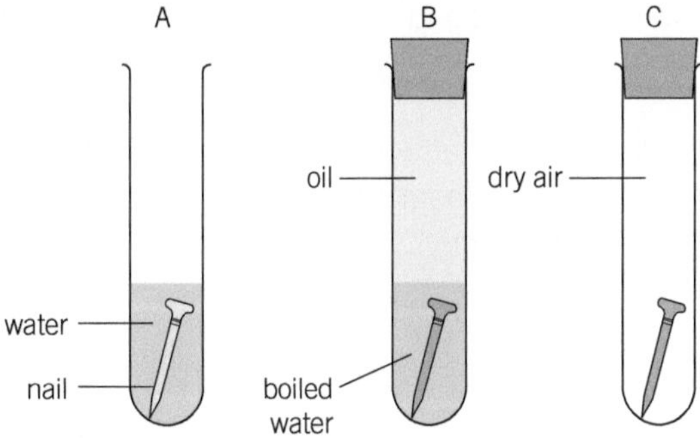


For each tube state if the iron rusts or not. For each tube explain your answer. [3]

The nail in tube A rusts because there is water present as well as air dissolved in the water. ✓

The nail in tube B does not rust because there is no air present because the water has been boiled and the air cannot get through the oil. ✓

The nail in tube C does not rust because there is no water. ✓

Explain why a clean iron object when painted does not rust. [2]

The paint acts as a barrier ✓ to stop the air and water getting through. ✓

S **Sacrificial protection** *prevents rusting* because a more reactive metal on the surface of the iron corrodes instead of the iron. This is because the more reactive metal loses electrons more easily than iron.

**Galvanising** (the covering of iron with a layer of zinc) protects iron from rusting by both a barrier method and sacrificial protection.

**Exam tip**

**Watch out**

In questions about sacrificial protection never write 'the zinc rusts **X** instead of the iron'. Only iron rusts!

**Recap**

- Oxygen and water are needed for rust (hydrated iron(III) oxide) to form.
- Rusting can be prevented by coating iron with various substances.
- S Sacrificial protection prevents rusting because a more reactive metal corrodes instead of iron because it forms positive ions more easily.

**Worked example**

Iron roofs are often galvanised with a layer of zinc. Explain two ways in which galvanising reduces rusting. [4]

S The layer of zinc acts as a barrier ✓ which prevents air and water from reaching the surface ✓ of the iron. If the roof is scratched, it still does not rust because zinc is more reactive than iron ✓ so it corrodes first ✓ instead of the iron.

Explain how the zinc prevents the iron from rusting in terms of electron transfer. [2]

Zinc loses electrons more easily than iron. ✓ Therefore the electrons are not lost from iron and iron does not get oxidised to iron ions. ✓

## Apply

2. a. State two substances needed for rusting.
   b. State the chemical formula for rust.
   c. Suggest why an iron object in the desert rusts very slowly.
   d. Explain how a plastic coating on an iron object prevents it from rusting.
   S e. A bar of magnesium is attached underwater to the side of an iron ship. Explain how the magnesium stops the side of the ship from rusting in terms of reactivity and electron transfer.

# 15.3 Alloys

**You need to:**

- Know that alloys can be harder, stronger and more resistant to corrosion than pure metals.
- Identify representations of alloys from diagrams of their structure.
- **Explain why alloys can be harder and stronger than pure metals.**

**Alloys** are mixtures of metal atoms with atoms of other elements.

*The properties of a metal are changed by making it into an alloy*. Alloys are stronger, harder and more resistant to corrosion than the pure metal.

**Worked example**

Which one of these structures best represents an alloy? Give a reason for your answer. [2]

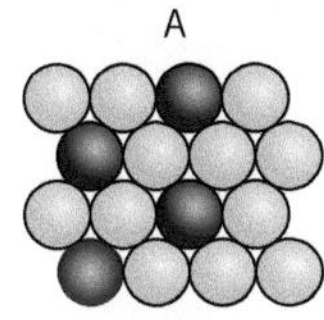


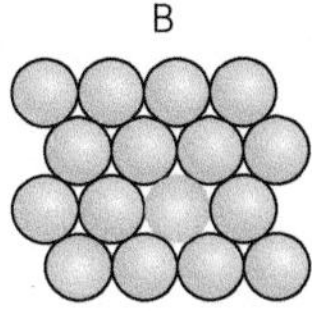


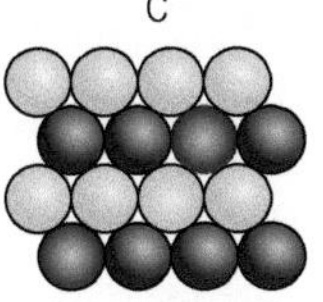


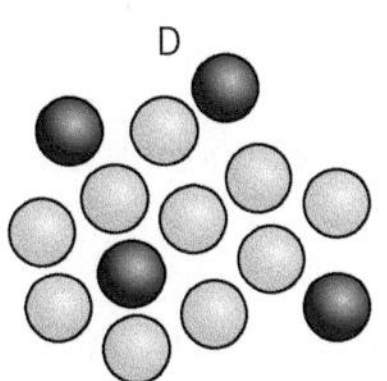


Structure A ✓ because it is the only one in which there is a mixture of atoms in layers ✓.

Explain why each of the other structures is not an alloy. [3]

B is not an alloy because all the atoms are the same type. ✓ It is an element. C is not an alloy because the atoms are not completely mixed up ✓ as in a true mixture. D is not an alloy because the atoms are not touching as in a solid ✓ and are not in layers.

*Alloys are stronger and harder* because the different sized atoms in the alloy prevent the layers of metal atoms from sliding over each other easily.

**Worked example**

Brass is a mixture of copper and zinc. Explain why brass is stronger than either pure zinc or pure copper. [4]

S The layers of atoms ✓ of pure copper and pure zinc are able to slide over each other easily ✓ when a force is applied. The layers in brass do not slide easily ✓ because the atoms of copper and zinc are different sizes. ✓

**Exam tip**

**Watch out**

When discussing the strength of alloys, make sure that you don't write 'the atoms slide'. Remember it is the *layers* of atoms which slide.

**Exam tip**

When writing about the structure of alloys it is acceptable to use the term atoms. But remember that when discussing metallic structure, the particles are positive ions.

**Recap**

- Alloys are mixtures of metal atoms with atoms of other elements.
- Alloys are stronger and more resistant to corrosion than the pure metals.
- S The different sized atoms in an alloy prevent the layers of metal atoms from sliding over each other easily.

## Apply

3. a. Why are alloys used for the body of an aircraft instead of pure metals? Give two reasons.

   b. Which two of these structures are **not** alloys of iron, carbon and nickel? For each structure give a reason.

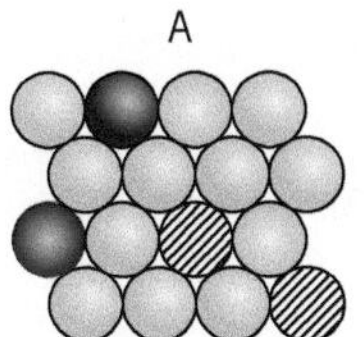


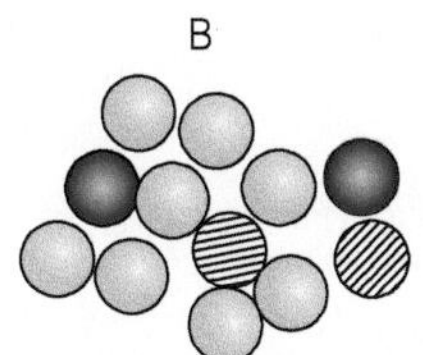


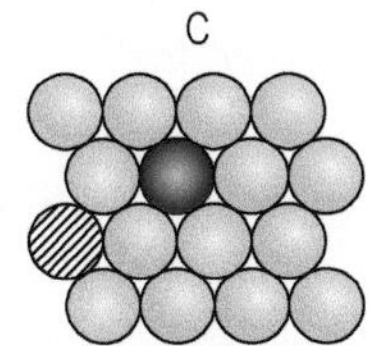


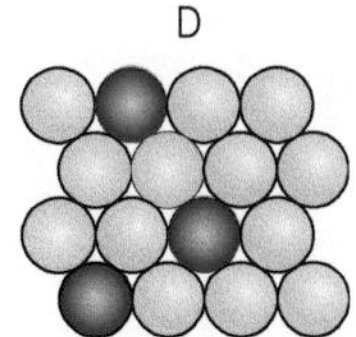


S c. (i) Describe the structure of an alloy.

   (ii) Explain why many alloys are hard by referring to their structure.

# 15.4 Uses of metals

**You need to:**

- Describe the uses of aluminium and copper in terms of their physical properties.
- Know that brass is a mixture of copper and zinc and that stainless steel is a mixture of iron and other elements.
- State that alloys are often more useful than the pure metals.
- Describe the uses of stainless steel.

### Exam tip

When writing about metals with *low density* don't use the terms 'light' or 'lightweight'.

### Exam tip

When discussing properties related to uses, don't write a whole list of properties. Select the ones which you think are most important, e.g. electrical conductivity or ductility for copper wiring.

### Recap

- Aluminium has a low density and is resistant to corrosion.
- Copper is a good conductor of electricity and very ductile.
- Stainless steel is resistant to corrosion and is hard.
- Brass is an alloy of copper and zinc.

*Aluminium* is used to make aircraft because of its low density and is used for food containers because of its resistance to corrosion.

*Copper* is used for electrical wiring because it is a good conductor of electricity and is very ductile.

**Steel** *is an alloy of iron* made by adding controlled amounts of other metals or by adding or removing carbon.

**Stainless steel** is used to make cutlery because it is resistant to corrosion and is hard.

**Brass** is an alloy of copper and zinc.

### Worked example

Name these metals or alloys:

an alloy of copper and zinc [1]

brass ✓

an alloy of iron with other elements such as nickel and chromium [1]

stainless steel ✓

a metal used to make food containers. Give a reason for your answer. [2]

Aluminium ✓ because it is resistant to corrosion. ✓

Copper conducts electricity. Give one other physical property which makes copper suitable to use for electrical wiring. Explain your choice. [2]

Copper is ductile, ✓ so it can be drawn into wires ✓ which bend without breaking.

## Apply

4. Choose suitable metals, compositions, uses or properties **V** to **Z** to complete the table.

| Metal | Composition | Use | Property which makes it suitable for the use |
|---|---|---|---|
| aluminium alloy | Al + Mg | aircraft body | **V** |
| brass | **W** | musical instruments | hard |
| copper | Cu | **X** | ductile |
| **Y** | Fe + Ni + Cr | cutlery | **Z** |

## Questions

1. **a.** Give the name of the main ore of iron. [1]

   **b.** Apart from the ore of iron, name two other raw materials which are put into the blast furnace in order to extract the iron. [2]

   **c.** The equation shows one of the reactions taking place in the blast furnace.

   $$Fe_2O_3 + 3CO \rightarrow 2Fe + 3CO_2$$

   **(i)** Write a word equation for this reaction. [1]

   **(ii)** Explain how you know that the $Fe_2O_3$ is reduced by CO. [1]

   **d.** **(i)** Calcium carbonate added to the blast furnace undergoes thermal decomposition to form calcium oxide. State the meaning of the term *thermal decomposition.* [2]

   **(ii)** Explain the importance of the further reaction of calcium oxide in the blast furnace. [3]

   **e.** **(i)** Iron rusts in the presence of oxygen and water. State the chemical name for rust. [1]

   **(ii)** Steel is an alloy of iron. Define the term *alloy.* [1]

   **(iii)** Give two reasons why stainless steel is used for cutlery rather than iron. [2]

   S **f.** Explain how galvanising an iron object provides sacrificial protection. [3]

## Sample question

1. **a.** **(i)** Name an alloy other than steel or stainless steel. Name the elements present in this alloy. [2]

   **(ii)** Give two reasons why alloys are more useful than pure metals. [2]

   **b.** The diagram shows an iron nail which has been left for 1 week at the bottom of a test tube.

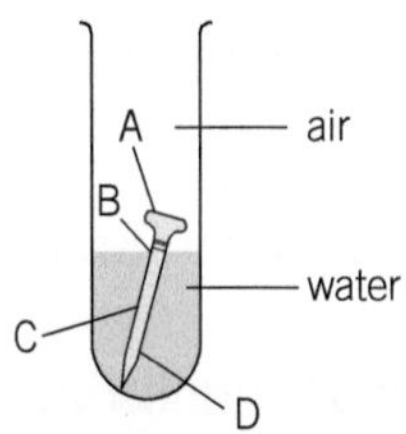


   Where is the nail most rusted? Choose from **A**, **B**, **C** or **D**. Explain why. [3]

   **c.** Iron is extracted in a blast furnace. Explain the purpose of the air added to the blast furnace. [2]

   **d.** **(i)** Explain how carbon monoxide is produced inside the blast furnace by a two-step process. [3]

   S **(ii)** In hotter parts of the blast furnace carbon reduces iron(III) oxide. Carbon monoxide is produced. Write a symbol equation for this reaction. [2]

   **(iii)** Explain how slag is produced inside the blast furnace by a two-step process. Include a chemical equation in your answer. [4]

   **e.** **(i)** Draw a diagram of a typical alloy containing two metals. [2]

   **(ii)** Explain why alloys are stronger than the pure metals from which they are made. [4]

   **f.** Pieces of magnesium are attached to an iron pipeline to prevent it from rusting. Explain how magnesium stops the pipeline from rusting. In your answer include ideas of electron transfer including a relevant ionic equation. [5]

# Compounds of nitrogen and sulfur

## Revision checklist

Tick these boxes to build a record of your revision. Columns 2 and 3 can be used if you want to make a record more than once.

| Core/**Supplement** syllabus content | | 1 | 2 | 3 |
|---|---|---|---|---|
| 16.1 | State the chemical equation for the Haber process and state the sources of the hydrogen and nitrogen used. | | | |
| 16.1 | State the essential conditions in the Haber process and explain why these conditions are used. | | | |
| 16.1 | Predict and explain how the position of equilibrium is affected by changes in reaction conditions. | | | |
| 16.2 | State that ammonium salts and nitrates can be used as fertilisers. | | | |
| 16.2 | Describe the need for NPK fertilisers. | | | |
| 16.3 | **Describe how sulfuric acid reacts with metals, metal oxides, metal hydroxides and carbonates.** | | | |
| 16.3 | **Predict and explain how the position of equilibrium in the Contact process is affected by changes in reaction conditions.** | | | |
| 16.4 | Describe the origins of nitrogen dioxide and sulfur dioxide in the atmosphere. | | | |
| 16.4 | Describe the formation of acid rain and its adverse effects. | | | |

# 16.1 Making ammonia

**You need to:**

- State the chemical equation for the Haber process and state the sources of the hydrogen and nitrogen used.
- State the essential conditions in the Haber process and explain why these conditions are used.
- Predict and explain how the position of equilibrium is affected by changes in reaction conditions.

The **Haber process** used to make ammonia uses nitrogen from the air and hydrogen obtained by reacting steam with methane.

The *conditions for the Haber process* are 20 000 kPa (200 atm) pressure, 450 °C and an iron catalyst.

An *increase in temperature decreases the* **yield** of ammonia because the forward reaction is exothermic.

An *increase in pressure increases the yield* of ammonia because there are fewer moles of gaseous products than moles of gaseous reactants.

A *compromise temperature* (not too high or low) is used in the Haber process which gives a good yield of ammonia with a fast enough rate of reaction.

**Worked example**

The Haber process is used to make ammonia.

$$N_2(g) + 3H_2(g) \rightleftharpoons 2NH_3(g) \qquad \Delta H = -92 \text{ kJ/mol}$$

State two conditions used in the Haber process. [2]

temperature of 450 °C ✓ and 20 000 kPa (200 atm) pressure ✓ and an iron catalyst

Describe and explain what happens to the yield of ammonia when the pressure increases. [3]

The yield of ammonia increases ✓ because the reaction goes in the direction of fewer moles of gas ✓ (4 moles of gas on the left and only 2 on the right). It does this to oppose the increase in pressure. ✓

Describe how the yield of ammonia changes when the temperature decreases. Explain your answer. [3]

Yield of ammonia increases ✓ because the forward reaction is exothermic. ✓ Decreasing the temperature makes the reaction move in the direction of releasing thermal energy. ✓ This is in favour of the products.

**Exam tip**

Conditions are temperature, pressure and presence or absence of catalyst.

**Exam tip**

There may be two command words in a question. For example: 'describe and explain'. This means that you have to comment on what happens or what you see (describe) as well as giving a reason for it (explain).

**Key skills**

You need to be able to interpret information given in equations such as number of moles of gas and $\Delta H$ values.

**Exam tip**

When writing about exothermic or endothermic reactions at equilibrium you need to make the direction of the reaction clear, e.g. endothermic in the forward direction.

**Exam tip**

You need to remember the exact conditions and the equation for the Haber process.

**Exam tip**

In equilibrium questions, the equation often gives you a clue. Look out for the sign of the enthalpy change (effect of temperature on equilibrium) and the moles of gas on each side of the equation (effect of pressure on equilibrium).

**Exam tip**

Remember the effect of changing pressure on equilibrium depends on the moles of *gas* on each side of the equation, not just moles.

**Recap**

- The conditions for the Haber process are 20 000 kPa pressure, 450 °C and an iron catalyst. The forward reaction is exothermic.
- A compromise temperature is used in the Haber process which gives a good yield of ammonia with a fast enough rate of reaction.

## Apply

1. Ammonia is synthesised by reacting hydrogen with nitrogen.

$$N_2(g) + 3H_2(g) \rightleftharpoons 2NH_3(g) \qquad \Delta H = -92 \text{ kJ/mol}$$

   a. State one source of hydrogen for this synthesis.

   b. Describe and explain what happens to the position of equilibrium when the pressure decreases.

   c. Describe the effect of increasing the temperature on the position of equilibrium.

   d. Explain why the reaction is carried out at 450 °C and not at a higher or lower temperature.

# 16.2 Fertilisers

**You need to:**

- State that ammonium salts and nitrates can be used as fertilisers; describe the need for NPK fertilisers.

**Fertilisers** *are added to the soil to improve* plant growth and replace essential elements lost when plants are harvested.

**NPK fertilisers** are salts which contain nitrogen, phosphorus and potassium.

*Examples of fertilisers* include ammonium salts such as ammonium phosphate and nitrates such as potassium nitrate.

**Worked example**

A farmer grows crops on the same field for 20 years without adding a fertiliser.

Suggest why the yield of crop decreased gradually over 20 years. [2]

The plants take nitrogen and other minerals from the soil ✓ and these are not being fully replaced after crops have been harvested. ✓

Name three elements present in fertilisers which help to improve crop yield. [3]

nitrogen, ✓ phosphorus ✓ and potassium ✓

Many fertilisers are salts.

Name an acid and an alkali needed for the synthesis of ammonium sulfate. [2]

aqueous ammonia ✓ and sulfuric acid ✓

Write the formula for ammonium sulfate. [1]

$(NH_4)_2SO_4$ ✓

**Recap**

Fertilisers containing N, P and K improve plant growth.

**Exam tip**

Remember that a single exam question can include material from different areas of the syllabus.

## Apply

2. a. Give the symbols of the three main elements found in fertilisers which help plant growth.

   b. Sodium nitrate is a fertiliser.

      (i) Write the formula for sodium nitrate.

      (ii) Write a word equation for the synthesis of sodium nitrate from an acid and an alkali.

      (iii) Describe how to prepare pure dry crystals of sodium nitrate from aqueous sodium nitrate.

**Exam tip**

You may be asked to write word or symbol equations for the formation of salts used in fertilisers. For making ammonium salts from ammonia and an acid, remember that no water appears as a product.

# 16.3 Sulfuric acid

**You need to:**

- **Describe how sulfuric acid reacts with metals, metal oxides, metal hydroxides and carbonates.**
- **Predict and explain how the position of equilibrium in the Contact process is affected by changes in reaction conditions.**

S The **Contact process** to make sulfuric acid uses sulfur dioxide, $SO_2$, (from burning sulfur or roasting sulfide ores) and oxygen from the air to make sulfur trioxide, $SO_3$.

The *conditions for the Contact process* are 200 kPa pressure, 450 °C and a vanadium(V) oxide catalyst, $V_2O_5$.

An *increase in temperature decreases the yield* of sulfur trioxide because the forward reaction is exothermic.

An *increase in pressure increases the yield* of sulfur trioxide because there are fewer moles of gaseous products than moles of gaseous reactants.

The *pressure used in the Contact process* is just above atmospheric pressure because the yield of sulfur trioxide is high even at low pressures.

A *compromise temperature* (not too high or low) is used in the Contact process which gives a good yield of sulfur trioxide with a fast enough rate of reaction.

**Exam tip**

You need to remember the exact conditions and the equation for the Contact process.

**Exam tip**

Sulfuric acid has two $H^+$ ions that can be replaced. Make sure that you remember this when writing equations for the reaction of sulfuric acid with metals, metal oxides or metal carbonates.

Supplement

### Worked example

The equation shows the reaction in the Contact process for making sulfuric acid.

$$2SO_2(g) + O_2(g) \rightleftharpoons 2SO_3(g) \qquad \Delta H = -197 \text{ kJ/mol}$$

Describe two methods for obtaining the $SO_2$ for this process. [2]

Burning sulfur in air ✓ and roasting sulfide ores ✓

Describe and explain the effect on the position of equilibrium when:

The pressure is increased. [3]

Position of equilibrium moves to the right. ✓ It goes in the direction of fewer moles of gas ✓ (3 moles of gas on the left and only 2 on the right). It does this to oppose the increase in pressure. ✓

The concentration of oxygen is decreased. [2]

The position of equilibrium moves to the left. ✓ It goes in this direction to try and increase the concentration of the oxygen. ✓

Sulfuric acid is made from $SO_3$.

Write a chemical equation for the reaction of dilute sulfuric acid with zinc. Include state symbols. [2]

$H_2SO_4(aq) + Zn(s) \rightarrow ZnSO_4(aq) + H_2(g)$

Equation correct ✓ state symbols correct ✓

### Recap

- The conditions for the Contact process for making sulfuric acid are 200 kPa pressure, 450 °C and a vanadium(V) oxide catalyst, $V_2O_5$.
- A compromise temperature is used in the Contact process which gives a good yield of sulfur trioxide with a fast enough rate of reaction.

## Apply

3. a. Sulfuric acid is a strong acid. State the meaning of the term strong as applied to acids.

   b. Sulfuric acid is made by the Contact process.

   $$2SO_2(g) + O_2(g) \rightleftharpoons 2SO_3(g) \qquad \Delta H = -197 \text{ kJ/mol}$$

   (i) State the name of the catalyst used in the Contact process.

   (ii) Describe and explain the effect of this catalyst on the position of this equilibrium.

   (iii) Write a chemical equation for the formation of $SO_2$ in this process. Include state symbols.

   (iv) State and explain what happens to the yield of $SO_3$ when the temperature increases.

   (v) State and explain what happens to the position of equilibrium when $SO_3$ is removed from the equilibrium mixture.

# 16.4 Acid rain

**You need to:**

- Describe the origins of nitrogen dioxide and sulfur dioxide in the atmosphere.
- Describe the formation of acid rain and its adverse effects.

**Acid rain** is rain with a pH of less than about pH 5.

*Acid rain forms* when sulfur dioxide and oxides of nitrogen react with oxygen and water in the atmosphere to form dilute acids.

*Sulfur dioxide in the atmosphere is formed* by the combustion of fossil fuels containing sulfur and from volcanoes.

*Oxides of nitrogen (especially nitrogen dioxide) in the atmosphere are formed* by the combination of oxygen and nitrogen in car engines and from high temperature furnaces.

*Effects of acid rain on wildlife* include death of trees and acidification of lakes leading to the death of fish and other water animals.

*Effects of acid rain on buildings* include erosion of limestone buildings and corrosion of metalwork.

**Worked example**

Which one of these pH values represents the pH of acid rain? Explain why the other values are not the correct answer.

pH 1 pH 5 pH 7 pH 9 [4]

Acid rain is pH 5. ✓ pH 1 is the pH of a concentrated acid and acid rain is not concentrated acid. ✓ pH 7 is neutral so is not acidic. ✓ pH 9 is alkaline so is not acidic. ✓

One of the compounds responsible for acid rain is sulfur trioxide, $SO_3$.

Describe a source of sulfur trioxide in the atmosphere and explain how it is formed. [3]

Burning fossil fuels containing sulfur ✓ produces sulfur dioxide. ✓ The sulfur dioxide is oxidised in the atmosphere ✓ to sulfur trioxide.

Write a symbol equation for the reaction of one molecule of sulfur trioxide with one molecule of water to form an acid. Name this acid. [2]

$SO_3 + H_2O \rightarrow H_2SO_4$ ✓ $H_2SO_4$ is sulfuric acid ✓

Describe one adverse effect of acid rain on wildlife. [1]

Lakes get so acidic that fish cannot survive. ✓

**Exam tip**

**Watch out**

When writing about the source of sulfur dioxide in the air, the word burns is essential. 'From fossils fuels' is too vague. It should be 'from burning fossil fuels'.

**Exam tip**

It is a common error to suggest that sulfur ✗ rather than sulfur dioxide ✓ is responsible for acid rain.

## Apply

4. a. (i) State the name of one compound of a Group V element and the name of one compound of a Group VI element that is responsible for acid rain.

(ii) State a source of each compound that you named in part (a)(i).

**Exam tip**

In the formation of acid rain, the gases react with water to form $H^+$ ions. They do not just dissolve.

b. Describe one adverse effect of acid rain on buildings.

c. Explain how acid rain is formed from a named oxide in the atmosphere and explain why it is acidic.

**Exam tip**

**Watch out**

Remember that acid rain does *not* rust iron structures. It corrodes them.

**Recap**

- Acid rain forms when sulfur dioxide and oxides of nitrogen react with oxygen and water in the atmosphere to form dilute acids with a pH of about pH 5.
- Sulfur dioxide is formed by the combustion of fossil fuels containing sulfur and oxides of nitrogen are formed by the combination of oxygen and nitrogen in car engines.
- Effects of acid rain include death of trees, acidification of lakes and chemical erosion of limestone buildings.

## Questions

**1.** Complete these sentences about fertilisers using words from the list.

compounds decrease elements increase nitrates
potassium sulfides tin

Crop plants need three major ............ for healthy growth: nitrogen, phosphorus and ............ Fertilisers contain salts such as ............, phosphates and potassium salts. These are added to the soil to ............ plant growth. [4]

**2. a.** Complete these sentences about acid rain using words from the list.

burned condenses dioxide fossil oxidised
reacts solution sulfuric

When ............ fuels containing sulfur are ............, sulfur ............ is formed. This gas escapes into the atmosphere and ............ with water vapour to form a dilute ............ of sulfurous acid. Some of the sulfur dioxide is ............ further in the atmosphere to form sulfur trioxide which reacts with water vapour to form dilute ............ acid. The acidic water vapour ............ and falls as acid rain. [8]

**b.** Describe one adverse effect of acid rain on buildings made of limestone (calcium carbonate). Give details of the reaction taking place. [3]

**3.** Ammonia is synthesised from hydrogen and nitrogen in the Haber process.

S **a.** State the source of the nitrogen and hydrogen. [2]

**b.** Write a chemical equation for this synthesis. [2]

**c.** Describe and explain what happens to the position of equilibrium when the ammonia is removed. [2]

**4.** Sulfuric acid is produced by the Contact process.

$$2SO_2(g) + O_2(g) \rightleftharpoons 2SO_3(g) \qquad \Delta H = -197 \text{ kJ/mol}$$

**a.** State and explain what happens to the yield of $SO_3$ when the pressure increases. [3]

**b.** State and explain what happens to the position of equilibrium when more oxygen is added. [2]

**c.** Describe the effect on the yield of $SO_3$ when the temperature is decreased. [2]

## Sample question

1. **a.** Calcium phosphate can be made into superphosphate fertilisers. Deduce the formula of calcium phosphate. The formula of the phosphate ion is $PO_4^{3-}$. [1]

   **b.** Potassium sulfate fertiliser can be made from an acid and an alkali.

   **(i)** State the acid and alkali used. [2]

   **(ii)** Describe how a pure dry sample of potassium sulfate crystals can be prepared from an aqueous solution of potassium sulfate. [3]

   **c.** Describe and explain the effect of acid rain on a structure made of iron. [3]

   **d.** Farmers sometimes add calcium hydroxide to their fields where crops are to be grown. Suggest why calcium hydroxide should not be added at the same time as a fertiliser containing ammonium sulfate. [4]

   S **e.** The graph shows the effect of temperature and pressure on the yield of ammonia in the Haber process.

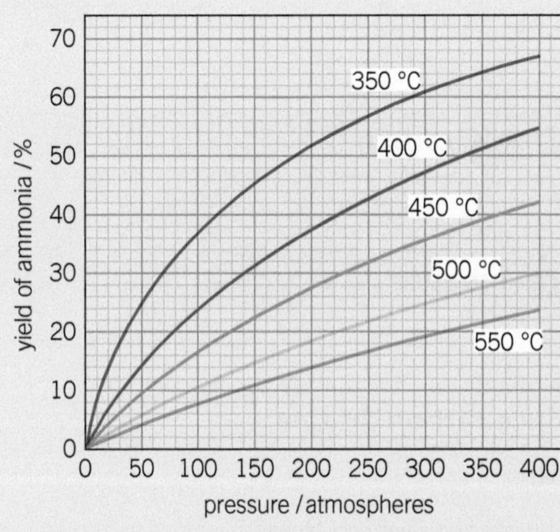

**Key skills**

You need to be able to interpret data from graphs.

   **(i)** Describe the effect of temperature on the percentage yield of ammonia. [1]

   **(ii)** Use the information in the graph to deduce the sign of the enthalpy change of the reaction. Explain your answer. [2]

   **(iii)** State one advantage and one disadvantage of using a temperature of 650 °C in this reaction. [2]

   **(iv)** The boiling points of hydrogen, nitrogen and ammonia are:

   hydrogen −253 °C, nitrogen −196 °C, ammonia −33 °C

   Suggest how ammonia can be removed from the equilibrium mixture. Explain your answer. [2]

   **f.** The equation for the essential stage of the Contact process is shown.

$$2SO_2(g) + O_2(g) \rightleftharpoons 2SO_3(g) \qquad \Delta H = -197 \text{ kJ/mol}$$

   **(i)** The sulfur dioxide can be produced from sulfur. Describe one other way of producing the sulfur dioxide for this process. [2]

   **(ii)** State and explain the conditions of temperature and pressure used in the Contact process. [5]

# Environmental chemistry

## Revision checklist

Tick these boxes to build a record of your revision. Columns 2 and 3 can be used if you want to make a record more than once.

| Core/**Supplement** syllabus content | | 1 | 2 | 3 |
|---|---|---|---|---|
| 17.1 | State the composition of clean, dry air. | | | |
| 17.1 | State the source of air pollutants including carbon dioxide, carbon monoxide and methane. | | | |
| 17.1 | State the adverse effects of these air pollutants. | | | |
| 17.2 | State the sources and word equation for reactions that produce carbon dioxide. | | | |
| 17.2 | Give the word equation for photosynthesis. | | | |
| 17.2 | **State the symbol equations for reactions that produce carbon dioxide.** | | | |
| 17.2 | Describe photosynthesis **including a symbol equation**. | | | |
| 17.3 | State that carbon dioxide and methane cause global warming which leads to climate change. | | | |
| 17.3 | **Describe how carbon dioxide and methane cause global warming.** | | | |
| 17.4 | State and explain how climate change and the emission of greenhouse gases can be decreased. | | | |
| 17.4 | State and explain how the formation and effects of acid rain can be decreased. | | | |
| 17.4 | **Describe the removal of oxides of nitrogen in car engines by catalytic converters.** | | | |
| 17.5 | State that water from natural sources contains a variety of substances some of which are beneficial. | | | |
| 17.5 | Describe the purification of the domestic water supply. | | | |
| 17.6 | State that water from natural sources contains a variety of substances some of which are harmful. | | | |
| 17.6 | State the harmful effects of substances found in the water (metal compounds, plastics, sewage, nitrates and phosphates). | | | |

# 17.1 Air pollution

**You need to:**

- State the composition of clean, dry air.
- State the source of air pollutants including carbon dioxide, carbon monoxide and methane.
- State the adverse effects of these air pollutants.

*Clean, dry* **air** contains 78% nitrogen, 21% oxygen, about 1% argon and 0.04% carbon dioxide.

*Carbon dioxide* (from combustion reactions) and *methane* (from the decay of vegetation and waste gases from animal digestion) both contribute to **global warming**.

*Carbon monoxide* (from incomplete combustion of carbon compounds) is toxic.

*Oxides of nitrogen* (from car engines) cause irritation of the lungs, eyes and throat and can be poisonous at higher concentrations. They are also responsible for acid rain and photochemical smog.

**Photochemical smog** is a smoky fog caused by reaction of oxides of nitrogen with ozone and hydrocarbons in the presence of light. It causes respiratory problems.

*Particulates* (from incomplete combustion of fossil fuels) cause respiratory problems and cancer.

*Sulfur dioxide* (from combustion of fossil fuels) is responsible for acid rain.

**Worked example**

The table shows the mass of air pollutants in samples of air over a 4-month period.

| | Mass of pollutant in 1000 $cm^3$ of air / nanograms | | | | |
|---|---|---|---|---|---|
| Month | Oxides of nitrogen | Sulfur dioxide | Carbon monoxide | Ozone | Particulates |
| July | 134.3 | 4.8 | 2.4 | 28.9 | 18.9 |
| August | 150.5 | 2.0 | 1.9 | 27.6 | 23.7 |
| September | 100.2 | 5.1 | 1.8 | 27.0 | 21.3 |
| October | 95.4 | 3.6 | 2.5 | 24.2 | 19.0 |

State which pollutant showed a continual decrease in concentration between July and October. [1]

ozone ✓

State which pollutant is present in the lowest concentration in August. [1]

carbon monoxide ✓

**Key skills**

You need to be able to analyse data from tables and carry out calculations using simple proportions.

**Exam tip**

Look out for double command words such as 'state and explain'. You have to do two things: state a fact then say how or why it happens.

**Exam tip**

In tables of data, look at each number in a column or row carefully to see if there is a trend.

**Exam tip**

Be prepared to do simple calculations in any subject area of chemistry; see the mathematical requirements in the syllabus.

**Exam tip**

If asked for *major* differences when comparing data, it generally means large percentage differences; for example, the percentage difference between 0.5 and 0.2 is large compared with the percentage difference between 82 and 79.

**Recap**

- Clean, dry air contains 78% $N_2$, 21% $O_2$, about 1% Ar and 0.04% $CO_2$.
- Carbon dioxide and methane contribute to global warming.
- Incomplete combustion of carbon compounds produces carbon monoxide and particulates.
- Oxides of nitrogen and sulfur dioxide are responsible for acid rain. Oxides of nitrogen also contribute to photochemical smog.

**Key skills**

You need to be able to develop strategies for memorising lists which link specific substances to their effects on the environment and health.

**Exam tip**

Make sure that you don't give vague answers about the effects of pollutants. Avoid statements such as 'harmful' or 'affects the surface'. When discussing the effects of acid rain on structures, scientific words such as 'erosion' or 'corrosion' should be used.

Calculate the mass of sulfur dioxide in 200 $cm^3$ of the sample of air taken in July. [1]

Using simple proportion: 1000 $cm^3$ air contains 4.8 g.

So, 200 $cm^3$ air contains $\frac{200}{1000} \times 4.8 = 0.96$ g ✓

Sulfur dioxide contributes to acid rain. State one other pollutant in the table which contributes to acid rain and state a source of this pollutant. [2]

Oxides of nitrogen ✓ from car exhausts ✓

State and explain one source of particulates. [2]

From car engines ✓ because of the incomplete combustion of fuel ✓

State one harmful effect of particulates on health. [1]

increased respiratory problems ✓ and cancer

## Apply

1. The table shows the percentage by volume of gases in the exhausts from a petrol engine and a diesel engine.

| Gas | Petrol engine percentage by volume | Diesel engine percentage by volume |
|---|---|---|
| nitrogen | 73 | 66.0 |
| carbon dioxide | 15 | 11.1 |
| water vapour | 11 | 10.0 |
| oxygen | 0 | 8.0 |
| oxides of nitrogen | 0.25 | 1.2 |
| carbon monoxide | 2.5 | |
| hydrocarbons | 0.25 | 0.2 |

a. Calculate the percentage by volume of carbon monoxide present in the exhaust gases of the diesel engine.

b. (i) State and explain the source of carbon monoxide in car exhausts.

(ii) State one effect of carbon monoxide on health.

c. State the names of two gases in the table that are present in clean, dry air. For each gas state their percentage composition in the air.

d. Give two major differences in the composition of the exhaust gases from the petrol engine and diesel engine.

e. Photochemical smog is a smoky fog caused by reaction of oxides of nitrogen with ozone and hydrocarbons from car exhausts. State one effect of photochemical smog on health.

f. Oxides of nitrogen react in the air to form acid rain. State one effect of acid rain on buildings.

# 17.2 Carbon dioxide in the atmosphere

**You need to:**

- State the sources and word equation for reactions that produce carbon dioxide.
- Give the word equation for photosynthesis.
- **State the symbol equations for reactions that produce carbon dioxide.**
- Describe photosynthesis **including a symbol equation.**

*Carbon dioxide is released* into the atmosphere by the complete combustion of fossil fuels and **respiration**.

**Photosynthesis** is the reaction between carbon dioxide and water to produce glucose and oxygen. **Chlorophyll** and light are needed for this process.

*Photosynthesis removes* carbon dioxide from the atmosphere.

*The concentration of carbon dioxide in the atmosphere is increasing* because more carbon dioxide is being released by burning fossil fuels than is being absorbed by photosynthesis.

**Worked example**

Carbon dioxide is produced by respiration.

State one other source of carbon dioxide in the atmosphere. [2]

complete ✓ combustion of fossil fuels ✓

Hydrocarbons such as methane, $CH_4$, undergo complete combustion. State the meaning of the term complete combustion. [2]

Burning in air or oxygen ✓ when the oxygen is in excess ✓ so that only carbon dioxide and water are formed.

Photosynthesis removes carbon dioxide from the atmosphere. Copy and complete the word equation for photosynthesis.

carbon dioxide + .................. → .................. + .................. [3]

carbon dioxide + water ✓ → glucose ✓ + oxygen ✓

S Explain why the concentration of carbon dioxide in the atmosphere is increasing, even though photosynthesis is removing it. [1]

more carbon dioxide is being released by burning fossil fuels than is being taken up by photosynthesis ✓

**Exam tip**

Candidates taking the core paper of IGCSE® are expected to complete chemical equations or construct simple chemical equations when given sufficient information.

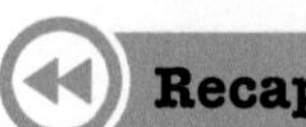

**Recap**

- Combustion of fossil fuels releases $CO_2$ into the atmosphere.
- Photosynthesis (the reaction between carbon dioxide and water to produce glucose and oxygen) absorbs $CO_2$ from the atmosphere. Chlorophyll and light are needed for this process.

**Key skills**

You need to be able to write word equations and construct symbol equations.

**Exam tip**

**Watch out**

It is a common error to muddle conditions with reactants. Remember that conditions are temperature, pressure or presence of light or catalyst.

**Exam tip**

Remember that incomplete combustion occurs when oxygen is limiting. It is incorrect to write 'oxygen is absent' or 'combustion without oxygen'.

## Apply

2. a. Hydrocarbons such as ethane undergo complete combustion. Write a word equation for the complete combustion of ethane.

   b. Write a symbol equation for the complete combustion of carbon. Include state symbols.

   c. (i) Copy and complete the symbol equation for the complete combustion of methane, $CH_4$.

   $$CH_4 + \text{.........}O_2 \rightarrow CO_2 + \text{.........}H_2O$$

   (ii) Name two substances formed by the incomplete combustion of methane.

   d. (i) Photosynthesis removes carbon dioxide from the atmosphere. State the conditions for photosynthesis.

   S (ii) Construct the symbol equation for photosynthesis.

# 17.3 Global warming

**You need to:**

- State that carbon dioxide and methane cause global warming which leads to climate change.
- **Describe how carbon dioxide and methane cause global warming.**

**Exam tip**

When discussing the effects of global warming statements such as 'ice melts' or 'floods' are too vague. 'Melting of ice caps' or 'increased risk of flooding' are more accurate.

*Methane and carbon dioxide are* **greenhouse gases** that cause global warming.

*Methane is produced* by decomposition of vegetation and formation of waste gases from digestion in animals.

The *effects of increased global warming* include: **climate change** (more extreme weather) and melting of the polar ice caps and glaciers leading to sea level rise.

S

**Greenhouse gases** are gases which absorb the thermal energy reflected or radiated from the surface of the Earth.

*Increased global warming* is caused by the increased thermal energy absorbed by greenhouse gases and the reduction of loss of thermal energy to space.

**Worked example**

Methane increases global warming.

State two natural sources of methane in the atmosphere. [2]

waste gases from digestion in animals ✓ caused by bacteria in the gut and bacterial decay of vegetation ✓

State the general name for gases which increase global warming. [1]

greenhouse gases ✓

State two effects of increased global warming. [2]

melting of polar ice caps ✓ and glaciers and more extreme weather ✓ such as floods and droughts

Explain how methane causes global warming. [4]

S Methane absorbs the thermal energy ✓ reflected from the surface of the Earth. ✓ So less energy is lost into space. ✓ This leads to an increase in atmospheric temperature. ✓

**Exam tip**

**Watch out**

Look out for the wording 'one *other*'. Don't write about something that has been covered in a previous part of the question.

**Exam tip**

You do not have to know the exact details about global warming but you should have an idea of (i) the absorption and reflection of thermal energy in the atmosphere and (ii) the reduction of thermal energy lost to space.

**Exam tip**

Many substances act as greenhouse gases but the two most important are carbon dioxide and methane.

**Recap**

- Methane and carbon dioxide are greenhouse gases that cause global warming.
- Increased global warming causes climate change and melting of the polar ice caps leading to sea level rise.
- Increased global warming is caused by the increased thermal energy absorbed by greenhouse gases and the reduction of loss of thermal energy to space.

## Apply

3. a. (i) State the meaning of the term greenhouse gas.

 (ii) Carbon dioxide is a greenhouse gas. Name and give the formula of one other greenhouse gas which is a compound containing one carbon atom.

 (iii) State one source of carbon dioxide in the atmosphere.

 (iv) Carbon dioxide increases global warming. Suggest the meaning of the term global warming.

 b. Explain how carbon dioxide increases global warming. S

# 17.4 Reducing environmental pollution

**You need to:**

- State and explain how climate change and the emission of greenhouse gases can be decreased.
- State and explain how the formation and effects of acid rain can be decreased.
- **Describe the removal of oxides of nitrogen in car engines by catalytic converters.**

### Exam tip

You need to know the chemistry of flue gas desulfurisation in terms of the neutralisation of sulfur dioxide by bases mixed with water.

### Recap

- Using non-carbon energy sources and reducing livestock farming reduces greenhouse gas emissions.
- Planting more trees absorbs more carbon dioxide from the atmosphere.
- Acid rain can be reduced by using low-sulfur fuels and flue gas desulfurisation.
- Oxides of nitrogen and carbon monoxide are removed from car exhausts by catalytic converters.

### Exam tip S

Be prepared to write equations for the overall reaction occurring in a **catalytic converter** (NO or $NO_2$ reacting with CO to form $N_2$ and $CO_2$).

*Carbon dioxide emissions can be reduced* by using alternative non-carbon energy sources (solar power, wind power, hydrogen).

*Methane emissions can be reduced* by reducing livestock farming.

*Planting more trees* absorbs more carbon dioxide from the atmosphere.

*Acid rain can be reduced* by using low-sulfur fuels, flue gas desulfurisation and the use of catalytic converters in cars.

**Flue gas desulfurisation** is the removal of sulfur dioxide from waste gases produced in furnaces by reacting the gases with calcium hydroxide or calcium oxide.

*Oxides of nitrogen and carbon monoxide can be removed* from car exhaust gases by a catalytic converter which converts these harmful gases into nitrogen and carbon dioxide.

### Worked example

Explain why planting more trees can help reduce global warming. [2]

Photosynthesis removes carbon dioxide ✓ which is a greenhouse gas ✓ from the atmosphere

Suggest one other way to reduce global warming. [1]

Use wind power or solar power instead of fossil fuels. ✓

Sulfur dioxide is a waste gas produced in furnaces.

State and explain the source of this sulfur dioxide. [2]

From sulfur in fossil fuels ✓ which when burned in air forms sulfur dioxide. ✓

A mixture of calcium oxide and water can be used to remove the sulfur dioxide. Explain how this mixture removes the sulfur dioxide. [3]

Sulfur dioxide is an acidic gas ✓ which is neutralised by calcium oxide ✓ (a base) to form a solid (calcium sulfite) ✓ which can be removed.

Explain how a catalytic converter removes oxides of nitrogen from a car exhaust. [3]

S The oxides of nitrogen react on the catalyst surface with carbon monoxide ✓ to form nitrogen ✓ and carbon dioxide. ✓

## Apply

4. a. (i) Explain why reducing livestock farming can help reduce global warming.
   (ii) Suggest one other way to reduce global warming.
   b. (i) Name the gas removed by flue gas desulfurisation.
   (ii) Name a substance used to remove this gas.
   (iii) Name the type of chemical reaction taking place.

   c. (i) Describe how oxides of nitrogen are formed in a car engine.
   (ii) Copy and complete the equation for one of the overall reactions taking place in a catalytic converter.

   $2NO_2$ + .................... → .................... + ....................

# 17.5 Clean water

**You need to:**

- State that water from natural sources contains a variety of substances some of which are beneficial.
- Describe the purification of the domestic water supply.

*Oxygen in unpolluted water* is needed for the respiration of aquatic organisms.

*Minerals in unpolluted water* are needed for healthy growth of aquatic organisms.

*In water treatment insoluble materials are removed* by **sedimentation** and filtration.

*Carbon is added during water treatment* to remove bad tastes and odours.

*Chlorine is added during water treatment* (**chlorination**) to kill bacteria.

### Exam tip

Be prepared to answer questions about extracting information from tables of data as shown in the worked example.

### Exam tip

**Watch out**

When answering questions about concentration of ions in a table, take great care in reading the question: make sure that you distinguish between the positive ions and negative ions.

### Worked example

The table shows the ions present in a sample of river water.

| Ion | Formula of ion | Mass present in mg/1000 cm$^3$ |
|---|---|---|
| calcium | $Ca^{2+}$ | 2.8 |
| chloride | $Cl^-$ | 1.2 |
| hydrogencarbonate | $HCO_3^-$ | 2.5 |
| magnesium | $Mg^{2+}$ | 1.5 |
| silicate | $SiO_3^{2-}$ | 6.0 |
| sodium | $Na^+$ | 10.0 |

**Exam tip**

Remember that tap water is not pure: it contains minerals and oxygen. That is why we do not use it in testing for ions (Chapter 12).

**Recap**

- Oxygen and minerals in unpolluted water are essential for the life of aquatic organisms.
- In water treatment insoluble materials are removed by sedimentation and filtration, carbon removes bad odours and chlorination kills bacteria.

State which negative ion is present in the lowest concentration. [1]

chloride ✓

State the name of the compound containing $Mg^{2+}$ and $SiO_3^{2-}$ ions. [1]

magnesium silicate ✓

Calculate the mass of solid formed when all the water is evaporated from 500 cm³ of the sample. [2]

Total mass of solid in 1000 cm³
= 2.8 + 1.2 + 2.5 + 1.5 + 6.0 + 10.0 = 24 mg ✓

So in 500 cm³ there will be $24 \times \frac{500}{1000} = 12$ mg ✓

State which one of these gases is present in unpolluted water and state why it is important.

ammonia hydrogen methane oxygen [2]

oxygen ✓ because it is essential for aquatic life ✓ – it is needed for respiration

Water treatment involves filtration, addition of carbon and chlorination.

The diagram shows part of a sand filter. Explain how this helps to purify the water. [3]

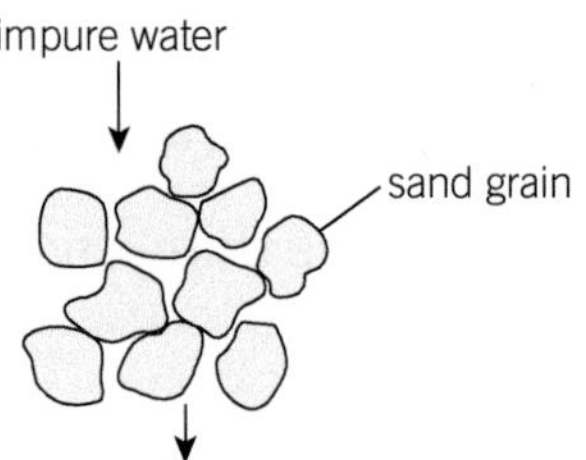


Pieces of insoluble material are trapped between the sand grains. ✓ Water molecules go between the sand grains ✓ because their molecules are very small. ✓

Give a reason for the addition of carbon and chlorination of the water supply. [2]

to remove bad smells ✓ to kill bacteria ✓

## Apply

5. a. Copy and complete these sentences about water treatment using words from the list.

carbon chlorine filter insoluble sedimentation solids

In the .............................. tank, larger particles of .............................. fall to the bottom. The water is then passed through a .............................. made of sand and gravel. This filters out smaller particles of .............................. material. .............................. is then added to the filtered water to remove bad odours. .............................. is added to kill harmful bacteria.

b. The list shows substances present in polluted water.

carbon dioxide oxygen calcium sulfate nitrogen

(i) Which one of these substances is a mineral?

(ii) State the importance of minerals in river water.

(iii) Which one of these substances is a gas which is essential for aquatic life?

c. Explain why tap water is not pure.

# 17.6 Water pollution

**You need to:**

- State that water from natural sources contains a variety of substances some of which are harmful.
- State the harmful effects of substances found in the water (metal compounds, plastics, sewage, nitrates and phosphates).

*Water from natural sources can be polluted* with metal compounds, plastics, sewage, harmful bacteria and nitrates and phosphates.

*Metal compounds* are often toxic.

*Plastics in the water* can trap or choke animals and fish. Microplastics can get into the bloodstream and cause harm.

*Sewage* is animal waste which often contains harmful bacteria.

*Excess nitrates and phosphates* from fertilisers can lead to **deoxygenation** of the water and the death of aquatic life.

**Worked example**

The list shows the compounds present in a sample of polluted water.

ammonium nitrate    carbon dioxide    mercury chloride
plastics    potassium phosphate    sewage    sodium chloride

Which compound is a toxic metal compound? [1]

mercury chloride ✓

Which two compounds lead to water becoming deoxygenated? [1]

ammonium nitrate and potassium phosphate ✓

State the source of these compounds. [1]

fertilisers ✓

State one harmful effect of plastics on aquatic life. [1]

Sea animals can't breathe when plastic gets stuck in their throat ✓

Explain why sewage is harmful to health. [1]

It contains harmful bacteria ✓ which cause disease

**Recap**

- Polluted water may contain metal compounds which are often toxic and nitrates and phosphates which can lead to deoxygenation of water.
- Sewage is animal waste which often contains harmful bacteria.
- Plastics in the water can trap or choke animals and fish.

**Exam tip**

You do not have to know the details of how the presence of nitrate and phosphate pollutants leads to deoxygenation of lakes and rivers and death of aquatic life.

## Apply

6. Link the pollutants in water, **A** to **D**, with their effects, **1** to **4**.

| | |
|---|---|
| **A** fertilisers | **1** they can block the digestive system of animals |
| **B** metal compounds | **2** they are very poisonous |
| **C** plastics | **3** they contain bacteria which cause disease |
| **D** sewage wastes | **4** they lead to the removal of oxygen from water |

## Questions

**1. a.** Link the pollutants **A** to **E** with their effects or properties, **1** to **5**.

**A** methane
**B** oxides of nitrogen
**C** particulates
**D** carbon monoxide
**E** sulfur dioxide

**1** contributes to acid rain **and** photochemical smog
**2** tiny solid particles from car exhausts
**3** contributes to acid rain
**4** hydrocarbon which contributes to global warming
**5** product of incomplete combustion of hydrocarbons [2]

**b.** For each of **B** to **E** in part **a**, state an effect on human health. [4]

**2.** Describe how flue gas desulfurisation removes sulfur dioxide from furnaces. [3]

**3. a.** Unpolluted water contains a variety of dissolved substances.

**(i)** Name a gas that is essential to aquatic life. [1]

**(ii)** Name one other group of substances dissolved in unpolluted water that is essential for aquatic life. [1]

**b.** State a harmful effect of each of these substances in polluted water.

**(i)** plastics **(ii)** sewage **(iii)** nitrates [3]

**c.** State the purpose of each of these processes in water treatment:

**(i)** sedimentation **(ii)** adding carbon **(iii)** chlorination [3]

**4. a.** State the names and sources of two greenhouse gases. [4]

**b.** Describe two effects of increased global warming. [2]

S **c.** Describe how greenhouse gases contribute to global warming. [3]

**5.** Explain why catalytic converters are attached to car exhausts and how they work. [4]

## Sample question

**1.** Air is a mixture of gases.

**a.** State the percentage composition of the three gases which make up most of clean dry air. [3]

**b. (i)** State the name of the gas in clean dry air which contributes to global warming. [1]

**(ii)** Describe and explain two things that can be done to reduce global warming. [4]

**c.** Carbon monoxide is an atmospheric pollutant.

**(i)** Describe a source of carbon monoxide and how it is formed. [2]

**(ii)** When propane, $C_3H_8$, is burned in limited oxygen a mixture of three compounds is produced.

Carbon monoxide and carbon dioxide are formed in a mole ratio of 2 to 1. Construct the chemical equation for this reaction. [2]

**d. (i)** Describe how oxides of nitrogen produce acid rain. [2]

**(ii)** Give one other environmental problem associated with oxides of nitrogen and state its effect on health. [2]

S **(iii)** Nitrogen(II) oxide, NO, is formed in car engines. Explain how a catalytic converter helps reduce the amount of NO put into the air. Include a chemical equation in your answer. [4]

# Organic chemistry and petrochemicals

## Revision checklist

Tick these boxes to build a record of your revision. Columns 2 and 3 can be used if you want to make a record more than once.

| Core/**Supplement** syllabus content | | 1 | 2 | 3 |
|---|---|---|---|---|
| 18.1 | State the type of compound present from a chemical name ending, e.g. -ene, -ol. | | | |
| 18.1 | Describe a homologous series as a family of similar compounds with similar chemical properties due to the presence of the same functional group. | | | |
| 18.1 | Write the general formulae for alkanes, alkenes, alcohols and carboxylic acids. | | | |
| 18.1 | **Describe the general characteristics of a homologous series.** | | | |
| 18.2 | Name and draw the displayed formulae of methane, ethane, ethene, ethanol and ethanoic acid. | | | |
| 18.2 | Draw and interpret displayed formulae and molecular formulae. | | | |
| 18.3 | **Draw structural formulae for organic compounds.** | | | |
| 18.3 | **Define structural isomerism.** | | | |
| 18.3 | **Name and draw structural and displayed formulae of alkanes and alkenes containing up to four carbon atoms per molecule.** | | | |
| 18.4 | Name the fossil fuels coal, natural gas and petroleum. | | | |
| 18.4 | Name methane as the main constituent of natural gas. | | | |
| 18.4 | Describe the separation of petroleum into fractions containing various hydrocarbons. | | | |
| 18.4 | Describe the physical properties of the fractions, e.g. relative volatility. | | | |
| 18.5 | Describe the fractional distillation of petroleum. | | | |
| 18.5 | Describe the difference in hydrocarbon chain length in the fractions from the top to the bottom of the distillation column. | | | |
| 18.5 | Name the uses of petroleum fractions. | | | |

# 18.1 A variety of organic compounds

**You need to:**

- State the type of compound present from a chemical name ending, e.g. -ene, -ol.
- Describe a homologous series as a family of similar compounds with similar chemical properties due to the presence of the same functional group.
- Write the general formulae for alkanes, alkenes, alcohols and carboxylic acids.
- **Describe the general characteristics of a homologous series.**

A **homologous series** is a family of similar compounds with similar chemical properties due to the presence of the same functional group.

A **functional group** is an atom or group of atoms that gives a compound particular chemical properties.

A **general formula** can be written for each homologous series: alkanes $C_nH_{2n+2}$; alkenes $C_nH_{2n}$; alcohols $C_nH_{2n+1}OH$; **carboxylic acids** $C_nH_{2n+1}$ COOH, where $n$ = number of carbon atoms in the hydrocarbon chain.

S *Other characteristics of a homologous series* are trends in physical properties and a difference in a $\_CH_2^-$ group between one member and the next.

### Exam tip

Not all compounds containing carbon are organic. CO, $CO_2$, carbonates and hydrogencarbonates are inorganic.

### Worked example

The structure of two organic compounds, **A** and **B**, are shown.

A: H—O—C(H)(H)—C(H)(H)—C(=O)—O—H

B: $H_2$C=C(H)—C(H)(H)—H

Name and give the formula of the two functional groups in compound **A**. [2]

alcohol –OH ✓ carboxylic acid –COOH ✓

Name the homologous series to which compound **B** belongs. [1]

alkene ✓

The members of a homologous series have the same general formula.

Write the general formula for the alkane homologous series. [1]

$C_nH_{2n+2}$ ✓

State two other characteristics of a homologous series. [2]

They have the same functional group ✓ and similar chemical properties. ✓ Their physical properties change in a regular way and each member differs from the next by a $CH_2$ group.

The first member of the alcohol homologous series is methanol, $CH_3OH$.

Write the formula of the next member of this homologous series in a similar way, showing the functional group. [1]

$C_2H_5OH$ ✓

**Recap**

- A homologous series is a family of similar compounds with similar chemical properties due to the presence of the same functional group.
- Each homologous series has a general formula, shows a trend in physical properties and a difference in a $-CH_2-$ group between one member and the next.

## Apply

1. a. The structures of two organic compounds, **A** and **B**, are shown.

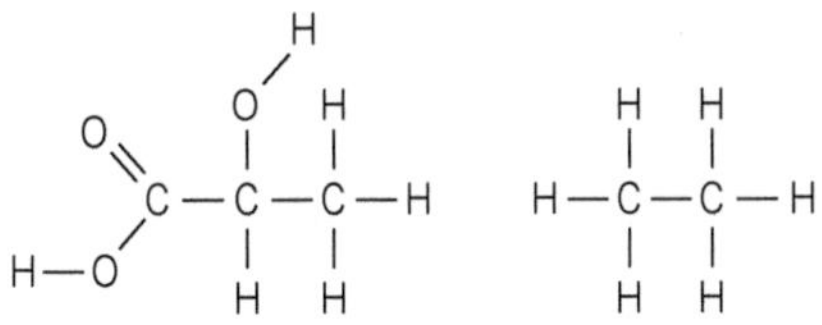

```
            H
           /
          O   H           H   H
  O       |   |           |   |
   \\     |   |           |   |
     C -- C -- C -- H   H -- C -- C -- H
    /     |   |           |   |
H--O      H   H           H   H
          A                   B
```

(i) Copy the structure of compound **A** and draw a circle around the alcohol functional group.

(ii) Name the homologous series to which compound **B** belongs.

b. The members of a homologous series have the same general formula.

(i) Write the general formula for the alkene homologous series.

(ii) Define the term homologous series.

c. The first member of the carboxylic acid homologous series is methanoic acid, HCOOH.

Write the formula of the next member of this homologous series in a similar way, showing the functional group.

**S** d. Describe how the physical properties and the formulae of the compounds in the same homologous series change from one member to the next.

**Exam tip**

**Watch out**

The OH in a carboxylic acid group COOH is *not* an alcohol functional group.

**Exam tip**

The chemical properties of the compounds in a homologous series are *similar*. It is a common error to suggest that they are 'the same' ✗.

# 18.2 Formulae of organic compounds

**You need to:**

- Name and draw the displayed formulae of methane, ethane, ethene, ethanol and ethanoic acid.
- Draw and interpret displayed formulae and molecular formulae.

*The prefixes meth-, eth-, prop-, but-* amongst others tell us the number of carbon atoms in the chain of the organic compound (meth- =1C; eth- = 2C; prop- = 3C; but- = 4C).

The *molecular formula* shows the number and type of each atom in a compound.

The *displayed formula* shows all of the atoms and all of the bonds in a molecule.

### Exam tip

Remember that each carbon atom has four bonds to other atoms and each hydrogen has one bond to another atom. It is a common error in exams to see carbon atoms with five ✗ bonds.

### Exam tip

You need to know the names and structures of the first four alkanes (or the first two for the core paper). But it is good to know the names up to six carbon atoms because you will come across them in data handling questions.

### Recap

- The prefixes meth-, eth-, prop-, but- tell us the number of carbon atoms in the chain of the organic compound.
- The displayed formula shows all of the atoms and all of the bonds in a molecule.

### Worked example

Draw the displayed formula and write the molecular formula for ethene and butane. [4]

$C_2H_4$ ✓

```
H   H
|   |
C = C ✓
|   |
H   H
```

$C_4H_{10}$ ✓

```
    H   H   H   H
    |   |   |   |
H — C — C — C — C — H ✓
    |   |   |   |
    H   H   H   H
```

The displayed formula for compound **C** is shown.

```
        H   H
        |   |      O
H—O—C = C — C //
                \
                 O—H
```

Write the molecular formula for compound **C**. [1]

$C_3H_4O_3$ ✓

Name compounds **D** to **G**. [4]

```
    H   H              H   H                 H       H              H   H   H
    |   |              |   |                  \     /               |   |   |
H — C — C — H      H — C — C — O — H           C = C            H — C — C — C — H
    |   |              |   |                  /     \               |   |   |
    H   H              H   H                 H       H              H   H   H
      D                  E                       F                      G
```

D ethane ✓ E ethanol ✓ F ethene ✓ G propane ✓

## Apply

2. a. Draw the displayed formula and write the molecular formula for (i) ethanoic acid (ii) propane.

   b. The displayed formula for compound **I** is shown.

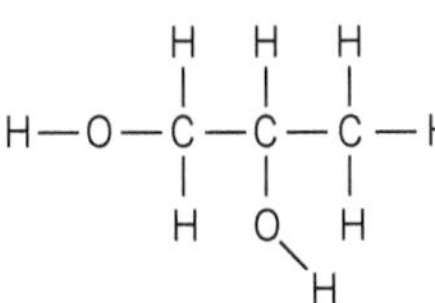

   Write the molecular formula for compound **I**.

   c. Name compounds **J** to **M**.

```
    H            H              H   H                H   H   H   H   H
    |            |              |   |                |   |   |   |   |
H — C — H    H — C — O — H  H — C — C — H        H — C — C — C — C — C — H
    |            |              |   |                |   |   |   |   |
    H            H              H   H                H   H   H   H   H
    J            K                L                          M
```

**Key skills**

You need to be able to use rules about combining powers of atoms to be able to write displayed formulae.

**Exam tip**

When drawing displayed formulae for alcohols, don't forget the O-H bond. It is a common error to write OH ✗.

# 18.3 Structural formulae and isomerism

**You need to:**

- **Draw structural formulae for organic compounds.**
- **Define structural isomerism.**
- **Name and draw structural and displayed formulae of alkanes and alkenes containing up to four carbon atoms per molecule.**

S A **structural formula** is an unambiguous (clearly defined) description of the way the atoms are arranged in a compound. For example, the structural formula of propan-1-ol is $CH_3CH_2CH_2OH$.

**Structural isomers** are compounds with the same molecular formula but different structural formulae. For example: $CH_3CH_2CH_2OH$ and $CH_3CH(OH)CH_3$ are structural isomers.

**Exam tip**

You do not need to know how to name branched chain isomers of alkanes and alkenes.

**Worked example**

Write the structural formulae for compounds **N** and **O**. [2]

```
    H   H   H    H             H   H   H
    |   |   |   /              |   |   |
H — C — C — C = C          H — C — C — C — O — H
    |   |       \              |   |   |
    H   H        H             H   H   H
          N                          O
```

**N** $CH_3CH_2CH{=}CH_2$ ✓ **O** $CH_3CH_2CH_2OH$ ✓

**Recap**

- A structural formula is a clearly defined description of the way the atoms are arranged in a compound.
- Isomers are compounds with the same molecular formula but different structural formulae.

Supplement

**Key skills**

You need to be able to see how to arrange carbon atoms in organic compounds in different ways.

Define the term structural isomer. [1]

Compounds with the same molecular formula but different structural formulae. ✓

Draw the displayed formulae for two structural isomers of butane, $C_4H_{10}$. [2]

```
 H  H  H  H               H
 |  |  |  |               |
H—C—C—C—C—H ✓           H—C—H
 |  |  |  |             H  |  H
 H  H  H  H             |  |  |
                      H—C—C—C—H ✓
                        |  |  |
                        H  H  H
     P                     Q
```

### Exam tip

When writing structural formulae take each carbon atom with its attached groups in turn. For compounds with side chains, the side chain is put in brackets after the carbon it is attached to, e.g. $CH_3CH(CH_3)CH_3$.

```
 H  H  H  H
 |  |  |  |
H—C—C—C—C—H
 |  |  |  |
 H  |  H  H
  H—C—H
    |
    H       R

H              H
 \            /
  C=C—C=C
 /  |  |  \
H   H  H   H
     S
```

### Exam tip

**Watch out**

Make sure that you do not draw the same isomer twice. These two are the same isomer:

$CH_3—CH_2—CH(CH_3)—CH_3$ and $CH_3—CH(CH_3)—CH_2—CH_3$

## Apply

3. a. Define structural formula.

   b Write the structural formulae for compounds **R** and **S**.

   c. Draw the displayed formulae for three isomers of butene, $CH_3CH_2CH{=}CH_2$.

# 18.4 Fuels

**You need to:**

- Name the fossil fuels coal, natural gas and petroleum.
- Name methane as the main constituent of natural gas.
- Describe the separation of petroleum into fractions containing various hydrocarbons.
- Describe the physical properties of the fractions, e.g. relative volatility.

### Exam tip

**Watch out**

Read questions carefully. For example in the worked example, the word 'gas' is easily missed out.

**Fossil fuels** include coal, natural gas (mainly methane) and **petroleum**.

A **fraction** is a group of molecules with a particular range of boiling points which distil at the same place during fractional distillation.

The *fractions produced by the fractional distillation of petroleum* provide us with a variety of hydrocarbon fuels.

**Hydrocarbons** are compounds containing only carbon and hydrogen.

*Heavier fractions from the distillation of petroleum* have higher viscosity and boiling points than lighter fractions.

### Worked example

Name a fossil fuel which is a gas at room temperature and state where it is found. [2]

Methane ✓ found in natural gas ✓ from under the ground.

When petroleum is distilled a number of different fractions are produced.

Name three of these fractions and place them in order of increasing number of carbon atoms. [2]

refinery gas, gasoline, diesel

(three correct fractions ✓ correct order ✓)

The table shows the number of carbon atoms in the molecules of particular fractions.

| Fraction | Number of C atoms in the molecules | State of fraction |
|---|---|---|
| **A** | 1–4 | gas |
| **B** | 5–10 | liquid |
| **C** | 10–16 | liquid |
| **D** | 16–20 | liquid |

Suggest how the boiling point of the fractions changes from fractions **A** to **D**. Give a reason for your answer. [2]

Increases from **A** to **D** ✓ because the size of the molecules gets bigger ✓ so there are more forces between the molecules.

Suggest how the viscosity changes from fractions **A** to **D**. [1]

Increases from **A** to **D** ✓ as the molecules get bigger.

Each fraction contains hydrocarbons. State the names and give the molecular formulae of two alkanes found in fraction **A**. [4]

methane ✓ $CH_4$ ✓ and ethane ✓ $C_2H_6$ ✓

Write a word equation for the complete combustion of the hydrocarbon hexane. [2]

hexane + oxygen $\rightarrow$ carbon dioxide + water

(hexane + oxygen ✓ carbon dioxide + water ✓)

## Apply

4. a. Name a fossil fuel which is a solid at room temperature.

   b. Sulfur is usually removed from fossil fuels before they are used. Explain why.

5. a. When petroleum is distilled a number of different fractions are produced.

   State the names of the fractions used (i) as aircraft fuel (ii) as fuel for home heating and ships.

### Key skills

You need to be able to interpret information from tables of data.

### Recap

- Coal, natural gas and petroleum are fossil fuels.
- A fraction is a group of molecules which distil at the same place during fractional distillation.
- Heavier fractions have higher viscosity and boiling points than lighter fractions.

### Exam tip

When defining the term hydrocarbon, the answer 'a compound containing carbon and hydrogen' is not sufficient. The essential word 'only' is missing. You could also add '... and no other elements'.

### Exam tip

Be prepared to write symbol equations for the combustion of fuels. For core candidates, suitable information such as relevant formulae will be given.

b. The table shows the number of carbon atoms in the molecules of particular fractions.

| Fraction | Number of C atoms in the molecules | Average boiling point of fraction / °C |
|---|---|---|
| L | 5–10 | 40–100 |
| M | 10–16 | 160–250 |
| N | 16–20 | 250–300 |
| O | 20–30 | 300–350 |

(i) Describe how the boiling point of the fractions changes from fractions **L** to **O**. Give a reason for your answer.

(ii) Suggest how the volatility changes from fractions **L** to **O**.

(iii) How does the chain length of the hydrocarbons change from **L** to **O**?

(iv) Each fraction contains hydrocarbons. Define the term hydrocarbon.

6. Complete the symbol equation for the complete combustion of pentane, $C_5H_{12}$.

$$C_5H_{12} + \dots\dots O_2 \rightarrow \dots\dots CO_2 + 6\dots\dots$$

# 18.5 Petroleum fractionation

**You need to:**

- Describe the fractional distillation of petroleum.
- Describe the difference in hydrocarbon chain length in the fractions from the top to the bottom of the distillation column.
- Name the uses of petroleum fractions.

**Exam tip**

Don't get petrol and petroleum mixed up! Petroleum is crude oil. Petrol is gasoline, a fraction from petroleum distillation.

*Each petroleum fraction* has a specific range of boiling points.

*Fractions with a higher boiling point* have molecules with longer hydrocarbon chains and higher molecular mass than fractions with lower boiling points.

*In a fractional distillation column*, there is a range of temperatures, high at the bottom and low at the top.

*Each fraction has a particular use*: for example, gasoline and diesel are used as fuels for cars and bitumen is used for making roads.

**Worked example**

Petroleum is separated into different fractions by fractional distillation.

Describe how the temperature varies in the distillation column. [1]

The temperature is high at the bottom and low at the top. ✓

Explain, in terms of molecular size and boiling points, how rapidly the different hydrocarbons rise up the fractionating column. [4]

Hydrocarbons with longer chains have higher boiling points ✓ and move up the column slowly. ✓ Hydrocarbons with shorter chains have lower boiling points ✓ and move more rapidly up the column. ✓

Explain why the different fractions come off at different parts of the column. [3]

The molecules rise up the column until the temperature falls to just below the boiling range ✓ of the fraction. At this point the vapour condenses ✓ to a liquid. They come off at different places because the molecules have different boiling points. ✓

Give one use for each of these petroleum fractions: [3]

naphtha

chemical feedstock ✓

kerosene

fuel for jets ✓

lubricating oil

polishes ✓

### Recap

- In a fractional distillation column, the temperature is high at the bottom and low at the top.
- Fractions with a higher boiling point have molecules with longer hydrocarbon chains and higher molecular mass than fractions with lower boiling points.
- Each fraction has a particular use.

### Exam tip

It is a common error to suggest that the fractions come off one by one at the top of the column in petroleum distillation. A better answer is that 'fractions come off at different heights in the column'.

### Exam tip

Make sure that you know the uses of each fraction and where they condense in the column. You do not have to remember the boiling range of each fraction.

## Apply

7. Petroleum is separated into different fractions by fractional distillation.
   a. State the physical property on which the separation of the fractions depends.
   b. Describe the difference in boiling point and size of the hydrocarbon molecules in the bitumen and in the refinery gas fraction.
   c. Describe the process of fractional distillation in an oil refinery.
8. Match the fractions **A** to **D** with their uses **1** to **4**.

| | |
|---|---|
| **A** kerosene | **1** making road surfaces |
| **B** bitumen | **2** fuel for ships and home heating |
| **C** gasoline | **3** fuel for jet aircraft |
| **D** fuel oil | **4** fuel for cars |

## Questions

**1. a.** Complete these sentences using words from the list.

ethanol functional general homologous physical similar

Methanol and ............ belong to the same ............ series. They have the same ............ group and the same ............ formula. They also have ............ chemical properties and show a trend in ............ properties. [6]

**b.** Draw the functional groups present in **(i)** alkenes **(ii)** alcohols. [2]

**c.** Define the term functional group. [2]

**d.** State the name of the homologous series to which these compounds belong:

**(i)** $CH_3CH_2COOH$ **(ii)** $CH_3CH_2CH_3$ [2]

**2.** The structures of five compounds are shown.

```
A                      B                        C
     H                     H   H     H              H
     |      O              |   |    /               |
H—C—C //            H—C—C=C                 H—C—O—H
     |    \                |       \                |
     H     O—H             H        H               H

D                      E
     H   H                H        H
     |   |                 \      /
H—C—C—H                     C=C
     |   |                 /      \
     H   H                H        H
```

**a.** Which two of these compounds belong to the same homologous series? Explain your answer. [2]

**b.** To which homologous series does compound **A** belong? [1]

**c.** Write the molecular formula for compound **C**. [1]

**d.** Draw the displayed formula for another compound in the same homologous series as compound **C**. [2]

**e.** Give the general formula for the homologous series that compound **C** belongs to. [1]

**3.** The diagram shows a fractionating column for the separation of petroleum fractions.

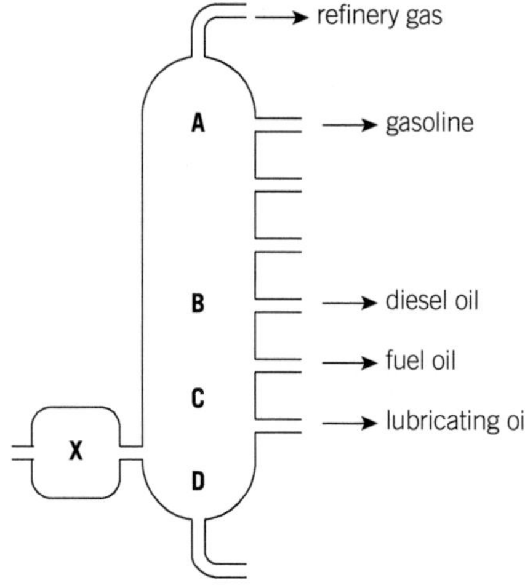


**a.** Where on the diagram, **A**, **B**, **C** or **D**, is the temperature highest? [1]

**b.** What happens at **X**, before the petroleum enters the column? [1]

**c.** Which labelled fraction on the diagram has the lowest boiling point range? [1]

**d.** State the name of two other fractions that are not labelled on the diagram. For each of these fractions, state where they condense in the column and what they are used for. [6]

**Key skills**

You need to be able to organise information when answering generalised questions, e.g. describing and explaining petroleum distillation.

## Sample question

**1. a.** Describe and explain how fractional distillation separates petroleum fractions. [5]

**b.** Refinery gas contains alkanes with 1–4 carbon atoms. Name and give the displayed formula for two alkanes present in refinery gas but not present in natural gas. [4]

**c.** One of the fractions is used for making other chemicals such as alcohols.

**(i)** Name this fraction. [1]

S **(ii)** Name the alcohol $CH_3CH_2CH_2OH$. [1]

**d.** Draw the displayed formula for propene. [1]

**e.** Determine the molecular formula of:

**(i)** a carboxylic acid with three carbon atoms [1]

**(ii)** an alcohol with two carbon atoms [1]

f. Pentane, $C_5H_{12}$, has several isomers. Draw two of these isomers which do not have just a single chain. [2]

**g.** Write the structural formula for compounds **X** and **Y**. [2]

**X**

$$\begin{array}{ccccccc} & H & & H & & H & \quad H \\ & | & & | & & | & \diagup \\ H- & C & - & C & - & C & = C \\ & | & & | & & & \diagdown \\ & H & & O-H & & & \quad H \end{array}$$

**Y**

$$\begin{array}{ccccccccc} & H & & H & & H & & & \quad O \\ & | & & | & & | & & & /\!/ \\ H- & C & - & C & - & C & = & C & - C \\ & | & & | & & & & | & \diagdown \\ & H & & H & & & & H & \quad O-H \end{array}$$

**h.** Construct the chemical equation for the complete combustion of propene, $C_3H_6$. [2]

# Some homologous series of organic compounds

## Revision checklist

Tick these boxes to build a record of your revision. Columns 2 and 3 can be used if you want to make a record more than once.

| Core/**Supplement** syllabus content | | 1 | 2 | 3 |
|---|---|---|---|---|
| 19.1 | Describe alkanes as being generally unreactive except for combustion and substitution by chlorine. | | | |
| 19.1 | **Describe the substitution reaction of alkanes with chlorine.** | | | |
| 19.2 | Describe the manufacture of alkenes and hydrogen by cracking alkanes. | | | |
| 19.2 | Describe the reasons for the cracking of larger alkanes. | | | |
| 19.3 | Know that unsaturated hydrocarbons have C=C or C≡C bonds and that alkenes have C=C bonds | | | |
| 19.3 | Distinguish between saturated and unsaturated hydrocarbons by their reaction with aqueous bromine. | | | |
| 19.3 | **Describe the addition reactions of alkenes with bromine, hydrogen and steam.** | | | |
| 19.4 | Name and draw the structural and displayed formulae of alcohols. | | | |
| 19.4 | Describe the uses of ethanol and the combustion of ethanol. | | | |
| 19.4 | **Name and draw the structural and displayed formulae of alcohols including position isomers.** | | | |
| 19.4 | **Describe the formation of ethanoic acid by the oxidation of ethanol.** | | | |
| 19.5 | Describe the manufacture of ethanol by fermentation. | | | |
| 19.5 | Describe the manufacture of ethanol by the catalytic addition of steam to ethene. | | | |
| 19.5 | **Describe the advantages and disadvantages of the two methods of manufacturing ethanol.** | | | |
| 19.6 | Describe the reactions of ethanoic acid with metals, bases and carbonates. | | | |
| 19.6 | **Describe the reaction of a carboxylic acid with an alcohol to form an ester.** | | | |
| 19.6 | **Name and the draw the displayed formulae of esters.** | | | |

# 19.1 Alkanes

**You need to:**

- State that alkanes are saturated compounds.
- Describe alkanes as being generally unreactive except for combustion and substitution by chlorine.
- **Describe the substitution reaction of alkanes with chlorine.**

**Alkanes** *are* **saturated** hydrocarbons because they contain only single bonds.

*Alkanes are generally unreactive* except for combustion and substitution by chlorine.

*Alkanes undergo complete combustion* to form carbon dioxide and water.

*Alkanes react with chlorine* in the presence of ultraviolet light and chlorine by a substitution reaction.

A **substitution reaction** is one in which one atom or group of atoms replaces another.

A **photochemical reaction** is a reaction which depends on the presence of light, which provides the activation energy.

### Exam tip

You may be asked to deduce formulae for organic compounds given information such as in the worked example or from general formulae.

### Worked example

The table shows some information about alkanes.

| Alkane | Formula | Boiling point / °C |
|---|---|---|
| methane | $CH_4$ | −162 |
| | $C_2H_6$ | |
| propane | | −42 |
| butane | $C_4H_{10}$ | 0 |

Name the alkane with the formula $C_2H_6$. [1]

ethane ✓

Deduce the molecular formula of propane. [1]

$C_3H_8$ ✓

Estimate the boiling point of $C_2H_6$. Explain how you reached your answer. [2]

About −100 °C. ✓ The trend in boiling points is increasing so the value must be between −162 and −42. ✓

State two types of reaction which alkanes undergo. [2]

Combustion ✓ and substitution with chlorine ✓

Copy and complete this equation for the reaction of $C_2H_6$ with oxygen.

$2C_2H_6 + 7O_2 \rightarrow$ ..........$CO_2$ + ..........$H_2O$ [2]

$2C_2H_6 + 7O_2 \rightarrow 4CO_2$ ✓ $+ 6H_2O$ ✓

### Key skills

You need to be able to interpret data from tables and deduce patterns in formulae.

### Exam tip

When given tables of data about organic compounds, remember to look for the trends and then choose a suitable value by extrapolation or choosing a value in between two other values as in the worked example.

### Exam tip

**Watch out**

Take care with negative numbers. Remember that −20 is lower in value than −10.

**Recap**

- Alkanes are saturated hydrocarbons which are unreactive except for combustion and substitution by chlorine.
- Alkanes react with chlorine in the presence of chlorine and ultraviolet light (which provides the activation energy). This is a substitution reaction. S

Alkanes react with chlorine. State the essential condition for this reaction. S [1]

ultraviolet light ✓

Construct the equation for the reaction of one molecule of $CH_3CH_3$ with one molecule of chlorine, $Cl_2$. Draw the organic product as a structural formula. [2]

$CH_3CH_3 + Cl_2 \rightarrow CH_3CH_2Cl$ ✓ + HCl ✓

($C_2H_6 + Cl_2 \rightarrow C_2H_5Cl$ + HCl gets 1 mark)

**Key skills**

You need to be able to construct displayed formulae using combining powers of carbon and hydrogen (and oxygen).

**Exam tip**

For the core paper, you do not have to know the details of substitution by chlorine. For the supplement you will be expected to draw the displayed or the structural formula of the products.

## Apply

1. The table shows some information about alkanes.

| Alkane | Formula | Density of liquid in g/cm³ | Boiling point/°C |
|---|---|---|---|
| ethane | $C_2H_6$ | 0.57 | −89 |
| propane | $C_3H_8$ | 0.58 | −42 |
| butane | | 0.60 | 0 |
| pentane | $C_5H_{12}$ | | 36 |

   a. Draw the displayed formula of ethane.
   b. Deduce the molecular formula of butane.
   c. Estimate the density of pentane.
   d. Describe the trend in the boiling point.

2. a. Write a word equation for the combustion of butane.
   b. Chlorine reacts with ethane in the presence of light. Describe the type of reaction that occurs.

3. S a. One molecule of ethane reacts with one molecule of chlorine in the presence of light. Draw the products as displayed formulae.
   b. Explain why ultraviolet light is essential in this reaction.

# 19.2 Cracking alkanes

**You need to:**

- Describe the manufacture of alkenes and hydrogen by cracking alkanes.
- Describe the reasons for the cracking of larger alkanes.

**Key skills**

You need to be able to balance equations for unfamiliar reactions when given suitable information.

**Cracking** is the breakdown of long-chain alkanes into shorter-chain alkanes and alkenes.

*Cracking is carried out* because we need more shorter-chain alkanes and alkenes than can be supplied by the distillation of petroleum.

*Hydrogen can be produced* by cracking shorter-chain alkanes.

The *conditions for cracking* are high temperature and a catalyst.

**Worked example**

Hydrocarbons are cracked in an oil refinery.

Explain the meaning of the term *cracking* and explain why it is carried out. [4]

Cracking is the breakdown (thermal decomposition) of longer-chain alkanes ✓ into shorter-chain alkanes and alkenes. ✓ It is carried out because there is not enough petrol made by just distilling petroleum. ✓ By cracking we can make more petrol. ✓

State the conditions needed for cracking. [2]

High temperature ✓ and a catalyst ✓

Dodecane, $C_{12}H_{26}$, is cracked to produce an alkane and one other hydrocarbon, S. Write the molecular formula for hydrocarbon S.

$C_{12}H_{26} \rightarrow C_8H_{18} + S$ [1]

$C_4H_8$ ✓

Ethane, $C_2H_6$, can be cracked to produce a hydrocarbon and one other gas. Identify both the hydrocarbon and the other gas. [2]

ethene ✓ and hydrogen ✓

**Exam tip**

When describing cracking, you must state three things: (1) large alkane molecules broken down to small alkane molecules (2) by heating + catalyst and (3) alkenes (and sometimes hydrogen) are formed.

**Exam tip**

In questions such as the worked example you simply subtract the number of carbon and hydrogen atoms in the first product from the number on the left-hand side, e.g. C: 12 – 8 = 4 and H: 26 – 18 = 8.

**Recap**

- Cracking is the breakdown of long-chain alkanes into shorter-chain alkanes and alkenes / hydrogen. High temperature and a catalyst are needed.
- Cracking is carried out because we need more shorter-chain alkanes and alkenes than can be supplied by the distillation of petroleum.

**Exam tip**

**Watch out**

There may be two parts to answer in a question. For example in the worked example, 'explain the meaning' and 'explain why it is carried out'.

## Apply

4. Describe how shorter-chain alkanes and alkenes are produced from longer-chain alkanes in an oil refinery.
5. a. Tetradecane is cracked to produce an alkane and one other hydrocarbon. Copy and complete the equation for this reaction.

   $$C_{14}H_{30} \rightarrow C_9H_{20} + \text{..................}$$

   b. Cracking can also produce a gas which has a lower relative molecular mass than methane. Name this gas.

**Exam tip**

You do not have to know specific temperatures or name the catalysts used in cracking.

# 19.3 Alkenes

**You need to:**

- Know that alkenes are unsaturated hydrocarbons because they have a C=C bond or a C≡C bond; distinguish between saturated and unsaturated hydrocarbons by their reaction with aqueous bromine.
- **Describe the addition reactions of alkenes with bromine, hydrogen and steam.**

### Exam tip

When describing the results of the test for unsaturation do not use the word 'clear' to mean colourless.

**Unsaturated compounds** contain C=C **double bonds** or C≡C **triple bonds**.

**Alkenes** *are unsaturated hydrocarbons* because one or more of their bonds are C=C double bonds.

*Unsaturated hydrocarbons turn aqueous bromine* from orange to colourless when the hydrocarbon is in excess.

*Alkenes react with steam* to form alcohols. The conditions needed are 300 °C, 6000 kPa pressure and an acid catalyst.

An **addition reaction** is a reaction in which two or more compounds react to form only one product. 

*Addition reactions of alkenes* include reaction with bromine, steam or hydrogen.

*Hydrogen reacts with alkenes* in the presence of a nickel catalyst to produce alkanes.

### Worked example

Describe the difference between saturated and unsaturated hydrocarbons in terms of their bonding. [2]

Saturated hydrocarbons only have single bonds. ✓ Unsaturated hydrocarbons have C=C double bonds or triple bonds. ✓

Describe how aqueous bromine can be used to distinguish between saturated and unsaturated hydrocarbons. [3]

Add a drop of aqueous bromine to each hydrocarbon in a test tube. Stopper the test tube and shake. ✓ If the bromine water is decolourised, the hydrocarbon is unsaturated. ✓ If the bromine water remains orange, the hydrocarbon is saturated. ✓

Alkenes react with steam at 300 °C to produce alcohols. State two other conditions needed for this reaction. [2]

6000 kPa pressure ✓ and an acid catalyst. ✓

The reaction of steam with alkenes is an addition reaction. State the meaning of the term addition reaction. [1] 

Two or more compounds react but only one product is formed. ✓

Write an equation for the reaction of hydrogen with ethene. Show the reactants and products as displayed formulae.  [2]

```
H       H ✓                      H  H      ✓
 \     /                         |  |
  C=C       + H—H  ——→       H—C—C—H
 /     \                         |  |
H       H                        H  H
```

Name the catalyst used in this reaction. [1]

nickel ✓

## Recap

- Alkenes are unsaturated compounds which contain C=C double bonds.
- Unsaturated hydrocarbons turn aqueous bromine from orange to colourless.
- Alkenes react with steam to form alcohols at 300 °C, 6000 kPa pressure using an acid catalyst. The reaction is an addition reaction.
- Alkenes react with bromine or hydrogen (in the presence of Ni catalyst) by addition reactions. 

## Apply

6. a. The structure of compound **A** is shown.

```
       H     H
       |     |      O
H—O—C—C=C—C  //
       |  |        \
       H  H         O—H
          A
```

Which group of atoms in this compound shows that it is an unsaturated compound.

b. Describe a test for an unsaturated compound stating any colour changes.

7. a. Draw the displayed formula of ethene.

b. Ethanol can be produced from ethene and another reactant using an acid catalyst.

(i) Name the other reactant.

(ii) State two other conditions needed for this reaction.

 8. Propene, $CH_3CH{=}CH_2$, reacts with bromine.

a. Write an equation for the reaction of bromine with propene. Show the reactants and products as displayed formulae.

b. State and explain the type of reaction that takes place.

 **Key skills**

You need to be able to deduce the functional groups and molecular formula when given a displayed formula.

**Exam tip**

You need to know the specific temperature and pressure for the reaction of steam with ethene and that the catalyst is an acid.

**Exam tip**

Remember that the reaction of bromine liquid with ethene produces the product $BrCH_2$-$CH_2Br$. This is not the main product formed with aqueous bromine.

**Exam tip**

**Watch out**

In question 8b there are two command words. So there are two things for you do: state the type of reaction and explain the meaning of this type of reaction.

# 19.4 Alcohols

**You need to:**

- Name and draw the structural and displayed formulae of alcohols.
- Describe the uses of ethanol and the combustion of ethanol.
- **Name and draw the structural and displayed formulae of alcohols including position isomers.**
- **Describe the formation of ethanoic acid by the oxidation of ethanol.**

**Alcohols** contain the –OH functional group.

*Ethanol can be manufactured* by addition of steam to ethene or by fermentation.

*Ethanol undergoes complete combustion* to produce carbon dioxide and water.

S *We can draw isomers of alcohols* with three or more carbon atoms with the –OH group in different positions.

The *oxidation of ethanol* produces ethanoic acid. It is carried out (i) by heating acidified aqueous potassium manganate(VII) or (ii) by bacterial oxidation during vinegar production.

### Recap

- Ethanol can be manufactured by addition of steam to ethene or by fermentation.
- Ethanol is completely combusted to carbon dioxide and water.
- S Alcohols with three or more carbon atoms have isomers with the –OH group in different positions.
- The oxidation of ethanol by acidified potassium manganate(VII) or by bacterial oxidation produces ethanoic acid.

### Worked example

Alcohols have the –OH functional group.

Write the general formula for alcohols. [1]

$C_nH_{2n+1}OH$ ✓

Draw the displayed formula of ethanol. [1]

```
    H   H
    |   |
H — C — C — O — H ✓
    |   |
    H   H
```

Write a word equation for the complete combustion of ethanol. [2]

ethanol + oxygen → carbon dioxide ✓ + water ✓

(if oxygen omitted or another error 1 mark)

Ethanol can be manufactured by fermentation. State one other reaction which produces ethanol. [2]

Reaction of steam ✓ with ethene ✓

S Butanol is an alcohol with four carbon atoms. Draw the displayed formula for the straight-chain form of butanol. [1]

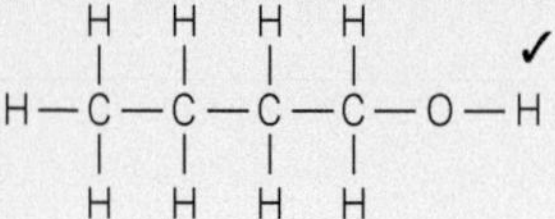

Draw the displayed formula for the other isomer of butanol which has a chain of four carbon atoms. Name this isomer. **S** [2]

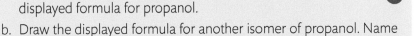

```
     H   H   H   H
     |   |   |   |
 H — C — C — C — C — H
     |   |   |   |
     H   O   H   H
          \
           H          ✓
```

Butan-2-ol ✓

The bacterial oxidation of ethanol produces ethanoic acid. State one other method of producing ethanoic acid from ethanol. [2]

Heat ✓ ethanol with acidified potassium manganate(VII). ✓

## Apply

9. a. Ethanol is an alcohol.
   Give the molecular formula for ethanol.
   b. State one use of ethanol.
   c. Copy and complete the equation for the complete combustion of ethanol.
   $C_2H_5OH$ + ..................$O_2$ → ..................$CO_2$ + 3..............................
   d. Ethanol can be manufactured by the reaction of ethene with steam. State one other method of manufacturing ethanol.
10. a. Propanol is an alcohol with three carbon atoms. Draw the displayed formula for propanol. **S**
    b. Draw the displayed formula for another isomer of propanol. Name this isomer.

11. Ethanoic acid can be produced by reaction of ethanol with potassium manganate(VII). State one additional reagent that is needed and state one condition for the reaction.

**Exam tip**

**Watch out**

In question 10b there are two command words: *draw* and *name*. Don't forget to do both.

**Exam tip**

You will often see the formula for ethanol written as $C_2H_5OH$ to show its functional group. Remember that this is *not* a molecular formula.

**Exam tip**

When balancing the symbol equation for the combustion of ethanol, remember that the ethanol contains an oxygen atom!

# 19.5 Fermentation

**You need to:**

- Describe the manufacture of ethanol by fermentation.
- Describe the manufacture of ethanol by the catalytic addition of steam to ethene.
- **Describe the advantages and disadvantages of the two methods of manufacturing ethanol.**

**Fermentation** *of glucose produces* ethanol and carbon dioxide.

The *conditions for fermentation* are yeast, a temperature of 25–35 °C and absence of air.

**Yeast** *contains* **enzymes** which are biological (protein) catalysts.

**S** *Production of ethanol by fermentation* is a low energy process, with a slow rate of reaction and forms impure ethanol.

*Production of ethanol by addition of steam to ethene* is a high energy process, with a fast rate of reaction and forms pure ethanol.

**Exam tip**

Make sure that you know the difference between conditions and reactants. Temperature, pressure, pH and absence or presence of catalyst are conditions.

### Exam tip

**Watch out**

It is a common error to suggest that oxygen is needed for the fermentation of glucose to ethanol. You need **anaerobic** conditions (absence of oxygen).

### Exam tip

Remember that fermentation uses yeast, which is a living organism. So the temperature must be 25–35 °C, otherwise the yeast will die. Make sure that you don't write 'high temperature'!

### Worked example

Write a word equation for fermentation. [2]

glucose ✓ → carbon dioxide + ethanol ✓

(both carbon dioxide and ethanol needed for second mark)

One of the conditions for fermentation is a temperature of 25–35 °C. Name two other conditions needed. [2]

yeast as catalyst ✓ and absence of air ✓

State one advantage and one disadvantage of producing ethanol by fermentation rather than by the reaction of ethene with steam. [2]

An advantage is that less energy is used ✓ because of the low temperatures needed. A disadvantage is that the ethanol is not pure. ✓ It needs to be distilled.

### Recap

- Fermentation of glucose by yeast in the absence of air at 25–35 °C produces ethanol.

- Fermentation is a low energy process, with a slow rate of reaction and forms impure ethanol.
- Production of ethanol from ethene is a high energy process, with a fast rate of reaction and forms pure ethanol.

## Apply

12. Fermentation produces ethanol and carbon dioxide. Yeast is a catalyst for this reaction.

**X** → carbon dioxide + ethanol

a. State the name of the reactant **X**.

b. State two conditions needed for fermentation other than the presence of yeast.

S c. State two advantages and one disadvantage of producing ethanol by the reaction of ethene with steam rather than by fermentation.

# 19.6 Carboxylic acids and esters

**You need to:**

- Describe the reactions of ethanoic acid with metals, bases and carbonates.
- **Describe the reaction of a carboxylic acid with an alcohol to form an ester.**
- **Name and the draw the displayed formulae of esters.**

*Ethanoic acid has the formula* $CH_3COOH$.

*Ethanoic acid reacts with reactive metals* to produce the salt of the carboxylic acid, $CH_3COO^-M^+$, and hydrogen.

*Ethanoic acid reacts with bases* to produce a salt and water.

*Ethanoic acid reacts with carbonates* to produce a salt, water and carbon dioxide.

*Salts of ethanoic acid* are called ethanoates. For example, magnesium ethanoate.

**Worked example**

Ethanoic acid reacts with metals. Write a word equation for the reaction of ethanoic acid with sodium. [2]

ethanoic acid + sodium → sodium ethanoate ✓ + hydrogen ✓

Name two other types of substance that react with ethanoic acid to produce a salt. [2]

Metal hydroxides ✓ and metal carbonates ✓

Draw the displayed formula for ethanoic acid. [2]

```
      H        O   ✓✓
      |      //
  H — C — C
      |      \
      H       O — H
```

(Correct structure of carboxylic acid group. ✓ Rest of molecule correct. ✓)

## Apply

13. a. Name the products formed when:
    (i) ethanoic acid reacts with magnesium carbonate
    (ii) propanoic acid reacts with potassium
    b. Give the formula for sodium ethanoate.
    c. Draw the displayed formula for the carboxylic acid functional group.

**Key skills**

You need to be able to construct displayed and structural formulae for esters from a given alcohol and carboxylic acid.

**Exam tip**

For the core paper you need only know about ethanoic acid, although you may be expected to handle data related to other carboxylic acids (see question 2c at the end of this chapter).

**Exam tip**

Carboxylic acids have typical acidic properties (see Section 11.2).

**Recap**

- Ethanoic acid reacts with reactive metals to produce a salt and hydrogen.
- Salts are formed when ethanoic acid reacts with bases and carbonates.
- Salts of ethanoic acid are called ethanoates.

**Exam tip**

When naming carboxylic acids the carbon atom of the COOH group is included. $CH_3COOH$ is ethanoic acid because organic compounds with two carbon atoms joined start with eth-.

Supplement

*Carboxylic acids react with alcohols* in the presence of an acid catalyst to produce an **ester** and water.

*When an ester is formed*, the OH is removed from the –COOH group of the carboxylic acid and the H is removed from the OH of the alcohol group to form an **ester linkage**.

### Exam tip

Remember that the salts of carboxylic acids end in -ate, e.g. sodium ethanoate.

### Worked example

Esters are formed from carboxylic acids.

Copy and complete the general equation for this reaction. [2]

carboxylic acid + .................... → ester + ....................

carboxylic acid + alcohol ✓ → ester + water ✓

Name a suitable catalyst for this reaction. [1]

sulfuric acid ✓

Draw the displayed formula of the ester formed when propanoic acid, $CH_3CH_2COOH$, reacts with ethanol, $CH_3CH_2OH$. [2]

```
                      ✓✓
    H   H   O       H   H
    |   |   ||      |   |
H — C — C — C — O — C — C — H
    |   |           |   |
    H   H           H   H
```

(if 2 marks not scored allow 1 mark for structure of COO group)

Name the ester formed in this reaction. [1]

ethyl propanoate ✓

Name the reactants used to make the ester methyl butanoate. [2]

butanoic acid ✓ and methanol ✓

### Exam tip

Remember that in naming esters the name begins with the alkyl group from the alcohol, e.g. methyl from methanol $CH_3OH$. The name ends with the part of the carboxylic acid, e.g ethanoate from ethanoic acid.

### Recap

- Carboxylic acids react with alcohols in the presence of an acid catalyst to produce an ester and water.
- In ester formation, OH is removed from the –COOH group of the carboxylic acid and H is removed from the OH of the alcohol group.

## Apply

14. a. Describe how the ester ethyl butanoate can be made from a named carboxylic acid and a named alcohol.
    b. Draw the displayed formula for methyl butanoate.
15. Name these esters.

```
(a)  H   O       H   H           (b)  H       O   H   H
     |   ||      |   |                |       ||  |   |
 H — C — C — O — C — C — H        H — C — O — C — C — C — H
     |           |   |                |           |   |
     H           H   H                H           H   H
```

16. Write the structural formula for **a** ethyl propanoate **b** propyl methanoate.

### Exam tip

When drawing structures of the ester remember that you remove the OH from the carboxylic acid and the H from the alcohol. Then join the parts together.

## Questions

1. The structure of two compounds, **S** and **T**, are shown.

```
    H   H     H              H   H   H
    |   |    /               |   |   |
H — C — C = C           H — C — C — C — H
    |        \               |   |   |
    H         H              H   H   H
       S                         T
```

   **a.** To which homologous series do each of these compounds belong? [2]

   **b.** Describe the effect of adding aqueous bromine to each compound, stating any colour changes. [3]

   **c.** State and explain which compound, **S** or **T**, is unsaturated by reference to its structure. [1]

   **d.** Write the molecular formula of compound **S**. [1]

   **e.** Write the general formula of the homologous series to which **T** belongs. [1]

2. The table gives some information about carboxylic acids.

| Carboxylic acid | Molecular formula | Density in g/cm³ | Boiling point/°C |
|---|---|---|---|
| methanoic acid | | 1.22 | 101 |
| | $C_2H_4O_2$ | 1.05 | 118 |
| propanoic acid | $C_3H_6O_2$ | | 141 |
| butanoic acid | $C_4H_8O_2$ | 0.96 | |

   **a.** Name the carboxylic acid with the formula $C_2H_4O_2$. [1]

   **b.** Deduce the molecular formula of methanoic acid. [1]

   **c.** Estimate **(i)** the density of propanoic acid **(ii)** the boiling point of butanoic acid. [2]

   **d.** Write a word equation for the reaction of ethanoic acid with sodium hydroxide. [2]

3. Copy and complete these sentences about ethene using words from the list.

   acid   addition   alkanes   catalyst   cracking   ethanol   hydrogen   pressure

   Alkenes and .................. can be produced by .................. long-chain .................. using a high temperature and a .................. The .................. of steam to ethene produces .................. The conditions are high .................., a temperature of 300 °C and an .................. catalyst. [8]

4. **a.** Give the formulae of the products of the combustion of ethanol. [2]

   **b.** State one use of ethanol. [1]

5. Methane reacts with chlorine.

   S **a.** Write a symbol equation for the reaction of 1 mole of methane with 1 mole of chlorine. [2]

   **b.** State the name of the type of reaction taking place and the conditions needed. [2]

6. Write an equation for addition reaction of propene, $CH^3CH{=}CH^2$, with steam, using displayed formulae. [2]

7. **a.** Describe how the ester ethyl propanoate can be made from a named carboxylic acid and a named alcohol. [3]

   **b.** Draw the displayed formula for ethyl propanoate. [1]

   **c.** Describe how butanoic acid can be produced from a named alcohol, stating the conditions and additional reactants. [4]

Raise your grade

### Exam tip

- Remember that in many questions you are expected to use your knowledge from other areas of the course. In question 1b it is from Chapter 4.
- Question 10b is best done by choosing a different ester as the isomer.

## Sample question

1. Ethane is an unsaturated hydrocarbon.
   - **a.** State the meaning of the term *unsaturated hydrocarbon*. [3]
   - **b.** Describe the structure and bonding in ethane. [2]
   - **c.** Copy and complete the symbol equation for the complete combustion of ethane.

     $2C_2H_6$ + ..............$O_2$ → ..............$CO_2$ + ..............$H_2O$ [3]
2. **a.** Explain the meaning of the term cracking including the substances formed. [4]
   - **b.** Explain why cracking is carried out. [2]
3. Ethene reacts with steam to produce ethanol.
   - **a.** Write a symbol equation for this reaction. [2]
   - **b.** State the conditions for this reaction. [3]
4. Write a word equation for fermentation and give three conditions required. [5]

S

5. Write a symbol equation using displayed formulae for the reaction of 1 mole of ethane with 2 moles of chlorine in the presence of ultraviolet light. [2]
6. Give three advantages of manufacturing ethanol by hydration of ethene rather than by fermentation. Give a reason for each advantage. [6]
7. Write a symbol equation for the reaction of propene with hydrogen, using structural formulae. [2]
8. Construct a symbol equation to show the cracking of 1 mole of the hydrocarbon $C_{14}H_{30}$ to produce only 1 mole of an alkane with eight carbon atoms and an alkene with two carbon atoms. [2]
9. **a.** Write a symbol equation for the reaction of magnesium with ethanoic acid. [2]
   - **b.** Name the organic product of this reaction. [1]
10. **a.** Draw the displayed formula of the ester ethyl ethanoate. [1]
    - **b.** Draw the structure of a different ester which is an isomer of ethyl ethanoate. Name this ester. [2]

# Polymers

## Revision checklist

Tick these boxes to build a record of your revision. Columns 2 and 3 can be used if you want to make a record more than once.

| Core/**Supplement** syllabus content | | 1 | 2 | 3 |
|---|---|---|---|---|
| 20.1 | Describe the terms monomer, polymer and addition polymerisation with reference to the formation of poly(ethene). | | | |
| 20.1 | Describe the environmental challenges caused by plastics. | | | |
| 20.1 | **Know that PET can be hydrolysed to its monomers and repolymerised.** | | | |
| 20.2 | **Identify the repeat units and linkages in addition polymers.** | | | |
| 20.2 | **Deduce the polymer structure or repeat unit for a given alkene.** | | | |
| 20.3 | **Describe the differences between addition and condensation polymerisation.** | | | |
| 20.3 | **Identify the repeat units and linkages in condensation polymers.** | | | |
| 20.3 | **Deduce the polymer structure or repeat unit for a given polyamide or polyester.** | | | |
| 20.4 | **Describe proteins as natural polyamides.** | | | |
| 20.4 | **Describe the general structure of amino acids.** | | | |
| 20.4 | **Describe the general structure of proteins.** | | | |

# 20.1 What are polymers?

**You need to:**

- Describe the terms monomer, polymer and addition polymerisation with reference to the formation of poly(ethene).
- Describe the environmental challenges caused by plastics.
- **Know that PET can be hydrolysed to its monomers and repolymerised.**

**Exam tip**

Remember that plastics only release toxic gases *when burned*.

**Polymers** are large molecules built up from small units called **monomers**.

An **addition reaction** is one where two or more molecules join together and no other product is formed.

In **addition polymerisation** the C=C bond between the carbon atoms of the monomer changes to a C–C bond when the monomers join together.

**Non-biodegradable** *plastics* are those that cannot be broken down by organisms in soil or water.

*Problems with plastic waste* include choking or strangling animals, blocking drains and litter.

*Methods of disposal of plastics* include landfill sites (but these are soon filled), burning to make electricity (but burning them produces toxic gases) and **recycling** by melting and remoulding to form new articles.

S *PET* is a plastic that can be hydrolysed to its monomers and then repolymerised.

**Hydrolysis** is the breakdown of a substance using water or dilute acid or alkali.

**Worked example**

Poly(ethene) is an addition polymer.

State the name and give the displayed formula of the monomer used to make poly(ethene). [2]

Ethene ✓

```
H   H
|   |
C = C ✓
|   |
H   H
```

Draw a section of the polymer chain of polyethene containing at least six carbon atoms. [2]

```
   H   H   H   H   H   H
   |   |   |   |   |   |
 — C — C — C — C — C — C —
   |   |   |   |   |   |
   H   H   H   H   H   H
```

Carbon and hydrogen atoms drawn correctly ✓ continuation bonds at the ends shown ✓

State two methods of getting rid of plastics other than by throwing them away as litter. Describe an environmental problem for each method that you choose. [4]

Burning ✓ the plastics produces poisonous gases or $CO^2$ which causes global warming ✓ Putting the plastic in landfill sites ✓ causes an eyesore ✓ and they are soon filled up.

PET is plastic. Describe how new samples of PET can be made from old samples of PET.  [3]

The PET is hydrolysed ✓ to its monomers. ✓ The monomers are then repolymerised. ✓

## Apply

1. Ethene is a small molecule which is polymerised to make poly(ethene).
   a. Give the general name for any small molecule that can be polymerised.
   b. What type of polymerisation produces poly(ethene)?
   c. Copy and complete part of the structure of poly(ethene) to show three ethene molecules polymerised.

H
|
—C—
|
H

2. Many plastics are non-biodegradable.
   a. State the meaning of the term non-biodegradable.
   b. Describe one environmental problem with non-biodegradable plastics thrown into the oceans.
   c. Describe one environmental problem with burning plastics.

**Recap**

- Addition polymers are produced from small monomers which join together to form a single product. The C=C bond in the monomer changes to C–C bond in the polymer.
- Plastic waste chokes animals, blocks drains and causes litter.
- Plastics are disposed of in landfill sites, burned or repolymerised from hydrolysed plastics.

**Supplement**

# 20.2 More about polymer structure

**You need to:**

- **Identify the repeat units and linkages in addition polymers.**
- **Deduce the polymer structure or repeat unit for a given alkene.**

*Addition polymers are named* after the monomers. For example, propene → poly(propene).

A **repeat unit** is the regularly repeating part of a polymer.

*To draw the structure of an addition polymer*: line up the C=C bonds with the side group(s) sticking up or down then join the monomers and change the C=C to C–C. Finally add continuation bonds to show that the carbon chain continues.

*To draw a simplified structure of an addition polymer*: draw the structure of the monomer with the side group(s) sticking up or down and change the C=C to C–C. Finally add brackets, an *n* and continuation bonds to show that the carbon chain continues.

**Key skills**

You need to be able to construct displayed formulae of unfamiliar compounds when given suitable information.

$$\left[ \begin{array}{cc} C_6H_5 & H \\ | & | \\ -C- & -C- \\ | & | \\ H & H \end{array} \right]_n$$

### Exam tip

Make sure that you draw the number of repeat units asked for in a question. For three repeat units (three C=C bonds in the monomer) you need to draw six carbon atoms in the chain.

### Exam tip

When drawing the structure of an addition polymer don't forget to change the C=C bonds to C–C bonds.

### Exam tip

Note that in the worked example, first rotate the Cl and H so they are at right angles to the C=C then make all the bonds between the carbon atoms single bonds.

### Recap

- A repeat unit is the regularly repeating part of a polymer.
- Addition polymer are drawn by lining up the C=C bonds and changing the C=C to C–C. Continuation bonds are added to show that the carbon chain continues.

### Exam tip

**Watch out**

When drawing polymer structure don't forget the continuation bonds!

### Worked example

The structure of a monomer is shown.

```
Cl     H
  \   /
   C=C
  /   \
H      H
```

Draw a section of the polymer chain formed from this monomer. Show three repeat units. [2]

```
  Cl H  Cl H  Cl H
  |  |  |  |  |  |
—C—C—C—C—C—C—
  |  |  |  |  |  |
  H  H  H  H  H  H
```

Either structure completely correct ✓✓ **or** structure without continuation bonds/wrong number of repeat units ✓

Draw the structure of this polymer as one repeat unit with brackets and *n*. [2]

```
 [ Cl H ]
 [ |  | ]
—[-C—C-]—
 [ |  | ]
 [ H  H ]n
```

Either structure completely correct ✓✓ **or** structure without continuation bonds/lacking brackets and *n* ✓

## Apply

3. The structure of a monomer is shown.

```
CH3    Cl
  \   /
   C=C
  /   \
H      H
```

a. Draw a section of the polymer chain formed from this monomer. Show two repeat units. [2]

b. Draw the structure of this polymer as one repeat unit with brackets and *n*. [2]

The *structure of a monomer from an addition polymer* can be deduced by drawing the repeat unit but removing the continuation bonds and changing the C–C to C=C.

### Worked example

The diagram shows polymer **A**.

```
  CN H  CN H  CN H
  |  |  |  |  |  |
—C—C—C—C—C—C—
  |  |  |  |  |  |
  H  Cl H  Cl H  Cl
```

polymer **A**

Draw the monomer of polymer **A**.

```
CN H
|  |
C=C
|  |
H  Cl
```

[2]

Double bond ✓ rest of structure correct ✓

## Apply

4. The diagram shows polymers **B** and **C**.

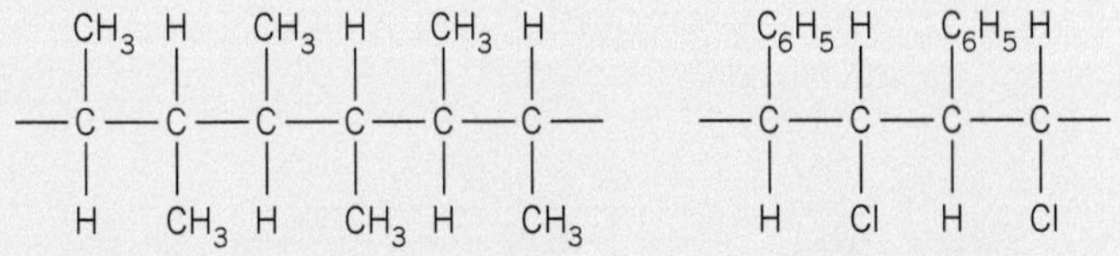

$$-\underset{\text{H}}{\overset{\text{CH}_3}{\text{C}}}-\underset{\text{CH}_3}{\overset{\text{H}}{\text{C}}}-\underset{\text{H}}{\overset{\text{CH}_3}{\text{C}}}-\underset{\text{CH}_3}{\overset{\text{H}}{\text{C}}}-\underset{\text{H}}{\overset{\text{CH}_3}{\text{C}}}-\underset{\text{CH}_3}{\overset{\text{H}}{\text{C}}}-$$

polymer **B**

$$-\underset{\text{H}}{\overset{\text{C}_6\text{H}_5}{\text{C}}}-\underset{\text{Cl}}{\overset{\text{H}}{\text{C}}}-\underset{\text{H}}{\overset{\text{C}_6\text{H}_5}{\text{C}}}-\underset{\text{Cl}}{\overset{\text{H}}{\text{C}}}-$$

polymer **C**

Draw the monomers of polymers **B** and **C**.

### Exam tip

Make sure that you can identify a repeat unit in a polymer. There is no definite place that a repeat unit starts but it must finish at the next identical place further along the chain.

### Exam tip

When drawing monomers from addition polymers don't forget to change the single C–C bonds to C=C bonds.

# 20.3 Polyamides and polyesters

**You need to:**

- **Describe the differences between addition and condensation polymerisation.**
- **Identify the repeat units and linkages in condensation polymers.**
- **Deduce the polymer structure or repeat unit for a given polyamide or polyester.**

A **condensation reaction** is one in which two molecules combine to form a larger molecule and a small molecule is eliminated (given off).

**Polyesters** and **polyamides** are **condensation polymers**.

*Polyesters* such as PET contain ester linkages:

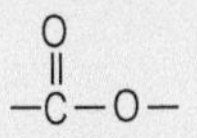

$$-\overset{\text{O}}{\overset{\|}{\text{C}}}-\text{O}-$$

*Polyesters* can be made by combining a dicarboxylic acid, HOOC–■–COOH with a **diol**, HO–□–OH. The –OH groups of the dicarboxylic acid are removed and the –H of the –OH groups of the diols are removed. Water is eliminated and the polymer shown is made.

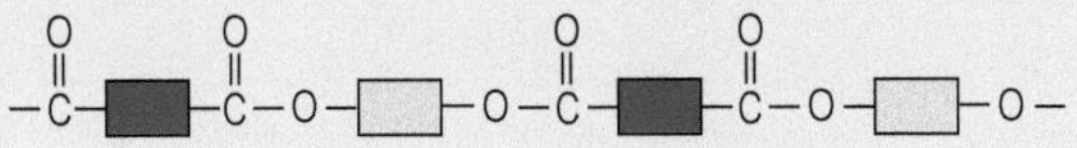

$$-\overset{\text{O}}{\overset{\|}{\text{C}}}-■-\overset{\text{O}}{\overset{\|}{\text{C}}}-\text{O}-□-\text{O}-\overset{\text{O}}{\overset{\|}{\text{C}}}-■-\overset{\text{O}}{\overset{\|}{\text{C}}}-\text{O}-□-\text{O}-$$

*Polyamides* such as nylon contain amide linkages:

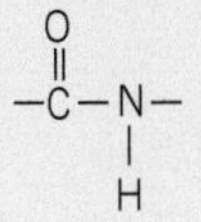

$$-\overset{\text{O}}{\overset{\|}{\text{C}}}-\underset{\text{H}}{\underset{|}{\text{N}}}-$$

Supplement

**Key skills**

You need to be able to interpret diagrams of polymers in terms of specific groups of atoms.

Polyamides can be made by combining a dicarboxylic acid, HOOC–■–COOH, with a diamine, $H_2N$–□–$NH_2$. The –OH groups of the dicarboxylic acid are removed and one –H of each $-NH_2$ group of the diamine is removed. Water is eliminated and the polymer shown is made.

### Exam tip

Remember that a repeat unit in a condensation polymer must include the main structures of both the monomers used.

### Exam tip

You should be prepared to draw diagrams of polyesters and polyamides using boxes as shown in the worked example.

**Worked example**

The diagram shows polymer **S**.

polymer **S**

On the diagram put brackets to show one repeat unit. [1]

polymer **S** ✓

Give the name of the linkage group in polymer **S**. [1]

amide ✓

Name and give the formula for the two functional groups which combine to make this linkage group. [4]

amine ✓ $NH_2$ ✓ and carboxylic acid ✓ COOH ✓

State the type of polymerisation reaction occurring when polymer **S** is made. [1]

condensation ✓

Name the small molecule which is eliminated when polymer **S** is made. [1]

water ✓

**Recap**

- In a condensation reaction, two molecules combine to form a larger molecule and a small molecule is eliminated.
- Polyesters and polyamides are condensation polymers.
- Polyesters contain ester linkages, COO, and polyamides contain amide linkages, CONH.

## Apply

5. The diagram shows polymer **T**.

   a. On the diagram put brackets to show one repeat unit.

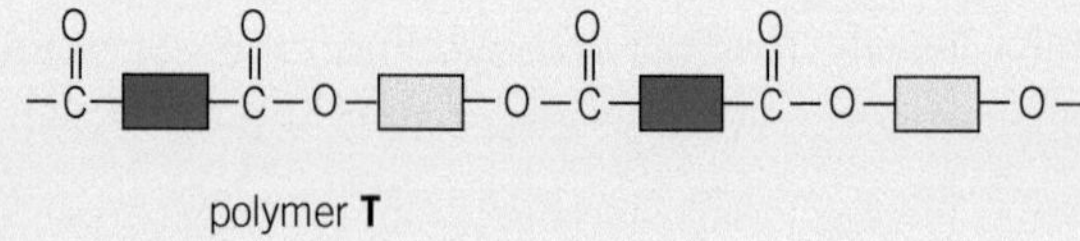

polymer **T**

   b. Give the name of the linkage group in polymer **T**.

   c. Name and give the formula for the two functional groups which combine to make this linkage group.

   d. The reaction to make polymer **T** is described as condensation polymerisation. Describe the meaning of the term *condensation polymerisation*.

### Exam tip

When drawing the structures of polyamides and polyesters take care to draw the linkages in the correct direction.

# 20.4 Amino acids and proteins

**You need to:**

- **Describe proteins as natural polyamides.**
- **Describe the general structure of amino acids.**
- **Describe the general structure of proteins.**

**Amino acids** have the general structure shown, where R represents different types of side chain.

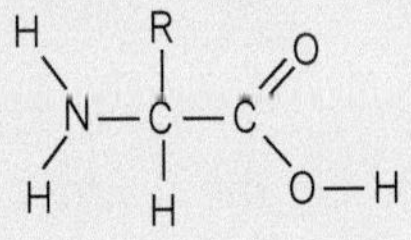

H₂N–CHR–COOH (structure: N bonded to two H atoms and to C; C bonded to R, H and to C(=O)–O–H)

**Proteins** have the same **amide linkage** as nylon-6,6 but they are arranged in the same direction: -$CONH_2$–CHR–$CONH_2$–CHR–.

*The structure of a protein* can be represented as shown, where the boxes represent different amino acids.

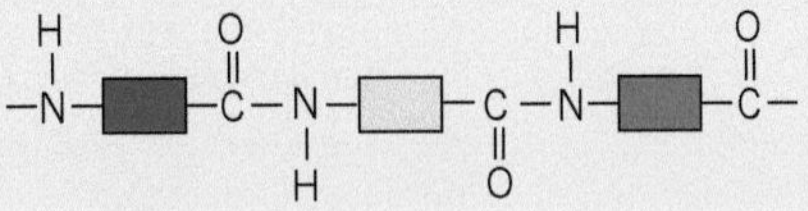

–N(H)–[■]–C(=O)–N(H)–[□]–C(=O)–N(H)–[■]–C(=O)–

## Worked example

The diagram shows part of a protein.

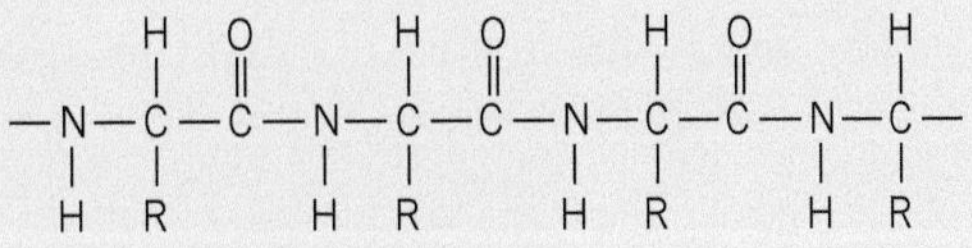

–N(H)–C(H)(R)–C(=O)–N(H)–C(H)(R)–C(=O)–N(H)–C(H)(R)–C(=O)–N(H)–C(H)(R)–

On the diagram draw a circle around the linkage group. [1]

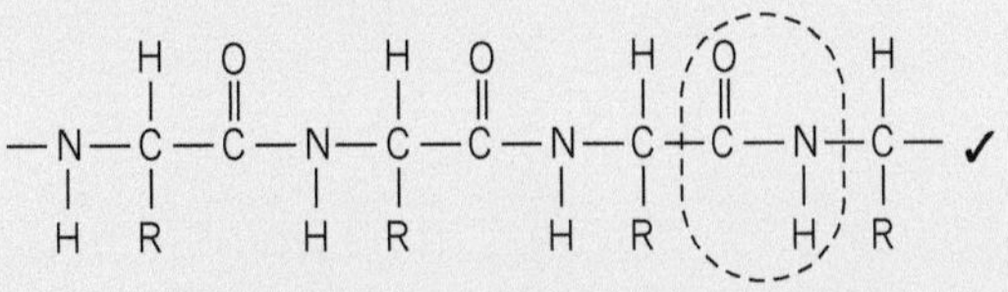

–N(H)–C(H)(R)–C(=O)–N(H)–C(H)(R)–C(=O)–N(H)–C(H)(R)–[C(=O)–N(H)]–C(H)(R)– ✓

Name the linkage group. [1]

amide ✓

Give the general name of the monomers used to make proteins. [1]

amino acids ✓

Complete the structure of one of the monomers used to make proteins. [1]

H₂N–C(R)– (incomplete)

H₂N–C(R)(H)–[C(=O)–O–H] ✓

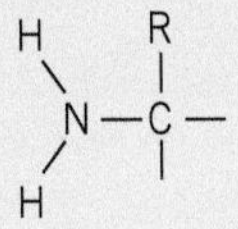

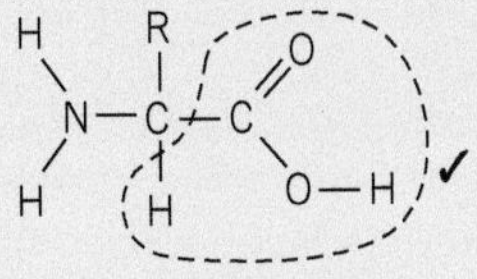

State two ways in which the structure of proteins differs from the structure of nylon. Assume that the nylon is made from two different monomers. [2]

Proteins are made from 20 different monomers. ✓ Nylon is only made from two. There does not appear to be any regular arrangement of the repeating units in the polymer ✓ but there is in nylon. The CONH groups are arranged in the same direction in proteins but alternate in opposite directions in nylon. (✓)

Supplement

## Exam tip

Note that sometimes you can write more points than the marks available.

## Exam tip

Make sure that you know the differences in the structures of a protein and a synthetic polyamide.

- Amino acids contain the functional groups COOH and $NH_2$ connected to a carbon atom with a side chain, R.
- Proteins have the same amide linkage as nylon-6,6 but they are arranged in the same direction.
- Some polyamides are natural, e.g. proteins. Other polyamides are synthetic e.g. nylon.

## Apply

6. Amino acids are the monomers used to make proteins.
   a. Copy and complete the structure of the amino acid alanine, which has a $CH_3$ side chain (R group).

      —C—C
      |

   b. Name the type of polymerisation when amino acids combine to make proteins.
   c. The structure of poly(glycine) is shown.

      —N(H)—C(=O)—$CH_2$—N(H)—C(=O)—$CH_2$—N(H)—C(=O)—

      (i) On the diagram, draw a circle around the amide linkage.
      (ii) Deduce the structure of the monomer used to make this polymer.
7. Complete these sentences about the difference between proteins and nylon-6,6 using words or formulae from the list.

   amino　condense　-CO-NH-　diamine　linkages
   monomers　-NH-CO-　regular　repeat

   There are about twenty different .................... acid monomers which .................... together when proteins are synthesised. Nylon-6,6 is formed from only two ...................., a dicarboxylic acid and a .................... In a protein, the amide .................... are in the same direction, -CO-NH- then ...................., but in nylon-6,6 the order alternates -CO-NH- then .................... In nylon, the repeat unit is in a .................... order but in proteins there is not regular order of the .................... units.

## Questions

1. Complete these sentences about addition polymers using words from the list.

   addition　double　join　long　monomers　polymer　two

   When small molecules containing carbon-carbon ________ bonds are polymerised, these small molecules, which are called ________, join together to form a ________ chain. No other molecule is formed apart from the ________. We call this type of polymerisation ________ polymerisation. In an addition reaction ________ or more molecules ________ together and no other product is formed.
2. There is a lot of waste plastic in the environment. Give two adverse effects of this plastic waste. [2]
3. The diagram shows the structure of monomer **G**.

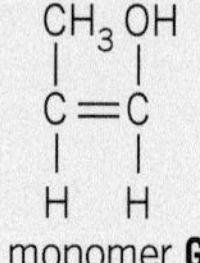


   **G** forms an addition polymer.
   a. Draw the structure of a section of this addition polymer to show three repeat units. [2]
   b. Explain why **G** does not undergo condensation polymerisation. [1]

4. A section of polymer **H** is shown.

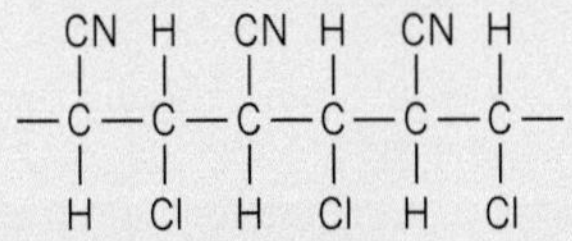

```
 CN H  CN H  CN H
 |  |  |  |  |  |
—C—C—C—C—C—C—
 |  |  |  |  |  |
 H  Cl H  Cl H  Cl
```

polymer **H**

Draw the displayed formula of the monomer used to make this polymer. [2]

5. PET is a polymer formed by a condensation reaction.

   a. Explain the meaning of the term condensation reaction. [2]

   b. The two monomers used to make PET are represented by **X** and **Y**.

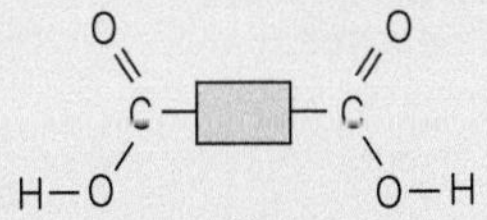

```
    O          O
    \\        //
     C—[  ]—C                H—O—[  ]—O—H
    /          \
 H—O            O—H
          X                        Y
```

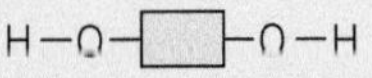

   (i) Name the functional groups in **X** and **Y**. [2]

   (ii) Draw the displayed formula for a section of PET to show two repeat units. [2]

## Exam tip

For question 3a, line up the C=C bonds with the side group(s) at right angles to the C=C then join the monomers and change the C=C to C—C. Finally add continuation bonds to show that the carbon chain continues.

## Sample question

1. Poly(ethene) is an addition polymer.

   a. Explain the meaning of the terms:

      (i) addition reaction [1]

      (ii) polymerisation [2]

   b. Draw the displayed formula for a section of a poly(ethene) chain containing six carbon atoms. [2]

2. The structure of part of poly(lactic acid) is shown.

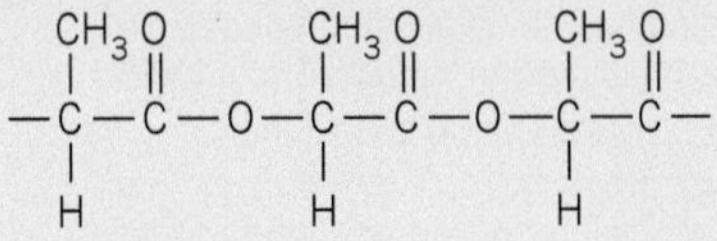

S

```
 CH3 O      CH3 O      CH3 O
 |   ||     |   ||     |   ||
—C—C—O—C—C—O—C—C—
 |          |          |
 H          H          H
```

Draw the displayed formula of the monomer used to make this polymer. [2]

3. The structure of alanine is shown.

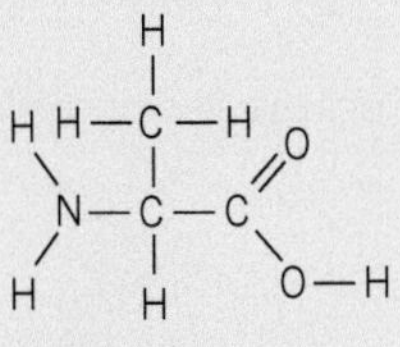

```
        H
        |
  H H—C—H  O
   \    |  //
    N—C—C
   /    |   \
  H     H    O—H
```

   a. To which group of organic compounds does alanine belong? Explain your answer. [3]

   b. (i) Draw the structure of a section of poly(alanine) to show two repeat units. [3]

      (ii) What type of polymer is poly(alanine)? Explain your answer. [3]

4. Draw the structure of a section of nylon to show two repeat units. In your diagram show the displayed formulae of the linkage groups and the rest of the molecule as blocks □ and ■. [3]

Raise your grade

# Glossary

**Accuracy** How close a measurement is to the true value

**Acid (Core definition)** A substance that forms hydrogen ions when dissolved in water. Acidic solutions have a pH less than 7.

**Acid (Supplement)** A proton donor

**Acid rain** Rain with an acidity below about pH 5 due to the reaction of sulfur dioxide or nitrogen dioxide with rainwater

**Activation energy, $E_a$** The minimum energy that colliding particles must have in order to react

**Addition polymerisation** The formation of polymers from monomers (having double bonds) where no substance other than the polymer is formed

**Addition reaction** A reaction where only one product is formed

**Air** The mixture of gases present in the atmosphere

**Alcohol** An organic compound with an –OH functional group

**Alkali** A soluble base which contains $OH^-$ ions in aqueous solution. An alkaline solution has a pH above 7.

**Alkali metal** The Group I elements in the Periodic Table. They have one electron in their outer shell.

**Alkane** A hydrocarbon having only single bonds

**Alkene** A hydrocarbon containing one or more C=C bonds

**Alloy** A mixture of a metal with other elements

**Amide linkage** The –CONH– formed when polyamides are formed from their monomers

**Amino acid** Molecules having the structure $H_2N$-CHR-COOH

**Amphoteric oxide** An oxide which reacts with both acids and alkalis separately to form a salt and water

**Anaerobic** Absence of oxygen

**Anhydrous substance** A substance containing no water

**Anode** The positive electrode in electrolysis

**Aqueous solution** A solution made by dissolving a substance in water

**Atom** The smallest part of an element that can take part in a chemical change

**Atomic number** The number of protons in the nucleus of an atom

**Avogadro constant** The number of defined particles (ions, atoms, molecules or electrons) in one mole of those particles

**Base (Core definition)** A metal oxide or hydroxide that reacts with an acid to form a salt and water

**Base (Supplement)** A proton acceptor

**Basic oxide** An oxide that reacts with an acid to form a salt

**Bauxite** The main ore of aluminium

**Binary compound** A compound containing just two types of atom or ion, e.g. NaCl

**Blast furnace** A furnace into which air is blown and in which a metal oxide is reduced using carbon

**Boiling** The change in physical state from liquid to gas

**Bond energy** The energy needed to break a mole of given bonds

**Bonding** The way the atoms or ions are held together in a substance

**Brass** An alloy of copper and zinc

**Burette** A piece of glassware for delivering a variable volume of liquid accurately (usually up to 50 $cm^3$)

**Carboxylic acid** A weak organic acid that contains the –COOH functional group

**Catalyst** A substance that increases the rate of a chemical reaction and is unchanged at the end of the reaction

**Catalytic converter** A piece of equipment put on a car exhaust to remove nitrogen oxides and carbon monoxide

**Cathode** The negative electrode in electrolysis

**Cation** A positive ion (which moves to the cathode during electrolysis)

**Chemical change** When substances react together and new substances are formed

**Chemical equation** A balanced equation showing the symbols for all reactants and products

**Chemical property** A property involving the formation of a new substance

**Chlorination** The addition of chlorine, especially in water purification

**Chlorophyll** A green plant pigment that catalyses photosynthesis

**Chromatogram** A piece of paper showing the separation of substances after chromatography has been carried out

**Chromatography** The separation of a mixture of soluble substances using filter paper and a solvent

**Climate change** The change in weather patterns that is linked to an increase in global warming

**Closed system** A reaction where there is no loss or gain of substances to or from the environment

**Coke** A form of impure carbon made by heating coal in the absence of air

**Collision frequency** The rate at which particles collide

**Collision theory** Using the idea of colliding particles to explain how reaction rates change with surface area, temperature and concentration

**Combustion** Burning (usually in a reaction with oxygen gas)

**Complete combustion** Combustion in excess air/oxygen

**Compound** A substance containing two or more types of atoms chemically combined

**Concentration** The amount of one type of substance dissolved in a specified volume of another. It is measured in mol/$dm^3$ or g/$dm^3$.

**Condensation** The change in physical state from gas to liquid

**Condensation polymerisation** Polymerisation reaction where a small molecule is eliminated

**Condensation reaction** A reaction where two or more substances combine and a small molecule, such as water or hydrogen chloride, is eliminated (given off)

**Condenser** A piece of apparatus for cooling a vapour and converting it to a liquid

**Conductor** A substance that allows thermal energy or electricity to flow through it

**Contact process** The industrial process for making sulfuric acid

**Cooling curve** A graph showing how the temperature changes with time when a substance is cooled at a constant rate

**Corrosion** The 'eating away' of the surface of a metal by a chemical, e.g. by acids

**Covalent bond** A pair of electrons shared between two atoms, usually leading to a noble gas electronic configuration

**Covalent compound** A compound having covalent bonds. They can be simple molecules or giant structures.

**Cracking** The thermal decomposition of an organic compound into smaller molecules by heating (or heating and a catalyst)

**Crystallisation** The formation of crystals when a saturated solution is left to cool

**Crystallisation point** The point at which crystals will form very quickly when a drop of saturated solution is placed on a cold surface

**Decimetre cubed** Unit of volume ($dm^3$) often used in chemistry. It has the same volume as 1000 $cm^3$.

**Decomposition** The breakdown of a substance into two or more products

**Delocalised electrons** Electrons that are not associated with any particular atom

**Density** The mass of a substance divided by its volume

**Deoxygenation** The removal of oxygen

**Diatomic** Molecules containing two atoms

**Diffusion** The gradual spreading out and mixing of different particles because of their random motion

**Diol** A compound containing two –OH functional groups

**Displacement** A reaction in which one atom or group of atoms replaces another in a compound

**Displayed formula** The formula of a substance which shows all of the atoms and all of the bonds

**Dissociated** (when referring to acids and alkalis) The breaking down of molecules into ions

**Distillation** A method of separating a liquid from a mixture by boiling the mixture then condensing the vapours

**Dot-and-cross diagram** A diagram showing the arrangement of the electrons in a molecule or in an ionic structure (usually only the electrons in the outer shells are shown)

**Double bond** Two atoms share two pairs of electrons between them

**Ductile** Can be pulled into wires

**Electrical conductivity** The ease with which an electric current can flow through a substance. Conduction is due to moving electrons in metals and moving ions in molten ionic compounds or ionic solutions.

**Electrode** A rod of metal or carbon (graphite) that leads an electric current into or out of an electrolyte

**Electrolysis** The decomposition of an ionic compound when molten or in aqueous solution by the passage of an electric current

**Electrolyte** A molten or aqueous substance that undergoes electrolysis

**Electron** A negatively charged particle in the atom found in electron shells outside the nucleus

**Electron shell** The energy levels at different distances from the nucleus where the electrons are found

**Electronic configuration** The number and arrangement of electrons in the electron shells of an atom (sometimes called the electronic structure)

**Electroplating** A process that uses electricity to coat one metal with another

**Element** A substance containing only one type of atom

**Empirical formula** The simplest whole number ratio of the different atoms or ions in a compound

**End point** The point in a titration when the indicator changes colour showing that the reaction is complete

**Endothermic** A transfer of thermal energy from the surroundings to a reaction mixture leading to a decrease in the temperature of the surroundings

**Enthalpy change, $\Delta H$** The transfer of thermal energy during a reaction

**Enzyme** A biological (protein) catalyst

**Equilibrium** In a reversible reaction, the point where the forward and backward (reverse) reactions are taking place at the same rate

**Ester** An organic compound containing the -COO- group, formed when a carboxylic acid reacts with an alcohol

**Ester linkage** The -COO- group found in polyesters

**Evaporation** The change from liquid to vapour state below the boiling point

**Excess** Being greater than something else in amount

**Exothermic** A transfer of thermal energy to the surroundings from a reaction mixture leading to an increase in the temperature of the surroundings

**Experimental yield** The amount in moles or grams of a specific product formed from a specific amount of reactants under experiment conditions

**Fermentation** Often refers to the breakdown of glucose by yeast in the absence of oxygen to form ethanol and carbon dioxide. Other fermentations can also occur.

**Fertiliser** A substance added to the soil to replace essential elements lost when crops are harvested

**Filtrate** The liquid or solution that has passed through a filter paper

**Filtration** Separating a solid from a liquid by using a filter paper

**Flue gas desulfurisation** The removal of sulfur dioxide from the waste gases produced in furnaces by reacting it with bases or carbonates

**Forces of attraction** Forces which tend to bring atoms, ions or molecules together

**Formula (chemical formula)** A representation of a compound or molecule using chemical symbols and numbers

**Fossil fuel** Fuel (coal, oil, natural gas) formed from the remains of tiny, dead, sea creatures or plants over millions of years

**Fraction** A group of substances with similar boiling points, distilling off at the same place in a fractionation column

**Fractional distillation (fractionation)** The separation of different substances in a liquid by their different boiling points

**Freezing (solidifying)** The change of physical state from liquid to solid

**Fuel** A substance that releases energy (usually when burned)

**Fuel cell** A cell where hydrogen and oxygen undergo reaction to produce an electric current

**Functional group** An atom or group of atoms that determines the chemical properties of a homologous series

**Galvanising** Coating a metal (usually iron) with a protective layer of zinc

**Gas syringe** A piece of glassware for measuring the volume of gases given off in a reaction

**General formula** A formula that applies to all the compounds in a particular homologous series of organic compounds

**Giant covalent structure** A structure with a continuous three-dimensional network of covalent bonds, e.g. diamond

**Global warming** The warming of the atmosphere due to greenhouse gases trapping infrared radiation radiated from the Earth's surface

**Graphite** A form of carbon that conducts electricity and is used for inert electrodes

**Greenhouse gas** A gas such as methane or carbon dioxide that absorbs infrared radiation radiated from the Earth's surface

**Group** A vertical column of elements in the Periodic Table

**Haber process** The industrial process for making ammonia

**Halide** A compound containing an ion formed from a halogen atom

**Halogen** An element in Group VII of the Periodic Table

**Heating curve** A graph showing how the temperature changes with time when a substance is heated at a constant rate

**Hematite** A common ore of iron

**Homologous series** A family of similar organic compounds with similar chemical properties due to the presence of the same functional group

**Hydrated substance** A substance chemically combined with water

**Hydrocarbon** A compound containing only carbon and hydrogen

**Hydrolysis** The breakdown of a compound by reaction with water. Acids or alkalis speed up hydrolysis.

**Impurity** A substance which contaminates a pure substance

**Incomplete combustion** Combustion when the oxygen supply is limited

**Indicator** A substance that has two different colours depending on the solution in which it is placed. It often changes colour according to the pH of the solution.

**Inert** Does not react

**Inert electrode** An electrode that does not react during electrolysis

**Insoluble** Does not dissolve

**Insulator** A substance that is a very poor conductor of electricity (or thermal energy)

**Intermolecular forces** Weak forces between molecules

**Ion** A species formed when an atom or group of atoms has become positively or negatively charged by loss or gain of electrons

**Ionic bond** The strong electrostatic attraction between the positive and negative ions in the crystal lattice

**Ionic equation** A chemical equation showing only the ions taking part in the reaction. The unchanged spectator ions are not shown.

**Ionic half-equation** Equation showing the oxidation or reduction parts of a redox reaction separately. Often used for reactions at the electrodes in electrolysis.

**Ionic lattice** A giant structure with a regular arrangement of alternating positive and negative ions

**Isotopes** Different atoms of the same element that have the same number of protons but a different number of neutrons

**Kinetic energy** Energy associated with movement

**Kinetic particle theory** The idea that the motion of atoms can explain states of matter, diffusion and rates of reaction

**Lattice** A continuous regular arrangement of particles

**Limiting reactant** The reactant that is not in excess

**Litmus** An indicator used to test if a substance is acidic or alkaline

**Locating agent** A compound that reacts with a colourless substance on chromatography paper to form a coloured spot

**Malleable** Can be hammered into shape

**Mass number** The number of protons plus neutrons in the nucleus of an atom

**Measuring cylinder** A piece of glassware to measure out liquids to the nearest 1 or 2 $cm^3$

**Melting** The change in physical state from solid to liquid

**Metallic bonding** The electrostatic attraction between the positive ions in a giant metallic lattice and a 'sea' of delocalised electrons

**Mixture** Two or more substances which are mixed but are not chemically combined and can be separated by physical means

**Molar gas volume** The volume occupied by one mole of any gas - 24 $dm^3$ at room temperature

**Mole** Unit of amount of substance that contains $6.02 \times 10^{23}$ specified particles (atoms, molecules, ions or electrons)

**Molecular formula** A formula showing the number and type of different atoms in a molecule, e.g. $C_2H_6$

**Molecule** A particle made up of two or more atoms held together by covalent bonds

**Monatomic** Consisting of one atom

**Monomer** A small molecule that combines to form a polymer

**Neutral** Neither acidic nor alkaline. A neutral solution has pH 7.

**Neutralisation** The reaction of an acid with a base to form a salt and water. For an acid reacting with an alkali this is represented by $H^+ + OH^- \rightarrow H_2O$

**Neutron** A particle in the nucleus of the atom which has no charge

**Noble gas** An element in Group 0 (Group VIII) of the Periodic Table

**Non-biodegradable** Not able to be broken down by organisms (especially microorganisms)

**NPK fertilisers** Fertilisers containing nitrogen, phosphorus and potassium

**Nucleus** The central part of an atom containing protons and neutrons

**Ores** Rocks containing a metal or metal compound from which a metal can be economically extracted

**Oxidation (Core definition)** The gain of oxygen by a substance

**Oxidation (Supplement)** The loss of electrons or increase in oxidation number of a substance

# Glossary

**Oxidation number** A number that describes how oxidised an atom is

**Oxidising agent** A substance that oxidises another substance by removing electrons, and is itself reduced in the process

**Percentage abundance** The percentage of each isotope in a given sample of an element

**Percentage composition by mass** The percentage by mass of each element in a compound

**Percentage purity** The mass of a given substance in a mixture divided by the overall mass of substances present, expressed as a percentage

**Percentage yield** The actual yield divided by the theoretical yield expressed as a percentage

**Period** A horizontal row of elements in the Periodic Table

**Periodic Table** An arrangement of elements in periods and groups in order of increasing proton number so that some elements with similar properties are arranged in the same groups

**Petroleum** A mixture of hydrocarbons present under the Earth's surface as a black sticky liquid.

**pH scale** A scale of numbers that describes how acidic (or alkaline) a substance is

**Photochemical reaction** A reaction that depends on the presence of light

**Photochemical smog** A smoky fog caused by the reaction of oxides of nitrogen, ozone and hydrocarbons in light

**Photosynthesis** The process by which plants make glucose (and oxygen) from carbon dioxide and water in the presence of sunlight

**Physical property** A property which does not involve a chemical reaction, e.g. melting point

**Pollutant** A substance that contaminates (makes less pure) the air, water or soil

**Polyamide** A polymer with -CONH- linkages

**Polyester** A polymer with -COO- linkages

**Polymer** A large molecule built up from many smaller molecules called monomers

**Polymerisation** The chemical reaction where monomers combine to form a polymer

**Position of equilibrium** How far the reaction goes towards the products or reactants side

**Precipitate** A solid formed when two solutions are mixed

**Products** The substances produced as a result of a chemical reaction

**Proteins** Natural polyamides made from amino acid monomers

**Proton** A positively charged particle in the nucleus of an atom. Also used as a term for a hydrogen ion.

**Proton acceptor** The definition of a base

**Proton donor** The definition of an acid

**Proton number** The number of protons in the nucleus of an atom

**Pure** There is only one substance present

**Purification methods** Methods used to separate the substance you want from mixtures, e.g. distillation, filtration

**Qualitative analysis** A way of identifying substances by observing the results of specific chemical tests

**Rate of reaction** The amount of product converted to reactants in a given time

**Reactant** A substance present at the start of a chemical reaction which reacts (usually with another substance) to produce a product or products

**Reacting mass** The amount of one reactant (in grams or moles) needed to react exactly with another reactant

**Reaction pathway diagram** A diagram showing the enthalpy change from reactants to products for exothermic or endothermic reactions (the activation energy can also be shown)

**Reactivity series** A list of elements (usually metals) in their order of reactivity

**Recycling** The processing of used materials to form new products

**Redox reaction** A reaction in which there is simultaneous reduction and oxidation taking place

**Reducing agent** A substance that reduces another substance by addition of electrons, and is itself oxidised in the process

**Reduction (Core definition)** The loss of oxygen from a substance

**Reduction (Supplement)** The gain of electrons or decrease in oxidation number of a substance

**Relative atomic mass, $A_r$** The average mass of the isotopes of an element compared to 1/12 th of the mass of an atom of carbon-12

**Relative formula mass** The sum of the relative atomic masses applied to all substances, both ionic and covalent

**Relative mass** The mass of one particle compared with another; used when the actual mass is very small, e.g. masses of protons, neutrons and electrons

**Relative molecular mass, $M_r$** The sum of the relative atomic masses of all the atoms in a molecule

**Repeat unit** A regularly repeating part of a polymer

**Residue** The solid that remains after carrying out evaporation, distillation, filtration or any similar process

**Respiration** The reactions that release energy in all living things. The overall reaction is glucose combining with oxygen to form carbon dioxide and water.

**Reversible reaction** A reaction in which the products can react together to re-form the original reactants

**$R_f$** The distance travelled by a substance during chromatography divided by the distance travelled by the solvent

**r.t.p.** Room temperature and pressure

**Rust** Hydrated iron(III) oxide formed when iron reacts with air and water. The term only applies to corrosion of iron and steel.

**Sacrificial protection** A more reactive metal is placed in contact with a less reactive metal. The more reactive metal corrodes and saves the less reactive metal from corrosion.

**Salts** Compounds formed when hydrogen in an acid is replaced by a metal or an ammonium ion

**Saturated compound** An organic compound made up of molecules in which all the carbon–carbon bonds are single covalent bonds

**Saturated solution** A solution which contains the maximum concentration of a solute dissolved in the solvent

**Sedimentation** The process where insoluble particles suspended in a liquid fall to the bottom

**Simple distillation** Purifying a liquid by first converting it into a vapour by heating and then condensing the vapour back into a liquid in a condenser

**Solubility** The amount of solute that dissolves in a given quantity of solvent

**Solute** A substance that dissolves in a solvent

**Solution** A uniform mixture of a solute in a solvent

**Solvent** A substance that dissolves a solute

**Solvent front** The furthest position the solvent reaches when moving up the chromatography paper

**Species** A general name for atoms, molecules, ions or electrons

**Spectator ions** Ions that do not take part in a reaction

**Stainless steel** A mixture of iron with other elements that does not rust

**State** The three physical states of matter are solid, liquid and gas

**State symbols** The letters (s), (l), (g) or (aq) placed after each formula in an equation to indicate the physical state of the reactants and products

**Steel** An alloy of iron containing controlled amounts of carbon and other metals

**Stoichiometry** The ratios of the reactants and products shown in a balanced chemical equation

**Strong acid/alkali** Acids or alkalis that are completely dissociated in aqueous solution

**Structural formula** A formula that gives an unambiguous description of the way the atoms in a molecule are arranged, for example $CH_3CH_2OH$

**Structural isomers** Compounds with the same molecular formula but different structural formulae

**Substitution reaction** A reaction in which one atom or group of atoms is replaced by another atom or group of atoms

**Surroundings** In energy transfers, anything that is not the reactants and products, e.g. test tube, air, solvent

**Theoretical yield** The amount in moles or grams of a specific product formed from a specific amount of reactants by calculation assuming a 100% yield

**Thermal decomposition** The breakdown of a compound into two or more substances by heating

**Titration** A method for finding the amount of substance in a solution using a burette to add one solution to another

**Transition element** A block of elements between Groups II and III in the Periodic Table with specific properties such as high density and formation of coloured compounds

**Triple bond** Two atoms share three pairs of electrons between them

**Unsaturated compound** An organic compound made up of molecules in which one or more carbon–carbon bonds are double bonds or triple bonds

**Volumetric pipette** A pipette used to measure out solutions accurately. A pipette for putting drops of liquid into a test tube is called a teat pipette.

**Water of crystallisation** The water molecules present in crystals

**Weak acid/alkali** Acids or alkalis that are partially dissociated in aqueous solution

**Word equation** An equation with the reactants and products written as their chemical names

**Yeasts** Single-celled microorganisms related to fungi

**Yield** The amount of product obtained in a reaction